The HARDNESS of the heart

Anthem

Words and Music by Alex Harvey, Hugh McKenna Copyright © 1992 Sony/ATV Music Publishing LLC All Rights Reserved – Permission Requested from Sony. Unless otherwise noted, Scripture quotations are from the Authorized (King James) Version.

Scriptures quotations marked (NIV) are taken from the Holy Bible, New International Version®, NIV®. Copyright © 1973, 1978, 1984, 2011 by Biblica, Inc.TM Used by permission of Zondervan. All rights reserved worldwide. www.zondervan.com. The "NIV" and "New International Version" are trademarks registered in the United States Patent and Trademark Office by Biblica, Inc.™

ISBN 13: 978-0-9846938-5-6

Library of Congress Control Number: 2014902374

Printed in the United States of America
First Printing: 2014/2017
21 20 19 18 17   5 4 3 2 1

Cover photo by Melissa Cary
Cover design by Rachel Abou-Zeid
Interior design by James Monroe Design, LLC.

SOMETHING
OR OTHER
PUBLISHING

Info@SOOPLLC.com
For bulk orders e-mail: Orders@SOOPLLC.com

For my family and friends

Contents

Foreword

In *The Hardness of the Heart*, the highly anticipated sequel to *The People of the Sign*, Wade Fransson encourages us to follow along on his quest for evidence of "pure religion" (James 1:27). But his journey, while undoubtedly spiritual, is not just an internal, philosophical one. Rather, it unfolds within the context of a unique, modern life, rife with conflict and competing priorities at home, in high-stakes corporate back rooms, and in other surprising locales. Wade's own haunted past makes this powder keg all the more explosive.

The book begins, as expected, where *The People of the Sign* left us dangling in Wade's life . . . with many unanswered questions about how his career as a minister of the Worldwide Church of God (WCG) would turn out and whether his marriage would survive. Both of these aspects of Wade's life seemed to be "near the end."

Wade takes us along on a "Magical Mystery Tour"—a compelling journey into his life, with an assist from The Beatles' song titles and lyrics, which he cleverly uses as chapter and section titles throughout the book. International travel piques the imagination as we are transported from Southern California to Egypt to Thailand to India . . . and back. As he struggles with serious illnesses, career triumphs and disappointments, and a failing marriage, Wade continues to search for ways to align with a church or ministry seeking to serve God and mankind in practical ways. Instead, he seems to find the same embodiment of hypocrisy Jesus often observed in the Pharisees and ministerial "teachers of the law" who appear more interested in fleecing the flock than in feeding it.

As Wade makes his way forward, often with his world crumbling around him, he experiences firsthand that the corporate world is generally driven by pure, intense greed. While struggling to forge a career at a high-profile consulting firm tasked with auditing other companies in the Enron era, Wade comes face-to-face with a dilemma—how to be true to his Christian morals and ethics and still keep his job. Wade describes the sense of "cognitive dissonance" he experiences when it finally sinks in that the "Almighty Dollar" is the driving force behind his company's (and many others') practices and policies. He comes to the sad realization that corporate and religious corruption are two sides of the same coin.

The book illustrates how greed is inherent in the "hard hearts" of all mankind. Without the guide of the Spirit of God in our lives, we are easily ruled by the love of money. At the end of the day, as one Beatles' lyric proclaims, "money can't buy [us] love."

If keeping the Sabbath was the sign of the people of the Old Covenant, then the sign of the New Covenant was provided by Christ in John 13:35, "By this shall all men know that ye are my disciples, if ye have love one to another." The new outward sign of God's people is simply **love in action**. As Wade puts it, "What we do is more important than what we profess." He takes this directive to heart as he struggles to help a fledgling group of new believers in India (putting his own health at great risk) by baptizing several converts in surroundings that are "less than hygienic," to put it mildly.

The Hardness of the Heart is a refreshingly frank, honest look at life from one very unique perspective. I encourage you to read it with an open mind and a "tender heart" as you follow Wade's thoughts and experiences. It is my sincere belief and desire that the epic quest described in the following pages may help all of us to find pure religion and love in action—a closer walk with God and neighbor.

– Laura Urista, Managing Editor,
The Plain Truth magazine, Christianity Without the Religion Journal

Preface

Dear Reader,

I poured my life into the pages of *The People of the Sign* in the hope that it might be of some use to those applying themselves to the work of seeking a path toward greater light. And I left my readers at a crossroad.

The Hardness of the Heart picks up at that crossroad. If you have not yet read *The People of the Sign*, I urge you to start there because these pages build on themes introduced in that volume, not to mention the names and positions of a few key players who reappear here. Myself included.

The second verse of Leonard Cohen's "Anthem" introduces chapter 1, as verse one did in *The People of the Sign*. That volume alternated between the yin and yang of two of my favorite songs by Talking Heads, "Warning Sign" and "The Good Thing." The tension between these opposing directions is a fitting backdrop to the unraveling of a carefully woven tapestry, and the tearing down of the strongholds of dogma. One of the early reviewers of *The People of the Sign* compared my mentality, as represented in that book, to that of a terrorist—a true believer, indoctrinated and believing whatever my holy book told me to believe, without questioning.[1] The review affirmed that I was on the right path with this work, presenting the past authentically, as it was, not coloring who I was then with the brush of who I am now.

As we become more adult, the stakes get higher, and the hard work really begins. This volume covers the latter, and more trying portion of what turned out to be forty years in the wilderness. But if you have come this far, I trust you'll find *The Hardness of the Heart* of greater value than *The People of the Sign*.

---

1. Speaking of holy books, all Scripture references are again from the King James Version, unless otherwise noted.

Many of the questions raised in *The People of the Sign* are answered herein. Many individuals and authors helped me gain the understanding needed, and I'll reference only two here. Daniel Boyarin's 2012 book, *The Jewish Gospels,* lends scholarly credibility to the religious context of Jesus taught during my years in the Worldwide Church of God (WCG), and the understanding the earliest believers had about who and what He represented. This is not to say I agree with all Boyarin's conclusions; only that his work enabled me to finally "put a fork in" mine—at least as far as the second volume of this trilogy is concerned. The other is a volume written by one of my early mentors, Henry Sturcke. His book *Encountering the Rest of God: How Jesus Came to Personify the Sabbath,* published in 2005, helps explain, using the techniques of biblical scholarship, what I apparently was only able to learn through the crucible of human experience.

My heartfelt hope in publishing these experiences—which brought me greater understanding, enlightenment, and ultimately the answers to a number of questions that plagued me at the end of *The People of the Sign*—is that they might provide some similar benefit to you, along whatever path you happen to be traveling at the moment.

In revisiting these events, a perspective developed that I sum up in the phrase "the Ego is the Antichrist." The irony in my satisfaction at having distilled such a potent sound bite is not lost on me, a point I request the reader remember throughout the volume. Documenting my beliefs and the actions taken because of them is a powerful mirror that has helped me continue to detach myself from who I was, in favor of who I might become.

It is my sincere belief that reflecting on whom and what we are can assist in purifying the heart to better reflect the light.

Sincerely,
Wade Fransson
September 21, 2015

Can I Take You Back

We asked for signs the signs were sent; the birth betrayed the marriage spent.
Yeah the widowhood of every government—signs for all to see.
I can't run no more with that lawless crowd while the killers in high places
say their prayers out loud. But they've summoned, they've summoned up a
thundercloud and they're going to hear from me.
Ring the bells that still can ring. Forget your perfect offering.
There is a crack in everything.
That's how the light gets in.

— LEONARD COHEN, "ANTHEM"

In October 1995, I was on a flight leaving the island of Maui, heading east. I had just spent eight days at a religious celebration, followed by a week of vacation, sun, surf, and golf. As the paradise of the fiftieth state to join the Union receded in the distance, I should have been relaxed and content.

Instead, I was craning my neck, peering through the glare on the little oval window, which seemed designed to obscure my view of the rapidly darkening night sky. I was scanning the stars as though they might reveal a sign. Their randomness seemed to signify that, however competent the pilot might be, we were all lost. When we landed, we'd find out just how far off course he'd taken us.

I had just resigned from my executive role with the Worldwide Church of God. I was educated at its university, ordained into its ministry, and climbed its ranks believing and teaching that we were the "One True Church"—the only church through which God was working.

Until it became obvious that we weren't.

Ask Me Why

The Worldwide Church of God (WCG) had been founded by a charismatic leader named Herbert W. Armstrong, the "Elijah to come," the prophesied announcer of Christ's return. He was God's Apostle—the one sent by Christ to this day and age. But he had now been dead for seven years, and the church he founded had shattered, along with any illusions about him occupying those roles. Despite resigning from my occupation within the church, his legacy still occupied me in a number of ways.

The most important of the many things that set the WCG apart from others was our adherence to the fourth of the Ten Commandments—the observance of the weekly and annual Sabbaths of God.[1] The symbolism inherent in the Sabbath—the weekly day of rest—was the Millennium, a thousand years of peace that Christ would usher in upon His return. And the seven annual Sabbaths laid out His prophetic plan for mankind. We were the remnant of the seed of the Woman of Revelation 12, the only ones on earth who both obeyed God's Commandments and had the testimony of Christ.[2] The Sabbath was the test commandment, and the sign between God and His Chosen Ones. We understood all this because we were the recipients of His Holy Spirit, which God gives to those who obey Him.[3]

The success of the WCG throughout most of the twentieth century helped make all this believable, until the institution to which we belonged came

---

1.   Exodus 31:13; Ezekiel 20:12, 20; Leviticus 23.
2.   Revelation 12:17.
3.   Acts 5:32.

crashing down around our egos. The first shock had been in 1986, when its founder, Herbert W. Armstrong, referred to as Mr. Armstrong or HWA, whom we had faithfully followed for decades, died. We papered over this problem by comparing him to Moses, who led the Children of Israel around in the desert for forty years. He, and HWA, had left their followers looking forward to the Promised Land without actually taking them there.

Just prior to his death, HWA had appointed Joseph Tkach as his successor. This had carried us forward for a few years until, unlike Joshua, who followed Moses, the teachings emanating from Tkach overturned his predecessor's teaching. When the central teaching on the Sabbaths fell, many felt kidnapped. We were taken hostage into the mainstream of Christianity—the home of all those doctrinally corrupt and spiritually bankrupt churches who claimed to be Christian but didn't understand the Bible.

The ministry and membership of the WCG were required to submit to their divinely authorized spiritual leaders (representatives in the Government of God) who were now teaching doctrine they had previously rejected. It was a shocking reversal for a church that prided itself on being different. The WCG had taught that all other churches were composed of deceived members who were not connected to the true God, YHWH, the God of Abraham, Isaac, and Jacob. The deceived members of those other churches were mercifully as unaware of their sins as they were of God's plan to save them. But for those of us who knew the truth, turning our backs on the Sabbath was a one-way ticket to the lake of fire.

And yet many members who initially disagreed had seemed to succumb to a mass outbreak of Stockholm syndrome, in which victims bond with those who kidnap them. More and more of them began to convert to the so-called new covenant as time went on. This spiritual erosion and the reversal on the issue of the Sabbath had provided justification for ten of twelve regional pastors in the United States to put aside their allegiance to the Government of God in favor of an organized walkout, taking a large portion of the WCG with them. This happened during the spring Holy Days in 1995 (Easter, for those outside the WCG). This breakaway group formed what became known as the United Church of God (UCG).

I had navigated the double bind by staying on after the organized rebellion of the UCG to complete my current assignments, then resigning to disconnect my paycheck from my faith. This gave me peace of mind, but also led to me being unemployed as I returned home from Hawaii after my last celebration of the Feast of Tabernacles with the WCG.[4] Unanswered questions about what to do next in terms of my finances, my career, and my spiritual journey were the primary reasons for my current angst. So I squinted through the less than transparent window of the plane heading east over the ocean and looked at the distant stars through a glass darkly. My wife and I had celebrated the Feast of Tabernacles on Hawaii's Kona coast, and I had stayed on another week, on Maui, while she returned to Los Angeles to work. This had been intended to bring clarity on what God wanted me to do next.

It hadn't work.

So I prayed that God would guide me through the debris created by the collapse of His One True Church, while floating, untethered from the earth. The vessel I was on headed away from the light, toward darkness, while the distantly blinking stars provided scant illumination—and no comfort.

It's not that I was unaccustomed to challenges. The mass kidnapping of my church had perversely mirrored my childhood experience of being kidnapped by my father. At age eight, I had been snatched away from my mother's legal custody and hustled out of the United States to Sweden, my father's homeland. There, I was deposited with relatives I didn't know, confronted with a language I didn't understand and a culture that was foreign to me. The trauma of those and subsequent events had set the stage for me to embrace the WCG and all it stood for. It had become my surrogate family, a tribe with which I strongly identified. The early death of my mother and my estrangement from my father—coupled with a miraculous near-death experience as a teenager—had led me to view myself as a spiritual orphan who had been adopted by God. The WCG was my spiritual mother.

After four and a half years at WCG's university, numerous international programs (including the prestigious City of David archaeological expedition in Israel), and foreign language studies, I had traveled the world doing God's Work. A string of accomplishments led me to an executive level position at the global headquarters. Now the church that had rescued me had split in half.

---

4.   The Feast of Tabernacles pictures the millennial rule of Jesus Christ, the Kingdom of God on earth. It was the annual highlight of the church I had just resigned from and was integral to who I became over the course of my life leading up to this point, as covered extensively throughout the prior volume, *The People of the Sign* (*TPotS*).

I was forced, in a new way, to experience a nasty divorce. I was once again a spiritual orphan. And I hadn't planned on being unemployed.

In preparing to leave my position with the WCG, I had applied for a highly visible position as the director of the official charity of the University of California, Los Angeles—a summer camp program for underprivileged children. It would have been a perfect career step, a transition with the benefit of continuing my education within the prestigious and respected UCLA system at a significant (employee) discount.

Hundreds of people had applied for this position, and I had successfully progressed through the four phases of the interview process. The search firm that had generated hundreds of candidates had proposed me as their all-around preferred candidate, with an unqualified recommendation to hire. I was ultimately rejected by the board in a decision delivered by its chairman, an African-American woman. She wanted someone with more "cultural diversity." I speak four languages, but this left me speechless. I had lived in seven countries and had participated in or directed summer and winter programs for teens in eight international locations across three continents and had broken down racial barriers in a multiracial camp in South Africa during apartheid.

My surprise might be surprising to minorities, which just illustrates that some groups are less accustomed to discrimination. Regardless, I had shaken this off with the understanding that God had other plans. Humility was a lesson one could not learn often enough, and increasingly I was seeing a need to overcome remnants of an inherent arrogance that generally had been accepted in ministers within the WCG.

In leaving the WCG behind, I was hesitant to join one of the splinter groups scrambling to claim its mantle of authority. I had been trying to find the balance between fanatical commitment to a calling as a minister, and my wife's resentment at taking a backseat to my focus on spiritual matters and service to the church. I was haunted by the words of the apostle Paul, who wrote, "An unmarried man is concerned about the Lord's affairs—how he can please the Lord. But a married man is concerned about the affairs of this world—how he can please his wife—and his interests are divided."[5]

I had dedicated my life to God, had been ordained into the ministry of His One True Church, and had made the work of that One True Church my

---

5.   I Corinthians 7:32–34 (NIV).

primary focus. That One True Church had been ripped in two, and my wife wanted to go along with the half that was issuing my paycheck. I wondered if compromising my beliefs in an effort to accommodate my wife was the reason my job offer with UCLA had fallen through. Our week together at the Feast had only seemed to highlight the increasing divide between us, and not just on the matter of doctrine.

I'm Down

It's hard to convey, to those without firsthand experience, the impact the breakup of the WCG had on its members, including my wife and me. Our attitudes and beliefs on almost every topic, large and small—from what we ate, to what we wore, how we spoke, where we went, when we went there, who we went there with, and what we did when we got there—had all been framed by the WCG and its belief system. The different ways in which we were changing cast shifting shadows over our relationship. Our WCG-influenced belief system was to hold each other on a very tight leash. The husband was saddled with the burden of being the primary breadwinner, and the wife had the responsibility to submit to this overloaded creature.

My plane landing in 1995 represented, so to speak, chickens coming home to roost. I hadn't figured out my next step, but I had reached one conclusion during my week away. Compromising with my beliefs wasn't going to help me save my marriage, which was looking shakier than ever. I needed to recommit myself to God, whether my wife liked it or not.

My first order of business upon arriving back in Los Angeles was to find a job, any job. We had recently bought a small, but (for us) expensive, house in Pasadena. When Joseph Tkach had announced that the new covenant negated the commandment to keep the Sabbath holy, I had joked that although WCG believed in the new covenant we had an old covenant mortgage. Our debt would not be forgiven.

So I quickly accepted the first opportunity that offered a way to pay the bills, a fourth- and fifth-grade-level teaching position at a private Armenian school. My brother-in-law began his teaching career there and was highly respected. He had moved on to the better-paying public school system, and recommended me to the administration. It paid about one-third the amount of the position I had been chasing at UCLA.

The resulting drop in pay and status—on top of our differences in opinion about changes within the WCG—had a negative impact on my marriage. My wife hadn't supported my resignation from the WCG and while my pay was reduced, hers was increasing. She had completed a legal assistant training course and landed a position with a respected law firm in Los Angeles. The new primary breadwinner was surrounded by high-powered alpha males—the kind she thought she had married, a man who had been developing into a mover and shaker in the WCG.

Before resigning, I had been able to bike to work. Now we needed a second car. The increase in my wife's income allowed me to buy one. This shift in roles was a misalignment with our views on men and women, which were shaped largely by the very traditional and patriarchal views of the WCG. In the transition, my wife opened a bank account to deposit her paychecks and began referring to it as "her" money.

My decision to buy a used but immaculate 1993 white Honda del Sol convertible aggravated the situation. This car was nicer, if not newer, than the 1994 plain gray Mazda Protégé base model that was now her car. In hindsight, deciding to drive a car that was outwardly more appealing than my wife's was not the smartest move I could have made under the circumstances.

But for me, this inexpensive little sports car brightened my perspective considerably. I remember the joy of driving my visiting niece down Santa Monica Boulevard while listening to Sheryl Crow rhapsodize that very road in "All I Wanna Do." It fit the image we had begun to adopt, that of a yuppie couple living the dream in Southern California.

She initially continued to attend the WCG, while I struggled with the decision of where to go next. There were now several other WCG splinter groups, some having formed in a prior schism from the 1970s and others more recently. The older groups were largely composed of people thrust out, carrying baggage created in the disagreements that had led to their ouster. The newer groups were comprised of people leaving voluntarily, with flimsily and hastily constructed theological positions for separating from the "One True Church" and positioning themselves as the new "One True Church." The UCG was the most acceptable of these to me because its ministers had stayed on long enough to prove loyalty to God and yet had left peacefully, rather than forcing the WCG to thrust them out.

In the end, I reluctantly joined the thirty thousand members of the UCG. My decision was influenced by the fact that some of the ministers I had respected had led in its formation, among them David Hulme. David was an intelligent and articulate Englishman who had studied philosophy at the University of Edinburgh and then graduated from Ambassador College. His success in the WCG's international regions had brought him a promotion to the rank of pastor and a move to Pasadena to take responsibility for international print advertising. There he further came to the attention of Herbert W. Armstrong, who promoted him to evangelist with the title of director of communications and public affairs.

It was around that time that David had hired me to assist him. His status as a rising star, with a high degree of political prominence, had given me the confidence and connections to move to Europe and assume an international role in promoting the goals of the WCG. Upon my return to headquarters in the midst of the doctrinal turbulence, I had benefitted from having David as a trusted mentor, seeking his counsel prior to resigning from the WCG. David Hulme had now been elected as the first UCG president, which made the transition easier.

Soon, my ministerial credentials were recognized by the UCG, making me a local church elder, the designation for an unpaid minister. I attended regularly, but found the overt corporate political spin being layered strategically throughout each sermon distasteful. As time went on, the spin gradually increased while I fumed in the back pews. After a few weeks of this, I found something that helped. As 1995 turned into 1996, I began to accompany my fourth-grade students to their art class where they were often frustrated by the expectations of their gifted but somewhat high-strung art teacher. She was just as frustrated at having to work with fourth graders, and was happy to have at least one adult student in the class. By focusing at church on making sketches of the various parts of the building and its people, I engaged parts of my brain I'd probably not used in decades, and this helped take the edge off, providing a release valve for the anger I felt at hearing things from the pulpit that I disagreed with.

My wife stopped attending the WCG soon after I joined the UCG, avoiding church activities and church people altogether. I can't comment on what her reasons were because we no longer discussed our religious beliefs. Most felt very betrayed by its collapse, but having been through something similar, my reaction was not anger; it was, where possible, to stay connected with people across the splintered groups.

This experience was just one more step on my path to recovery from relationship dysfunction. The WCG had undergone a long, slow process toward maturity that was helpful to my development. A toddler needs to be told no frequently, and needs clear, forceful commands and limits, having not yet internalized the principles and understanding needed to be self-directed in positive ways. WCG theology had given me that, but it left its members stuck in a juvenile state, not yet fully mature. For me it had been healthy to regress to a more childlike position and then grow slowly from there. Now my growth was accelerating.

The ministry of the UCG, however, was trying to reestablish loyal obedience—even if in a somewhat kinder, gentler format. I wasn't ready to carry on as though nothing had happened. I had walked away from the role of minister for reasons of conscience. Several fundamental concerns needed to be addressed before I could be convinced that God would bless the efforts of this new organization. The consciences of other UCG ministers might not be bothering them, but that didn't mean the situation wasn't fraught with the same ethical disconnects that I had identified in the WCG.

For example, the tithing system in which members contributed 10 percent (and more) of their gross income to the church enabled the men in leadership positions within the UCG to continue a standard of living that exceeded that of the membership by a significant margin. Despite this, UCG leadership tended to portray themselves as the heroes of the apostasy. However, the seamless formation of the UCG had enabled ministers to keep their jobs, which were dependent on tithe-paying Sabbath observers, many of whom had lost their jobs as a result of having begun keeping it, when they had joined the WCG. Portraying oneself as a hero made it easier to ignore questions one couldn't answer.

The WCG had claimed to be God's True Church, and Joseph Tkach was the duly appointed apostle under God. So what right did anyone have to leave it? Why hadn't we joined the so-called GRUMPs, those who claimed they were "God's Remnant Under Much Persecution" in the WCG, beseeching God to fix things, instead of taking matters into their own hands? It was hard to accept that a church that avoided these questions while ensuring a continuation of the physical well-being and status of the shepherds was really focused on the spiritual growth and development of the sheep.

While these nagging concerns bothered me, my primary focus was paying the bills. And there were more of them to pay as we became more integrated into the mainstream of the Southern California lifestyle. As summer approached, I had to find work during my time off from teaching. A temp agency shared a listing from Disney Interactive. They were looking for someone to test software in Norwegian. I didn't have any experience with Norwegian but felt that with my command of Swedish and experience with technology and software, I could still manage. I applied and got the job.

Within the first three weeks, my multilingual skills helped me isolate software issues that had been missed during the initial English-language testing, performed by more experienced people. This brought me a raise and boosted my confidence, which turned out to be the start of a transformation. During the next school year, I began working through a self-help program on cassette tape by motivation guru Anthony Robbins, *30 Days to Personal Power*.

He convinced me that my beliefs about money were keeping me from earning it. Attitudes and opinions about the way the rich and powerful ignore and even exploit those less fortunate, coupled with the teachings of the WCG and a one-sided reading of certain Scriptures, had led me to associate wealth with greed and oppression. A reasonable person understands the connection between these things but also that they don't necessarily have to go together. In my case, whenever financial success might present itself, my internal discomfort led to subtle, subconscious self-sabotage. I credit Anthony Robbins with my shift in attitude that enabled success. But it was my wife who brought opportunity to my doorstep.

She connected me with the owner of a small software-training company used by the lawyers at her firm. The owner was a recently divorced woman who had been ridiculed by her chauvinistic husband for daring to believe she could be successful at business. After having proved him wrong, she divorced him and was now an avid follower of Anthony Robbins, having participated in several of his retreats. When she learned that I had recently completed his *30 Days to Personal Power* course, she offered me a position.

During my next summer break, I worked for her as a contractor. By the end of the summer, I was offered a training assignment at a midsized reinsurance firm in New York that lasted several months and paid double my teaching salary.

Maxwell's Silver Hammer

I jumped at the offer, and my first trip to New York coincided with the Jewish New Year—Rosh Hashanah. In the WCG, Rosh Hashanah was the Day of Trumpets, announcing the terrible events of the Day of the Lord that would destroy human civilization and decimate mankind. This was symbolized by the seven trumpets of Revelation 8–10 announcing the return of the King of Kings and Lord of Lords. From the rubble, Christ would establish a millennial reign of peace and prosperity, lasting a thousand years. Despite these dire implications, the Holy Days were a highlight for us that usually found a number of congregations coming together for an all-day celebration.

These were mini–family reunions for members of the WCG movement. The pastor of the Long Island UCG congregation was a man whom I had known in Europe.[6] I suspected there would be others there that I had known during my time in the WCG. Having successfully transitioned into the corporate world from being a WCG minister, I was eager to present this new version of myself.

These thoughts went through my head as I stood at an intersection on Thirty-Fourth Street and waited for the pedestrian sign to turn from a red "Don't Walk" to the green "Walk." As the light turned, I took one step into the street before a loud noise to my right, on the uphill side of the crossing, stopped me in my tracks. A city bus had just sideswiped a taxi and I watched, stunned, as it barreled toward the intersection.

Time began to crawl and in the second it took the bus to reach our intersection, I could see the driver's face, twisted into a distorted mix of confusion and fear, through the large window. The look in his eyes was unmistakable. This bus wasn't stopping. The noise from the bus hitting the taxi had kept me out of the intersection, but an overeager Honda Accord driver was not so lucky. I watched in horror as the bus broadsided the Honda amidst a cacophony of

---

6. Paul Suckling, director of SEP Scotland, where I had spent six summers (see *TPotS*, chaps. 5–6).

crashing, squealing tires, and screaming pedestrians. The car spun around before coming to a steaming halt twelve feet from where I had shifted to catlike preparedness—ready for whatever urgent action might be needed. The time warp generated by my adrenaline drove my mind at a speed much faster than the bus.

Years of dedication to a cause bigger than me, a focus on announcing the impending collapse of civilization and the return of Jesus, the conquering King, to usher in a divinely structured utopia, immediately turned my thoughts to saving others. My calling was to warn those further down the street of the danger heading their way at a terrifying speed—a fifteen-ton, out-of-control beast wanting to put its deadly mark upon them. The pace of the bus was glacial compared to my racing thoughts. I envisioned launching my body down the street to shout out the advance warning.

As I was imagining myself as some kind of savior, the bus exploded out of the time warp. My legs, unlike my mental processes and my ambition, were constrained by the physical world, and in a nanosecond, I was no longer ahead of this disaster. My mind raced ahead again, and I realized that an agitated warning would only draw people's attention to me while the bus splattered them like flies—turning me from supposed savior into an accessory to their slaughter.

I aborted my attempt at warning those around me and stood riveted, like those next to me, watching the tragedy unfold. The bus continued down the street on a straight path, catching the next light green by chance before receding into the distance. As it moved farther away, there was nothing I could do to help that others surrounding the damaged Honda weren't already doing, I continued on my way to the Holy Day services.

The bus incident did not dampen the celebration. Yet in my conversations with old and new friends, at lunch between services and on into the evening, I asked if anyone else had heard about it. No one had. On the way back to my corporate apartment, I continued to ponder the disturbing parallels between my morning experience with the bus and the Day of Trumpets.

Arriving, I heard on the news that the bus had traveled about nine blocks, doing extensive damage before eventually running up on a curb and colliding with a building. There were injuries, but remarkably only one fatality. This was partially attributable to the reduced traffic, pedestrian and otherwise, given the Jewish observance of Rosh Hashanah.

There seemed to be a specific reason why I had been present to witness these events. I was certain there was an intended message hidden within the tragedy, but what was it? While drafting this book, I discovered a link to an account of the out-of-control bus (see appendix I). In reviewing the story in the *New York Times* fourteen years after the fact, it struck me (pun sadly intended) that the person killed in the accident was a messenger, making the experience eerily ironic.

One of the reasons for the success of the WCG from the 1930s through the 1980s was the urgency created by the belief in the need to warn the world of the unprecedented cataclysmic events accompanying the imminent return of Jesus Christ. HWA had defined himself as an apostle—"one sent"—a messenger. The WCG's divine responsibility was to deliver a warning message to a dying world. If we failed to do so, their blood would be on our heads.

I had contributed to this effort internationally. One area of involvement was organizing eight-day Feasts behind the Iron Curtain, made possible by covert negotiations with government agencies that bent the rules in order to obtain Western currency. I had operated with the attitude of a divine agent, imbued with an understanding of a divine message not generally understood by humanity at the time.

With my zeal, focus, and confidence fading since leaving Europe, I drew inspiration from my experience with the bus. It highlighted one of the biblical roles we had believed we were fulfilling in the WCG, that of the "Watchman."[7] God wanted us to warn the world before "the great and terrible" Day of the Lord, and the life-threatening event that happened right in front of me on Rosh Hashanah—while I was powerless to warn people about it—was significant.

Having solved my immediate financial problems, God was waking me up to the more important issue of warning the world about the imminent apocalypse. And yet this dramatic event had brought home the inherent challenge in trying to warn people from whom you are completely disconnected, and with whom you have no relationship whatsoever. Some of us in the WCG—my father being a prominent example in my life—seemed to eagerly anticipate the "rod of iron" coming down like Maxwell's hammer upon their heads.[8] This had always

---

7. Ezekiel 3 and 33, and elsewhere.
8. Psalm 2:9; Revelation 2:27; 12:5; and 19:15.

bothered me, and now it bothered me more than ever. The timing of this was important in light of what was happening in the UCG.

Dizzy Miss Lizzy

Dissatisfaction had been building over David Hulme's imperial style as president. Pasadena was the geographical focal point. The battle lines were drawn around the Great Commission to preach the gospel as a witness. David Hulme was a major proponent of this approach while the bulk of the UCG leadership, being from the regional pastor structure, wanted a focus on Christ's admonition to Peter to "feed my sheep."[9]

Living temporarily in New York, focused on career success, these rumblings from Pasadena seemed to reflect nothing but a political tempest in a teapot. As Christmas 1997 approached, I flew my wife to New York for a week of sightseeing. As we stood before the twin towers of the World Trade Center, marveling at their height, I thought of them as monuments to the global economic system, symbolized in the book of Revelation as Babylon the Great, which would be destroyed at the time of Christ's return.[10] We decided against the long holiday-season line for the ride to the top. My extended assignment would allow us to tour the inside and top of the twin towers in the near future. How could I know at the time that these towers would soon become symbolic of a global religious struggle?

And yet, the out-of-control bus became an illustration in a sermon I gave in Pasadena. My inability to warn others was a sign that we needed to regain our focus on warning the world, but with a twist. My sermon also addressed the similarities and differences between Matthew 24:14 and Matthew 28:19–20 in response to the political background noise in our church. The former was a touchstone Scripture for the WCG on its Great Commission to witness by warning the world, which appealed to the "doing God's Work" contingent. The latter was an even clearer mandate to make disciples, which aligned more closely with the "feed My sheep" crowd. The distinction here was that the

---

9.   John 21:15–17 records Christ repeating this instruction a numerically significant three times.

10.   Revelation 18 and elsewhere.

WCG message was not primarily intended to result in disciples. The warning message was a witness against those who weren't going to listen, freeing us from responsibility for their fate.

My reflections on the event in New York suggested a more integrated approach to these two activities: John the Baptist had warned; Christ had saved. This was aligned more closely with what my experience as a minister in Germany had taught me about being our brother's keeper, including a broader definition of who our brother is. A tendency of WCG members and ministers to abdicate personal responsibility for contributing to solutions to society's problems was a longtime pet peeve of mine. Many resorted all too readily to the cop-out answer that problems would only get worse until Christ returned. This conveniently covered up that the speaker either had no solution to the problem, or was unwilling to go to the effort to implement it. My New York experience with the bus further shifted my focus to finding meaningful ways to educate people about the calamities ahead, rather than assuming they were destined not to listen. After all, Christ expanded our conception of who our brother is, as well as our responsibility to him.

Many listeners praised this sermon, but some in the audience, including Mark Kaplan, seemed to feel that my message had been politically motivated.

I had known Mark Kaplan ever since he was my academic advisor upon my arrival at Ambassador College years earlier.[11] He was a well-educated minister of Jewish background whom I had always liked and looked up to as a sterling example. His grasp of the Bible and rabbinical traditions, coupled with a readily apparent humility, had led me to view him with a great deal of respect. But he had recently launched into an angry attack on David Hulme during a discussion in the church parking lot after our weekly Sabbath service. I had listened politely, but was unnerved by the interaction. Mark suddenly seemed to view me as some kind of political enemy.

Mark had exchanged pleasantries with me after the sermon before lodging a complaint against me to the regional pastor in the area. Without informing me, much less getting my side of the story, the UCG removed the sermon from its library and me from the speaking list.[12] I was floored.

---

11. See *TPotS*, chap. 5, "Blue Jay Way."
12. I informed Mark Kaplan that I was planning to include him in this section and invited him to review it and provide input, but he declined.

Despite my involvement in a variety of important areas within the WCG, I had never been considered a political player. My sermon was intended to be a nonpolitical encouragement to look to the Bible to bridge the perceived gap in our understanding, and to get on with the work of both preaching the gospel and feeding the flock in unity and with a renewed zeal. My goal was to assist members (and ministers) in focusing on the spiritual implications of Christ's desire to find his servants "so doing" across all of these activities.[13]

Unlike with the issues behind the split between the UCG and the WCG, ample middle ground seemed to be available on this point. Apparently, others couldn't find it. David Hulme was removed as president of the UCG and soon formed his own group.

During the split that resulted, members worldwide—but especially in the Pasadena/Los Angeles area—were forced to take sides. As had been the case with the formation of the UCG, whether you stayed or left, you were once again taking a spiritual position and making a political statement. It was another painful spiritual divorce, forced upon members who had just been through one during the formation of the UCG.

Forced to make a choice, it was a natural decision for me to align with David Hulme. In my view, he stood for a focus on "doing the Work," whereas his opponents seemed to be building a structure for the benefit of the "old boys' club." What convinced me were David's initial communications, in which he voiced a willingness to deploy a nonpaid ministry in order to spend the tithe on preaching the gospel.

I was very conscious of the need for the ministry to gain insight into their culpability in the collapse of the WCG. The ministry as a whole hadn't been forced to walk away from their salaries over the issue of the Sabbath during the formation of the UCG, but with David Hulme's departure, a subset appeared willing to do so.[14]

In the newly formed church, led by David Hulme and titled "the Church of God, an International Association," I gave a beefed-up version of the sermon

---

13. Matthew 24:46; Luke 12:43.
14. This was written fourteen years after the events, based on personal recollection. As with the split from the WCG, I avoided involvement in the debate at the time, making an independent choice on where to attend. In doing research for this book, I located and reviewed, for the first time, an interview with David Hulme. It is included as appendix II.

with the story about the bus. It was turned into a video and played in all of David's churches. The response was very positive. For the first time in a year, I had a platform to preach to an audience that was open and eager to hear the insights God was granting me.

Then I was fired.

Not from the church.

From my job.

I remember the pain of yet again being severed from something to which I had devoted myself—this time even more abruptly and against my will. There was also the devastation of having to return home to inform my wife that, once again, our financial future was at risk. I broke down in tears on the long flight home from New York.

I Am the Walrus!

One reason this affected me so powerfully, was because the firing was unjust and unwarranted. My boss (the owner of the company) and her client used a very minor incident as an opportunity to quickly resolve a project budget problem. I felt my boss had chosen me as the sacrificial lamb because I had offered to bring in a Danish company as a client but wanted to benefit from the deal. She had been offended at my presumptuousness.

The injustice bothered me less than my recognition that it was due to my tendency to come across as arrogant and uncooperative. Years of believing I had unique insights of divine origin unavailable to my fellow humans contributed to this. Coworkers, managers, and supervisors were often irritated or even threatened by their interpretation of my attitudes and perspectives.

A typical response to this by those of us trained in the WCG—or what was now becoming known, due to the growing number of splinter groups, as the "Church of God" (COG) movement—was to believe that we were being persecuted for righteousness's sake.[15] This was a cop-out. I was trying to look in

---

15. WCG splinter groups had the name "Church of God" in common, and were differentiated legally, and among the members, by descriptors such as "United," "Global," and "International." Members used initials (UCG) or the descriptor (Global) to refer to these churches. David Hulme's choice seemed a clever use of British understatement, establishing a primacy by not using such a descriptor. If this was indeed his purpose, it backfired, as nonmembers avoided referring to his church as "the Church of God"—calling it "Hulme's group."

the mirror to figure out what changes we needed to make to stop the pattern from recurring. But such change is difficult, and progress was slow.

Another reason I reacted emotionally to being fired was that I was genuinely worried about my marriage. I was trying to improve our standard of living in the hopes that my wife would view my success in this area as evidence that I cared about her and to enable me to provide her with more of the things that were important to her. On the long plane ride home, I imagined the discussion I would be having with her and realized any remaining respect for me would be vaporized by this latest setback.

Not one to wallow in defeat, I was already laying out a plan by the time the flight landed. I had learned the ropes of this business and would pursue the Danish client I had tried to bring to my former employer before she fired me. I reached out to one of my fellow trainers who had also had enough of the antics and approach of the owner of the company; he let me know that should I be able to land this client, he would join me. I arranged to fly him to Denmark to scope out the project, and together we won the business.

In an embarrassingly cocky display of ego, I named my new company Business Education and Software Training (BEAST). This wicked little bit of humor irreverently mocked the Beast referenced in the book of Revelation who combines the power of religion and commerce to fight Christ at his return. My visit to New York, and the connection between the World Trade Center and what the book of Revelation calls Babylon the Great was occupying my thoughts. But there were other reasons for the name as well.

Naming my company BEAST was a defiant celebration of not having my paycheck tied to my faith, and no longer living off the sacrificial donations of the faithful. It was also my own strange way of thanking God for blessing my efforts to obtain a higher standard of living and further distancing myself from the COG ministry. Naming my business BEAST Inc. was a public rejection of the limitations of fear and control and an ironic expression of a more confident faith.

My business venture was immediately successful, as I added a couple of clients and additional contractors to deliver these services. One of these contractors was my wife, as a part-time editor. We were suddenly earning an annual income in the six figures. But it wasn't all rainbows and sunshine. My insistence on investing this money in the business, rather than enabling a spending spree, led to arguments about money. The tension reached a climax one day, in the wood-paneled hallway of our little cottage.

This location already had bad Karma because she had wanted to rip out the paneling, and I had refused, believing it would result in having to replace the interior wall. According to WCG-defined marital roles, the woman might voice her opinion or perspective, but the man—the head of the house in God's authority structure—would make the decision. Neither of us really believed in this model any more. She was as unwilling to submit as I was to continue claiming divine authority. Yet I had more experience with home construction, real estate values, and what we could and couldn't afford.

So I pleaded with her to be patient with my efforts to get onto a more solid financial footing, one in which I could accommodate her requests without taking on more debt. She accused me of not keeping past promises related to money and held me responsible for her general dissatisfaction. With increasing intensity and earnestness, I asked her—begged her—to be reasonable. She doubled down, demanding that I admit to and take responsibility for things that either were not true or were completely outside my control.

I knew I was doing the best I could, and I can still remember the painful rush of emotions and the anguish in my voice as I begged her to believe my intentions and motives, only to see her face grow ever colder, harsh and stony. An air of condemnation permeated the narrow, confined space. In frustration, I blurted out, "How can you be so cold?"

She said nothing in response, her face like chiseled rock, conjuring up the image of Pharaoh's heart being hardened. She was stubborn and unrelenting while I faced a God-given mandate to reach agreement with her. I burst into tears in front of her, which I can't recall ever having done previously.

Her expression changed from stubbornness to disgust.

Suddenly, I realized she no longer loved me and that I was going to lose her. Something inside me snapped.

I collapsed on the floor in what I can only describe as a hopeless puddle of despair.

The seconds seemed to drag on for hours as I lay first howling and then whimpering, unable to get up and with the frightening realization that I was having a nervous breakdown.

It was an eternity that may have lasted from one to ten minutes—I honestly cannot say.

During this time, she stood motionless.

In utter humiliation, I slowly struggled to stand, while she stared at me in disgust and pity. I was overcome with a deep sadness, realizing that I was not the man I thought I was. I was vulnerable in a way I had never imagined, susceptible to a mental breakdown that left me helpless.

Once it let go of me, this intense emotional attack began to fade almost as quickly as it had hit. Yet it had stamped an indelible impression into my psyche. The feeling that I was going to be unable to save my marriage was hard to shake. Neither of us ever mentioned this episode again, but it had changed the nature of our relationship for the worse.

Perhaps influenced by this experience, I began to worry that I lacked the business training needed to manage the legal, tax, accounting, and human resource / hiring issues I was now facing. I was leery of hiring experts in these fields given my own inexperience and my generally negative view of human nature. Those more experienced in business than I was would take advantage of me. Even though I was experiencing success, I was haunted by a fear of failure and a general distrust of my fellow man.

When a friend told me about a corporate position he wanted me to interview for, I jumped at the chance. A salary and the opportunity to get an inside view of the world of business were equally important. The most important benefit may well have been the boost to my ego. A large corporation with offices in downtown LA wanted to hire me. I might actually be what I was pretending to be.

The position was with CB Richard Ellis, which had recently achieved the status of the world's largest commercial real estate services firm when CB (Coldwell Banker) Commercial acquired Richard Ellis International Limited in May 1998. I joined the Madison Advisory services group, a boutique consulting company that had also been acquired.

While there, I saw an opportunity to turn a minor product line into a software consulting practice. The challenge had some similarity to one I had faced in founding my own business, so although it was a stretch for me to suddenly become an expert on corporate real estate software, I threw myself into the opportunity with confidence.

Money (That's What I Want)

When I shifted my focus to a corporate career, BEAST died a gradual death. While it did, I was double-dipping financially. And the timing of my entry into the corporate world coincided with Y2K mania. This was the fear that the earlier programming practice of using only the last two digits of the year was going to cause a systems meltdown and a mini-Armageddon at the turn of the millennium.

By now, the evidence that many in the U.S. tend to react with fear and hype to doomsday scenarios should not be surprising. Knowing this didn't stop me from searching for answers to why prophecies, which were clearly overdue, had not yet come to pass. The bus incident in New York, and now Y2K, brought these questions to the forefront of my awareness. I embraced them in semi-ironic ways, such as naming my company BEAST or joking about launching a turn-of-the-century cruise on the International Date Line to escape the Y2K meltdown. But the sense that the fulfillment of prophecy was closer than we could imagine was always present.

In the meantime, information technology professionals experienced a lucrative boost in income, and my career was springboarded by the brouhaha. CB Richard Ellis (CBRE) had been using homegrown software that was not Y2K compliant to serve its clients. Initially, a large part of my job was to assist CBRE's biggest corporate customers in finding and implementing an alternative to soon-to-be-obsolete software. CBRE's Lease Administration software solution was named Asset Control for Executives, or ACE. I created a tongue-in-cheek summary of the situation and called them to say, "There's a new version of ACE; it's called Replace."

And just like that, I was suddenly progressing nicely in a career with a respected company. A promotion and a raise followed this initiative. Next, I was invited to take on a challenging assignment with a leading consulting group on a prestigious project.

Chris Corpuz, a managing director in the Madison Advisory group, was a young, Harvard-educated hotshot. He, along with a senior leader in another division, had brokered CBRE's involvement in what was called the Corporate Real Estate Portfolio Alliance. Companies like Microsoft, Fidelity Investments, State Farm Insurance, and Boeing, among others, had agreed to fund a yearlong research project to benchmark best practices across their sizable real estate portfolios. Wharton School of Business; UC, Berkeley; and Cambridge University were involved, as well as a variety of real estate industry experts from companies like CBRE, Johnson Controls, and Jones Lang LaSalle. Chris Corpuz had originally planned to have two consultants from an outside boutique shop perform the technology research, but when they burned through the entire budget just doing the interviews with the participant companies, my manager suggested me as an alternative.

I jumped at the chance to be involved, but soon found that the consultants resented having been pulled off the project and were less than cooperative at passing on the results of their initial research. When the documentation finally arrived, the information across the participant companies was inconsistent and incomplete. There was not enough time to turn it into the presentation Chris was scheduled to deliver at an executive summit at Harvard University. To make matters worse, my skills at using PowerPoint were a bit lacking. I wasted time futzing with the software instead of turning the research into a compelling presentation. When the stakeholders began asking me for a draft, my stall tactics did not help the rookie's reputation with the A-players.

Early one morning, on the tail end of an all-nighter on the Harvard presentation, I had to admit I was in over my head. How had I, in such a short time, become responsible for CBRE's contribution to a major, corporate-funded research project on a subject in which I was a novice? My degree was in theology from a now-defunct college while the professionals heading up the other research areas had advanced degrees and years of deep experience in their respective areas of responsibility. They had arrived where they were through hard work and by consistently delivering results. I had stumbled largely unprepared into this role. I was way out of my depth—and the stakes were high.

What I did have going for me was a liberal arts education, a spiritual foundation, and international experience. I applied myself diligently, worked to understand, and questioned everything from the perspective of an outsider. So, at 4:30 a.m., with a looming deadline, I crawled under my desk to pray to God for assistance. This was partially desperation and partially due to my firm belief that it was God's will for me to be successful in business.

I drew inspiration from God's rescue of Israel from slavery. His plan was to transform them from a nation of slaves making mud bricks for their taskmasters into a nation of kings and priests. God gave them the Sabbath, a day of rest, as a sign between Him and His people. Under my desk at CB Richard Ellis, I asked God for assistance with creating a presentation for an executive session at Harvard that would help me rise in my career the way He had elevated them. I got off my knees determined not to be intimidated by the research conducted by my peers or by my distinguished audience, all of whom had much more business experience.

And I had an inspired idea.

I would make the presentation as simple as possible, as though it was to be delivered to my fourth graders. I would also weave in humor and simple examples to tell the story. This allowed me to summarize the more basic elements of what I had learned and uncovered rather than stretching to achieve more advanced findings. In football terms, I was going to punt, and I was going to do it proudly.

To say Chris was disappointed with the presentation I created would be an understatement. He was kicking himself for not having had more experienced help, but it was too late. So he decided to have me present the material instead of him, which I presume was to distance himself from me and my work. This was actually good news. Ambassador College had many weak areas in its liberal arts curriculum, but public speaking was not one of them. We had been grilled and drilled in all aspects of presenting and teaching, and I had fifteen years of international experience in presentations of all kinds, including almost two years of full-time teaching.

When the day arrived, I was scheduled as the last presenter. I watched the other research chairs give their presentations. The executives were engaged. They challenged the speakers on their conclusions and assumptions. I began to get nervous. Chris, who sat next to me, was fidgeting. He leaned over a few minutes prior to my presentation and stated that due to his flight schedule he would have to leave right after introducing me to the group. He stood up, mumbled an apologetic introduction, focused on his need to catch a flight, and headed for the door.

As it shut behind him, I confidently delivered my overview and a couple of jokes. The jokes drew the audience into the presentation, and I relaxed as I spoke directly to them—not at them, or above their heads. They appreciated my direct, friendly, and colloquial approach. As I proceeded through my simple slides, they welcomed my simplification of a complex topic. Rather than debating my findings, as they had done with the other presenters, they were agreeing and contributing ideas, advancing the limited initial conclusions that I had been able to summarize and articulate visually in PowerPoint. They were excited by the collaborative approach, and the presentation was very well received.

I had scored a home run and driven in the others who had been stuck on their bases.

The organizers and participants, who had previously treated me with a degree of condescension and suspicion, congratulated me warmly after the event. On the elevator down to the lobby and the big celebratory dinner, I stood next to the director of the International Center for Facilities, with offices in London, Paris, and San Francisco. He had always reminded me of Winston Churchill. In his thick British accent, he proclaimed, "I'd like to congratulate you on a presentation of absolute clarity."

I had arrived.

With A Little Luck

He that is of the opinion money will do everything may well be suspected of doing everything for money.

– BENJAMIN FRANKLIN, FROM POOR RICHARD'S ALMANACK

The success of the Harvard presentation turbocharged what was suddenly a growing professional reputation. Chris, upon hearing the praise of his customers and the colleagues he respected, reembraced me as "his boy." I was officially granted the mantle of technology chair for the Corporate Real Estate Portfolio Alliance. As a result, I continued working with the Alliance executives, their company representatives, and the very bright people in the other research disciplines. While delivering our individual findings at a variety of venues, such as a workshop at Boeing and a round of presentations at Sun Microsystems, we developed a coherent story. Soon, I was a nationally known expert in my field, cited in several publications, publishing a white paper in a respected business journal.[1]

---

1. This article, coauthored by David Nelson, "Management Information Systems for Corporate Real Estate," appeared in the *Journal of Corporate Real Estate* 2, no. 2 (2000): 154–69.

I Wanna Be Your Man

My progress in the business world accelerated as I focused on the intersection of technology and strategy. Next, CBRE's chief information officer (CIO) sponsored my acceptance into the Regional Leadership Forum (RLF)—a one-year training program put on by the Society for Information Management (SIM). SIM was a CIOs-only club, open to RLF graduates. I was a willing sponge and thrived on the experience, insights, and skills that I was accumulating. After completing the program, I became a member of SIM and began to rub shoulders with CIOs and other technology executives from a variety of organizations. I won an important system selection and implementation engagement with Sun Microsystems.

To keep economic score, I created a spreadsheet to manage our family's finances and track our net worth. It captured our assets, the house in Arizona, our house in Pasadena, our respective retirement funds, bank accounts, and the stocks that I had started buying. Nineteen ninety-eight's entry was a net worth of $85,500, which grew by 70 percent in 1999 to $145,540. But I couldn't please my wife.

CBRE moved my office from LA to Irvine, near Newport Beach, ninety-plus minutes away. The decision of where to move was a painful one because my wife and I disagreed on that all-important real estate aspect—location. I picked a house in a previously depressed area because of the potential for it to increase in value. She told me that if I bought it I'd be living in it by myself.

She wanted a house by the beach. This might have also worked from a property appreciation perspective, but the homes she wanted weren't within our price range. In the end, we settled on a small two-bedroom, one-and-a-half-bathroom house with a humble kitchen in Long Beach. This was LA's harbor town, with some of Southern California's least desirable beaches, which would still be just outside of walking distance.

I made my peace with it because of a rooftop deck from which you could imagine, but not quite see, the beach. With its beachfront pedestrian area, bike paths, beach volleyball, restaurants, and an Olympic-sized pool for swimming, it represented an upgraded, pleasant lifestyle. This house would also appreciate nicely, so giving in to my wife's version of a dream home was actually not a bad move, all things considered.

A chunky raise followed the move to our new offices, and since wearing a suit while driving without air-conditioning in Southern California had become unbearable, I decided now was the time to get myself a car with air-conditioning. Following through on a recommendation from our realtor, I managed to get a new Mustang convertible at the price usually reserved for corporate leasing programs. With a temporarily happy wife in a new house by the beach and a new Mustang convertible to drive along Pacific Coast Highway to my office, the California dream seemed to be coming true.

Underneath the surface of our improved lifestyle, however, was a growing tension about finances. Materialism is insidious: the more we had, the more we both wanted. We were doing well, but the house had been at the top of our price range. The transformation from idealistic volunteers to yuppies was rapid, and whether it was our money, or just her money, we were spending it as fast as we made it.

For the moment, success kept my nervousness at bay. In the process of winning the engagement with Sun Microsystems, I had outbid the respected consulting firm, Deloitte & Touche. They responded by recruiting me, offering a significant pay increase, along with the chance to work with "the best and the brightest." At the same time, I was offered an even better option as an industry expert with the federal government in Washington, DC, reporting to the CIO of the General Services Administration, at the GS-13 level, a prestigious position.

This was a dramatic transformation. Suddenly, I had two attractive offers, each representing a highly desirable career path, and both paying six figures. As I pondered the decision, my wife signaled her refusal to move to DC, which was puzzling to me since she worked for the federal district court in LA, and the folks in DC were offering to help her with contacts to find a comparable position there. I was torn. The position in DC paid better, and I would be reporting high up in the federal government. Although it was tempting to try to talk my wife into it, I had two concerns, both related to working for the government.

The first was that some of the folks I met during my interviews reminded me of zombies. When I asked the CIO what my initial responsibilities would be, he said, "Attend some meetings, and make some recommendations." He may have been trying to reassure me that it would not be too difficult or stressful, but it had the opposite effect. I imagined being sucked into a vortex of inertia in which I would not grow personally or professionally.

The second concern was due to my belief in belonging to a spiritual kingdom not of this world.[2] Though I was cheeky enough to label my company BEAST Inc., working for the government was outside my comfort zone. Revelation 18 calls the intersection of government and commerce "Babylon the Great," and says that "all the nations had drunk the wine of the wrath of her fornication." God proclaims, "come out of her, my people, that ye be not partakers of her sins, and that ye receive not of her plagues.[3]

Still, if my wife had been willing to relocate to DC, I would have chosen that route, adding proximity to the center of political power to my rising financial fortunes. In this regard, it was tempting to compare myself to Joseph and Daniel, both of whom had been very connected to God while obtaining high positions in Egypt under Pharaoh, and Babylon under Nebuchadnezzar, respectively. At the time, it seemed that God was granting me favor for some yet unknown reason that He would unveil in his own good time. The position in DC, reporting to the CIO of the General Services Administration, appeared to be the path God wanted me to take. And yet I knew that if I insisted on what I wanted as opposed to what my wife wanted, my marriage would end in divorce, as had the marriage of my parents.

So I convinced myself that the Deloitte opportunity was more in line with where I perceived myself to be in my career. At Deloitte, I would be working with talented colleagues and would become a more accomplished and capable individual, which God could use even more effectively in the future. And with Deloitte, I was now a professional—a management consultant with a respected firm. My transformation from minister to business professional was complete.

---

2.   John 18:36: "Jesus answered, My kingdom is not of this world: if my kingdom were of this world, then would my servants fight, that I should not be delivered to the Jews: but now my kingdom is not from hence."

3.   Revelation 18:1–5: "And after these things I saw another angel come down from heaven, having great power; and the earth was lightened with his glory. And he cried mightily with a strong voice, saying, Babylon the great is fallen, is fallen, and is become the habitation of devils, and the hold of every foul spirit, and a cage of every unclean and hateful bird. For all nations have drunk of the wine of the wrath of her fornication, and the kings of the earth have committed fornication with her, and the merchants of the earth are waxed rich through the abundance of her delicacies. And I heard another voice from heaven, saying, Come out of her, my people, that ye be not partakers of her sins, and that ye receive not of her plagues. For her sins have reached unto heaven, and God hath remembered her iniquities."

Old Brown Shoe

I had escaped from the corrupt economic system in force within the WCG. My life was now aligned with the American Dream. I could now shift my attention to catching up with the pillars of cloud and fire.[4] It seemed as if they were quite far ahead, up in the distance, but I had begun to discern the direction they had taken. The path forward, however, appeared to be a lonely one.

There had been no right side in the breakup of the WCG. None of the groups had the answers to the questions posed by the shattering of the hermetically sealed set of beliefs caused by the split of the church. Even so, in my discussions with others, they all seemed certain that they had made the right decisions.

Those who stayed with the WCG seemed to go along with the organization's historical claim to divine authority to interpret and deliver God's message for today. But their revised interpretations destroyed their claim to exclusive divine understanding and authority. Those who left the WCG to form new organizations also generally appealed to the divine authority claimed by HWA and the WCG, but this was not transferrable to anyone except HWA's authorized successor, which they were not. Some bolstered their succession claim by proof texting and applying obscure Scriptures to current events, Nostradamus style, while others deployed a murky, unexplainable theology in the form of vague political slogans in sermons.

My personal experience had been that when I actively sought God's will through diligent prayer, study of His Word, and fasting, I had repeatedly gained what I believed were clear answers. Health problems had often helped keep me honest in this regard, as I had wrestled within myself. Sadly, with my health issues largely behind me, and having resigned from a corrupt version of God's one true church, it was easier to sit on the sidelines and watch the spectacle of the collapse of the WCG and the creation of the splinter groups than to actively and diligently engage with God to seek out His will.

---

4. Ancient Israel, under Moses, followed pillars of cloud and fire through the desert, en route to the Promised Land. In the previous volume I explained how this metaphor, which signifies closeness to God, and a willingness to follow His lead, was important to me.

At the same time, I did spend a lot of time pondering the question of what God was doing. There were no answers available at that time and no good decision available, so I chose not to make one. The role the COG movement played in my life was slowly receding, while my new path was paying off physically. I had left the WCG to avoid getting lost in mainstream religion, and now I was enjoying closer alignment with mainstream America. My newfound success in business was delivering both financial rewards and greater respectability. Like Tevye in *Fiddler on the Roof*, I had asked God if He would be so kind as to make me "just a little rich" and—against all odds—He seemed to be saying, with a Jewish shrug, "Sure, why not?"

We'd cleared the Y2K hurdle, and in the year 2000, the Internet gold rush was at its peak. The NASDAQ was pushing 5,000 and the dot-com boom was turning America into a nation of trickle-down believers, chasing the riches offered to them through their online stock-trading accounts. We were reading about "the Millionaire Next Door," and even billionaires were being minted regularly. Many who weren't at the top of the corporate feeding troughs were quitting their jobs to become day traders. As the rising tide of the tech bubble floated my boat, my material success was in rather stark contrast to many of my former colleagues. My growing financial independence and my increasing confidence empowered me to challenge the self-proclaimed COG leadership

In my mind, the UCG had already failed my personal litmus test; a political struggle at the top had resulted in me being silenced for speaking the truth. As a result, I opted to affiliate with the group headed up by the UCG's former president, David Hulme. But a disturbing trend was evident there as well. Shortly before leaving the UCG, one minister (David Hulme's brother-in-law) had spoken out against what he termed the "mind control" taking place in the UCG. Yet he was guilty of this within the new group. Believing he was right seemed to justify the same kind of doctrinal clampdown he had decried within the UCG.

After two big, painful church splits, I was not willing to simply go along. I tried to broach this topic in a variety of ways, privately and in the messages I delivered in church. The sermon I gave on Pentecost 2000, if I have my dates correct, is a good example. In the sermon titled "Change, the Church, and the Comforter," I emphasized the need to follow the Holy Spirit by reading relevant Scriptures in context. Jesus's emphasis was unmistakable. His church and its individual members should look to the Spirit for guidance, and He held them accountable for doing so. The Spirit, not men or human authority, was the source of guidance.

The reaction of the leadership, ministry, and most of the membership in Hulme's group was uncomfortable silence. Following the lead of the Spirit was apparently not something they were interested in doing. COG leaders were able to identify pulpit-driven mind control in other groups, but not in their own, and members wanted an authority figure to tell them dogmatically what to think. God had allowed, or perhaps even caused, these splits. We were being forced to learn a lesson common to spiritual seekers throughout history—God operates outside religious orthodoxy. The religion of Christianity had long ago succumbed to so much corruption and schism that those individuals most connected to God could be found any- and everywhere, but could not be identified as being within any specific group.

I was not bothered by my declining reputation in the COG universe. The out-of-control bus on the streets of New York on Rosh Hashanah, which had literally killed the messenger, was a mini-wake-up sign for me. The death bus of the Great Tribulation and the Day of the Lord was just up the road a bit, and it was coming for all of humanity. This was the beginning of the end of my Jonah phase. God had helped me put my life back together in a way that was more mature, more useful to Him. He wanted people of faith who were able to make their faith work for them in the real world. People who were lights that He could display prominently, rather than curiosities He might do well to hide.

God had no time for those whose focus was on creating boundaries, defining who was in and who wasn't.

Spirits of Ancient Egypt

Despite the growing tension between me and those in David Hulme's group, in 2000 I kept the Feast of Tabernacles with them in Jordan. Prior to the feast, my wife and I went on a weeklong excursion to Egypt, touring all the main attractions, including the pyramids, Valley of the Kings, Luxor, Abu Simbel, and more.

My wife's interest in the pyramids had been the driving force behind the trip to Egypt. My step-uncle, who had been doing our taxes for us, was an avid student of the pyramids and shared books with her about the many theories related to them. These outlined the amazing evidence of a superior civilization with knowledge and understanding that even today we struggle to replicate in some ways. I was not overly interested in those theories, but once we arrived, I was drawn—like so many travelers before—into the mystery represented by the ancient civilization and the unanswered questions about the construction of the monuments. There did not seem to be a logical explanation for how and why they were built, but our tour guide provided some fascinating perspectives. His amazing grasp of the history of Egypt brought fact and context to bear on our visit.

Over the better part of a week, he explained the development of hieroglyphics and how they were used in tombs, such as in the Valley of the Kings. In contrast, he felt that the strange writings in one of the oldest step pyramids described energy patterns that may have been tapped to build the later and greater pyramids. After that pyramid, no subsequent ones had any writings in the inner chambers. He therefore believed the pyramids were not tombs at all but that they functioned as giant astrological instruments wielded by the priesthood who were the learned class at the time. This correlated with specific hieroglyphics the guide showed us elsewhere, in which the ancient Egyptians showed themselves capable of calculating the exact square footage of the land of Egypt, a feat of mind-boggling complexity. The only way we know that this could have been accomplished would have been to use coordinates a great distance away, such as could only be obtained by coordinated instruments in other parts of the world.

My mind worked overtime on the puzzle of how these edifices, and the society they represented, aligned with the events of the Bible and others not featured in the Bible. I reflected on what I had learned from history, biblical archaeology, my tour of Israel, and participation in the City of David project.

A number of ideas and possible connections presented themselves, one of which was related to discussions on the Tower of Babel, and the city of Jericho. I had been curious about remains uncovered near Jericho, which I had viewed in 1981. They had opened questions that nobody could answer to my satisfaction at the time. Now I was getting a sense that the answers were tantalizingly close.

So I paid close attention, with an eye to piecing together the puzzle of how these monuments fit in to where and how to get to the pillar of cloud and fire today.

This further opening to a new interpretation of history corresponded to my growing disillusionment with the COG movement. It was locked into ideas introduced by HWA and others decades earlier. Many of these were myopic and had been disproved by subsequent events and discoveries. I had a growing willingness to consider the evidence objectively, without forcing it into a predetermined mental framework.

It would take years of travel and study before these ideas could mature into anything worth sharing in print. During our tour of Egypt, one of the experiences that contributed to this maturing occurred on what was advertised as a four-star cruise on the Nile. Upon boarding the boat, we were struck by how small and relatively dirty it was. As we wound our way through several narrow passageways, and down a dank, carpeted staircase, which had seen better days, the sounds and smells of the engine began to invade our senses.

By choosing one of the less expensive rooms, assuming that anything on a four-star liner would be acceptable, we were trapped on the bottom deck nestled right up against the noise and fumes emanating from a rather loud and noxious engine. The room itself was cramped, and it was difficult to get in and out of the tiny shower and bathroom. To get in, I had to wedge myself between the toilet and open door of the shower, then step sideways to enter the tiny chamber. In doing so, it was virtually impossible not to step on the sticky caulk surrounding the drain. Aside from it sticking to your feet, the embedded dirt and hair from the prior occupant was but one reason the bathroom was unpleasant to use.

I had visited some forty countries by this time, and in the Caribbean, Israel, behind the Iron Curtain, and most recently in Mexico, I had become acquainted with that exquisite traveling companion known as Pharaoh's revenge. Here, on the Nile, we were on Pharaoh's home turf, and I was determined to show proper deference. Egypt was just the first leg of a journey that would continue to Jordan for the Feast of Tabernacles, and I wanted to avoid ruining my trip by foolishly thinking I wouldn't succumb to it. My caution had paid off so far. We had traversed Egypt and visited pyramids, tombs, and monuments to the gods, and I had not been forced to bend my knees to their oppression.

But on the second day of the cruise, I drank some juice that must have been reconstituted with water from the Nile. Within the space of a couple of hours, I was hit by a wave of agony. The debilitating stomach cramps were worse than anything I had ever experienced. Within the space of a couple of hours, I had become seriously ill and began running a high fever.

My experience was psychedelic in its intensity as the dreaded bacteria affected my mind and perceptions as well as my body. I soon became intimately acquainted with that sticky drain on the floor of the shower; it was more appealing to face than the abominable toilet bowl since I was now exploding at both ends. Without anything safe to drink, I knew I was becoming dehydrated as well. In the darkness of the night, in that tiny room next to the pounding and grinding of the engines, in the dank inner bowels of a vessel taking me deeper into the heart of Egypt, that proverbial and perennial nemesis of the people of God, I began to wonder if this was where I was going to die.

My wife obtained some pills from the ship's doctor designed to reverse stomach ailments. These I pounded back—taking perhaps more than the maximum recommended dosage—and after sixteen awful hours, the worst of it had subsided. However, for the next thirteen days (three in Egypt and ten in Jordan), the ghost of Pharaoh haunted me, and it took a couple of weeks back in the States for me to fully recover.

Probably due to the sermon I had delivered earlier (about the Holy Spirit being our teacher), I had not been invited to speak at the Feast in Jordan. This was the first time since well before my ordination to the ministry more than a decade earlier that I had no speaking assignment during the Feast. I had taken it in stride, believing that focusing more exclusively on my wife would help our relationship. But we were both equally frustrated at having to listen to sermon after sermon designed to bring straying sheep back into line with the Government of God as practiced in His True Church. These seemed designed to shut down any openness to the kinds of insight I had been advocating. In Hulme's group, there was no consideration of the possibility that we might *not* already have all the answers or that God might be trying to get our attention to move us in a different direction.

Readers will likely recognize the typical male tendency to be blissfully ignorant of just how empty the life of a female companion can be when her significant other is happily pursuing his own interests. I had been confident that my wife was in agreement with me, if not openly supportive. More recently, I had assumed she was content to enjoy our newfound freedom to pursue our own interests in parallel.

The truth was that my heart was in need of some serious softening. I had critical, painful lessons ahead if I was ever going to find my way back to the pillar of cloud and fire. I was blind, and God was going to use my relationship with my wife to begin the process of opening my eyes. I apparently wouldn't learn any other way.

I'm Looking Through You

My wife and I agreed on one thing at this point: the pursuit of material success. However, there was a difference in the way we approached this goal. While I pursued a lucrative new career, she was taking hypnotherapy classes. After some time practicing on fellow students in the program, she was assigned to experiment on a guinea pig outside the class. Guess who she chose?

I was not exactly a fan of the idea of hypnotism. Letting someone else control your mind was not an idea those of my religious persuasion warmed up to, to say the least. Yet it was a practical program designed to help others stop smoking, lose weight, or handle other issues they had been unable to overcome.

She asked me what I wanted help with. I didn't smoke or need to lose weight, but as we sat in bed and discussed this, I remembered an upcoming golf outing planned as a team-building event for our practice area within Deloitte, the audit and consulting firm I had joined the previous fall. So I halfheartedly said, "OK, help me improve my golf game," and she went to work. She had me settle back on the bed, propped up with an extra pillow, and had me imagine a series of boring repetitive and confusing actions, such as repeatedly descending and ascending a complicated series of flights of stairs. The last thing I remember is falling asleep out of sheer boredom.

The next morning, I awoke refreshed and headed to the office, where my colleagues and I gathered to form teams for the golf outing at the Arroyo Seco par-three Golf Course in South Pasadena. My familiarity with the course helped reduce my angst about my colleagues discovering what a pathetic golfer I was. This was a friendly competition with seven teams of four players each: a beginner, an advanced, and two average players per team. I was really a beginner but counted as average since Michelle on our team had never golfed. The other average golfer was Mark, the practice leader, and a partner within Deloitte. The expert on the team was Jeff.

The outing format was "Best Ball," so each person teed off separately, but everyone used the location of the best ball for their own subsequent shot. There was some good-natured ribbing going on as we gathered at the first tee and commented as the teams, one by one, tackled the hole. With Mark on our team, we brought up the rear and got to have the most fun in that regard.

When our turn finally came, Michelle was first up, and she set a low bar for our team. Her shot careened to the left, coming to rest about fifty yards down, halfway to the cup, between the two short, scrawny trees. This was disappointing, especially in light of the trash talk we had all engaged in. As Michelle moved away from the four-foot square piece of Astroturf and I bent over to place my ball on it, she muttered that nobody should be surprised. The surprise came when my tee shot landed within a couple of feet of the cup.

I was the one most surprised by this. I had played this course a half-dozen times and would usually land one or two out of the eighteen tee shots on a green. My first shot of any golf day had never flown a hundred yards, straight as an arrow, in the proper direction. And rarely had I landed a tee shot so close to the cup. Mark's shot came close to the green, and Jeff landed his shot on the green, but several yards further away from the flag than mine. I had the honor of putting my ball into the cup, giving us a birdie.

Several high fives later, I found myself teeing off first on the second hole, and against all odds, a similar situation unfolded. To my astonishment, the pattern remained unbroken after three holes. I had driven three consecutive balls to the green, achieving best ball for our group on all three holes, resulting in three under par. Mark and Michelle were patting me on the back, but Jeff, was riding me about pretending to be a below-average golfer. He was struggling with having represented himself as advanced, only to be shown up by someone who took a more humble approach.

It was a gorgeous Southern California day, and I was playing the best golf of my life, but I was uncomfortable with the attention and notoriety of having delivered three birdies in a row. To mitigate this, I apologized for playing so well, enabling Jeff to adopt a humorously antagonistic stance more readily, regarding me as a sandbagger. This smoothed over the awkwardness I felt at performing so well at a sport at which I typically sucked.

That was the dynamic as we approached the fourth hole, which stretched out to 136 yards, the longest drive so far. A large screen to the right of the tee protected players at the adjacent hole. To the left was a fenced-in pump house powering an artificial stream that ran through the course. The screen and the trees protecting the pump house created a narrow corridor to the green. Usually, on this hole, I would hit the screen or bounce it off the roof of or the trees surrounding the pump house. Instead, I was stunned as, on completion of my swing, the ball sailed in a perfect arc, again landing on the green and once again within a few feet of the cup. This sent me into an introverted daze, in which I struggled to understand what to me was a mystifying and quite difficult to handle situation. Why was I suddenly doing so well at this challenging sport?

The fifth and sixth holes had the stream on the right and a road to the left, making them narrow and—for golfers like me—problematic. But the inexplicable pattern of perfect shots continued, with the only notable difference being the increase in the intensity of my discomfort at my own success. It was as though I could not miss, no matter what I did. Even stranger, it was happening despite the banter my superior performance was causing within the team. Previously, my ability to focus in golf had always been adversely affected by the moods and attitudes of other players. And Jeff, the crack player on our team, was visibly unhappy.

He, unlike me, had not been immune to the effect of the whims of the golf gods, who had caused Michelle, Mark to a lesser degree, and even him, either to fail to clear thirty yards or to land balls in the stream, on the road, and out of bounds in adjacent fairways. Those golf moves normally featured frequently in my repertoire, but not on this day. The fact that I made it look easy was causing Jeff to flounder.

As the first two teams wound their way past us on the back nine, we compared scores, which caused no small amount of trash talk back and forth. Mark and Michelle enjoyed the banter with the other teams, who were learning that we were five strokes under par. Mark was touting me as the team's secret weapon while I racked my brain for an explanation for what the heck was going on.

It was not only improbable, it was impossible. We were winning this competition because of me, but I had never been a good player. Even on a good day, I was very inconsistent, and this situation was not limited to golf. I had never been an MVP on a sports team. Somehow I felt like I was cheating Jeff out of his rightful position. The only reason we hadn't birdied on the sixth hole was that we had started choosing tee shots other than mine (the only one on the green), due to the requirement to use at least two tee shots from each member of the team. This put Jeff in a position he was not accustomed to either.

As I stepped up first to the tee on the seventh hole, the tension was unbearable. My self-talk was now angry chatter that all but ordered me to hit a bad shot. It would be worth it, just to break the spell and the tension I felt from everyone watching me to see how I would perform. Looking down 122 yards to the flag, I was so agitated that I was certain I'd miss the ball entirely or knock it into the creek off to the left. Lifting the club back for the swing, I was wondering how bad the stroke would be and which wrong direction the ball would take upon impact. I brought my swing forward and watched in near shock as the ball, once again, flew in a perfect arc, straight as an arrow toward the flag, clearly landing on the green. When the other three had swung, mine was again the only ball on the green, within five feet of the cup.

The team decided to play my ball, and we cashed in on another birdie, bringing us to six under par on seven holes. Mark and Michelle were jubilant, Jeff was quiet, and I was deeply troubled.

This was bizarre. I couldn't relate to what was happening. It was unlike anything I had ever experienced.

My early life had been filled with unpleasant events, largely outside my control, followed by my own self-destructive behavior, which had nearly killed me. With God's help, and two decades of active self-criticism, I had learned not only to color successfully within the lines, but also how to objectively achieve a measure of success, first in the nonprofit religious world and now in business. But my obsessively self-controlled efforts were usually erratic and mixed, at best.

This was unqualified mastery—something completely unfamiliar—and I was trying to figure out what had possessed me. I had always wanted to golf well but had not believed I ever would. I had mastered foreign languages and certain other matters within my personal control, but my fledgling efforts at golf were not serious. I believed that I possessed no natural talent for the game, and was usually lucky to hit fours and fives on these three-par holes, Even that would normally be beyond me on a day like this, where competition and group dynamics were involved.

It all seemed almost supernatural. Something was driving me, almost against my will, to perform better than I had ever imagined. I couldn't figure out what was wrong with me. I was embarrassed at my sudden ability, and I was embarrassing myself with my increasing apologies after every shot, as I agonized within myself about what had come over me.

As we approached the eighth hole and I started to hunch over at the tee, it finally hit me. I bolted upright in one movement, turning to the team, literally slapping my head, cartoon-style.

"I was hypnotized!" I shouted.

My teammates looked at me as if I were nuts.

With a mixture of surprise and relief, I excitedly confessed that my wife had hypnotized me the evening before to improve my golf game, ending with, "That's why I was playing so well."

My teammates reacted with disbelief.

"You can't be serious." they retorted.

And then they started with the jokes.

The jokes relieved the tension somewhat as I stepped back up to the eighth tee. Now that I knew what had happened, I was excited to play the rest of the round.

This hole was 128 yards, slightly uphill, but unlike my experience at the seventh hole, I stood with supreme confidence at the tee, certain I'd deliver an above-average drive. The ball, however, seemed to have a mind of its own. It veered off to the left, landing short and a good thirty yards away from the flag.

It was the first time I had expected a good drive, and the result had been my first bad shot of the day. I was surprised that what had felt so certain had gone so wrong. After that, I began playing terribly.

Stroke after stroke, I sent balls into the woods, over the neighboring fairway, and even missed the ball entirely. Sad to say, I was actually more comfortable now, despite being irritated with myself. I wondered what all this meant. My teammates were demanding the "old Fransson" back, as we began to see our score deteriorate.

Having heard my wife talk about the techniques for hypnosis, and that self-hypnosis was possible, I managed to recover somewhat using focused breathing. By the last two holes, I was back in control of my normal bad game, which kept alive, barely, the glow of possibility that had been created by hypnosis.

This was quite a feat in itself, given that my mind was racing faster than the balls off the tee. I had never given hypnotism much thought, other than the general opinion that 90 percent of it was probably fraudulent. How could my wife's subliminal suggestions turn me into a completely different (and much better) golf player, literally overnight? Regardless of my performance on the back nine, the lead we had off the front nine proved unassailable. Unlike the kind of hypnosis where the subject has no recollection of what he did, the first eight holes had indelibly imprinted themselves into my memory.

Although I don't remember the final score, we did win, resulting in much banter in the clubhouse afterwards. The comic notoriety helped me to fit in at Deloitte, despite my very unusual background and recent conversion to the world of business.

That old adage "we are our own worst enemy" was validated by this incident. That and a newly gained insight that there was no physical reason my golf game should not dramatically improve. The ideas we hold in our head hold us back.

My initial golfing difficulties had convinced me that I would never be a good golfer: I had started too late, I had a bad back, I wasn't flexible or muscular enough, and I was too short. Any excuse would do. My recent experience brought to the forefront of my consciousness that I was afraid of appearing "too good" in front of others—at least in golf.

What other areas of life were like this for me, I wondered?

My wife and I often listened to books on tape and sometimes discussed them. Her study of hypnotherapy led her to Freud and Jung. I've mentioned the anti-intellectual bias in the COG movement; Freud and Jung were among those held in low esteem. Psychoanalysis and dream interpretation were considered enemies of faith, with those who went that route certain to end up confused and deceived, like everyone else in "the world"—that is, those not called by God. But I was beginning to abandon such views.

Learning about Freud and Jung was an important educational step. I could readily identify and understand some of their key insights as original sources of scientific and popular thought that influenced and shaped our society and the world. I was particularly fascinated by Jung's work in the areas of archetypical dream imagery, our consciousness, and the shared consciousness we have as a species. All of these inputs and related insights would soon bloom and bear the fruit of a slowly increasing open-mindedness.

It was fascinating to learn how these men had influenced society, yet I was still skeptical about some of their specific theories. I no longer held them in contempt, but I compared their conclusions to the Bible and what I understood, rather than blindly accepting what they put forward as accurate. Changes in my own beliefs, at least initially, were incremental and minor. On the other hand, my wife seemed to set aside critical analysis, swallowing whole everything we were reading and listening to. While I was integrating it into aspects of what I thought had been our common faith—which to me was bedrock, foundational, undeniable—she, in my view, seemed to have lost all interest in religion, the Bible, and even God. We were moving so far apart, in fact, that my next encounter with a hypnotist would be far less pleasant.

Paperback Writer

With my marriage crumbling under my feet, I reached out to God for help through prayer and study. One of the outcomes of this was a different understanding about the relationship God intended between men and women. My insights came when I was meditating on how male/female relationships were affected by sin in the Garden of Eden.

God explained to Eve that "thy desire shall be to thy husband, and he shall rule over thee."[5] In reflecting on this being God's judgment against her, it seemed undeniable that God's original intent had not been for Adam to rule over her in this way. It was a result of her behavior. Likewise, Adam's decisions had led to the ground being cursed, giving him a very long row to hoe, as they say. His responsibility to protect and provide for himself in a now hostile world would be extended to the woman and the rest of his family. He would have to struggle and fight for survival on a daily basis.[6]

---

5. Genesis 3:16.
6. Genesis 3:17b–19: "Cursed is the ground for thy sake; in sorrow shalt thou eat of it all the days of thy life; thorns also and thistles shall it bring forth to thee; and thou shalt eat the herb of the field; in the sweat of thy face shalt thou eat bread, till thou return unto the ground; for out of it wast thou taken: for dust thou art, and unto dust shalt thou return."

This conflicted with the traditional view of male/female relationships and marriage within many Christian churches, including the COG movement. COG theology emphasized Paul's declaration that the husband was the head of the wife in the same way that Christ was the head of the church.[7] This was viewed as an expression of the ideal, established by God at creation. Various Scriptures from Genesis and elsewhere were combined to support this construct. It was taken seriously in COG circles, and numerous doctrines rested on this foundation.

This divinely ordained hierarchy, went the teaching, was an expression of God's government for all mankind. The wife was to submit to the authority of the husband, as a basic building block in the Government of God structure. We were being judged on our acceptance of, and performance under, this hierarchy—even if others were not. Upon Christ's return, He would deploy it across the planet, ushering in the Millennium—a thousand years of peace, prosperity, and happiness for all.

But now my Bible was telling me that it was not God's original intent for men to have authority over women. It was a judgment against Eve that resulted from her sin. Because of his sin, Adam would also suffer, even though (or, perhaps, because) he was assuming the role of ruler.[8]

The insights gained from my study are critical to understand the journey I was on, even though I had no idea where all this was leading at the time. For that reason, it's important to spend some time on it here.

The Genesis creation story reveals that both the man and the woman were created perfect, in God's image, imbued with divine capacity, and given dominion over the earth, under the rulership of the heavenly lights.[9] This original, pristine state of humankind's creation was one of earthly dominion. They were sovereign on the earth, prevented only from tampering with the sources of light, including the "signs, seasons, days, and years," which were to rule them.

---

7. Ephesians 5:23.
8. I'll revisit this topic to explain the apparent disconnect between Genesis and Paul.
9. Genesis 1:14–16: "And God said, Let there be lights in the firmament of the heaven to divide the day from the night; and let them be for signs, and for seasons, and for days, and years: And let them be for lights in the firmament of the heaven to give light upon the earth: and it was so. And God made two great lights; the greater light to rule the day, and the lesser light to rule the night: he made the stars also." See also Genesis 1:26–28. in which both the man and woman ("mankind") are given dominion.

Whatever they needed was easily available, with limits on what was to be eaten.[10] They were to be vegetarians, as part of the original, natural order that God established. Then there was that one tree and its fruit.

Eve desired that fruit. As with our English word *desire*, the Hebrew word *chamad* can mean "to take delight in," in a positive sense, but also, negatively, "to covet." [11]

In Genesis 3:16 God explains that after eating the forbidden fruit, Eve's "desire" would be to her husband. The Hebrew word here for desire is *tĕshuwqah*, a rare word appearing only three times in the Bible.[12] In addition to describing the illicit longing of a man for a woman or a woman for a man, it also is used for a beast's craving to devour. It ominously portends how human and beast begin to devour each other both literally and figuratively. The use of two different words is poetic and powerful.

The similarity between *tĕshuwqah* (desire) and the Hebrew word *teshuvah* (turning) also seemed important. These concepts, even down to specific words, are woven into the narrative in an astounding feat of literary tapestry making. Eve's turning away from the instructions of God toward the fruit she desired mirrors the turning away of her affection from God toward the man. The stamp of these few verses is indelibly imprinted upon the entire narrative of the Bible. Their influence is like a fractal pattern woven into the DNA of the overall message. There is so much packed into these few verses that we can but scratch the surface. What we find when we do is fascinating.

A well-known feature of God's judgment on Eve is the increase of sorrow in childbirth and its messianic implications. The whole process, starting with conception, is implicated: "Unto the woman he said, I will greatly multiply thy sorrow and thy conception; in sorrow thou shalt bring forth children."

---

10. Genesis 1:29–30: "And God said, Behold, I have given you every herb bearing seed, which is upon the face of all the earth, and every tree, in the which is the fruit of a tree yielding seed; to you it shall be for meat. And to every beast of the earth, and to every fowl of the air, and to every thing that creepeth upon the earth, wherein there is life, I have given every green herb for meat: and it was so."

11. *Strong's Hebrew Lexicon (KJV)*, s.v. "H2530, *chamad*," accessed September 26, 2017, https://www.blueletterbible.org/lang/lexicon/lexicon.cfm?Strongs=H2530&t=KJV.

12. *Strong's Hebrew Lexicon (KJV)*, s.v. "H8669, *tĕshuwqah*," accessed September 26, 2017, https://www.blueletterbible.org/lang/lexicon/lexicon.cfm?Strongs=H8669&t=KJV.

Eve conceived and bore Cain and his brother Abel. She surely understood that the prophetic nature of the curse indicated resolution would come through her offspring, as outlined in Genesis 3:15. God proclaimed that judgment on the serpent would come through Eve's children: "And I will put enmity between thee and the woman, and between thy seed and her seed; it shall bruise thy head, and thou shalt bruise his heel."

Instead, Cain proceeded to become the first murderer, and his victim was Abel, his righteous brother who had brought an offering that was pleasing to God. Eve had surely hoped that her sons would turn out right, and her sorrow was truly great, far beyond the pain of childbirth. Imagine how crushed she must have been when the prophecy seemed to fail and deliver only further grief.

And note how Cain's failure was similar to her own. Consider God's admonition to Cain in Genesis 4:7: "If thou doest well, shalt thou not be accepted? and if thou doest not well, sin lieth at the door. And unto thee shall be his desire, and thou shalt rule over him." Desire is again central, and Cain, like Eve, did not do well. God's judgment upon her had resulted in Adam ruling over her, and now sin has assumed rulership over her son. Adam's life as a sinner was hard with the burden he now carried, but Cain instinctively claims his to be beyond his capacity to bear.[13] The weave of these fractal patterns is jaw dropping, as the abdication of responsibility leads to unbearable oppression within a single generation.

Eve lived to see her hopes dashed as Cain fell victim to an Achilles' heel of human ego—envy— and failed to fulfill the prophecy to bruise the head of the serpent. It would be thousands of years until the dramatic fulfillment of this, in the form of Jesus's victory over sin and temptation, giving His life, as Abel had done, and in the process vanquishing Satan. Throughout history, there are countless recurrences of this example: Noah, who saved humanity in the ark; Job, the perfectly righteous man who suffered; Abraham, who was willing to sacrifice his son; Joseph, betrayed by his brothers only to find them bowing to him in Egypt; and Moses, who prayed that God would spare Israel, and, as a result of carrying their burdens, fell short of entry into the Promised Land.

All of this is built into the story of Adam, Eve, and their sons. The story itself becomes a seed. Every letter, phrase, word, and pattern in the Hebrew language is carefully chosen, and it unfolds as the seed germinates, grows, and

---

13.   29 Genesis 4:13

flowers. Another Hebrew word that impacted my shifting understanding was *mashal.* It is the word chosen to describe Adam's rule over Eve.

Eve turning her desire away from God to the man represents a form of idolatry—an abdication of her sovereignty. It illustrates how we bow down to the creation instead of ruling over it. Adam's life has also been turned into a sorrowful struggle with the increased responsibility represented by the burden of a woman who looks to him, instead of to God, for protection, sustenance, emotional nurturing, and many other needs. Because of this, a dominion is established that did not previously exist, to which Eve willingly subjects herself, and Adam willingly assumes over her.

But there is another connection.

In Genesis 1:14–16 God established the rulership of the heavenly lights, forming an intricate clockwork that perfectly governs the prophetic timeline. God declares their sovereignty and purpose, to govern "signs, seasons, days, and years." They perform this function by spinning in their interrelated orbits. A prophecy in Daniel 7 reveals that an opponent to God's people will challenge the rule of the lights God established in Genesis 1:14–16 by seeking to change "times and laws."[14]

Students of prophecy will note the reference to the Times of the Gentiles here, a prophetic timeline that subjugates the people of Israel until their restoration in the Holy Land in the end times. What may not have been apparent is the tie-in of the fractal pattern of *teshuvah*—turning away from the light, and truth. The lights turn in their assigned orbits, providing prophetic signs and the light to understand them, and marking the time at which they are to be fulfilled. Daniel 7 describes a turning from this divinely ordained rule toward a humanly devised order.

This provides an overview of the downward spiral humans experience when turning away from God. By turning away from the heavenly sovereignty of the divine lights, we become enmeshed in darkness and sin. So it is with the earthly sovereignty God has granted each individual. When one abdicates a responsibility to rule over self, personal sovereignty is traded for slavery— to one's own desires, to sin, and to others.

---

14.   29 "And he shall speak great words against the most High, and shall wear out the saints of the most High, and think to change times and laws: and they shall be given into his hand until a time and times and the dividing of time."

James 1:14–16 reinforces this: "But every man is tempted, when he is drawn away of his own lust, and enticed. Then when lust hath conceived, it bringeth forth sin: and sin, when it is finished, bringeth forth death." The next verse echoes the creation account, that of the rulership of the divine lights. It shows the path out of such darkness. The last phrase from the prior verse is the introduction, "Do not err, my beloved brethren. Every good gift and every perfect gift is from above, and cometh down from the Father of lights, with whom is no variableness, neither shadow of turning." The path out of slavery is a turning back to the One who has ultimate sovereignty over that appointed order. While the divine light, the heavenly signs of God can, from our human perspective, have that variability or refraction—a "shadow of turning"—the One who established them does not. Christ gave one sign that He was who He said He was—the sign of the prophet Jonah, who spent a full three days and three nights in the belly of a great fish. This is the same sign that Judaism explicitly denied in its outright rejection of the Messiah and that Christian orthodoxy implicitly denied with its Friday afternoon crucifixion and Sunday morning resurrection.[15] As I contemplated this I was on the verge of an important breakthrough in my understanding.

The sign of the Sabbath, under Moses, was a two-way sign, identifying both the giver of the sign and its recipients, based on their response to it. Christ gave a sign to identify Himself; Judaism and Christianity rejected this sign, and the Church of God movement fully embraced it, on the surface. But what identified His disciples? Was it, as the COG movement (broadly speaking) felt, their keeping of the Mosaic sign of the Sabbath and annual Holy Days, which demonstrated their understanding of Christ's three days and three nights? What we do is, in fact, more important than what we profess, another truism that the WCG had understood. But was what we were doing the right expression of our understanding of the sign Christ gave of who He was?

I had struggled for a decade with both formulating and answering this question, given the prominence of the Sabbath in COG theology. In allowing the Sabbath to recede in the background, the question became more important, and the answer became obvious. Christ had provided a clear and emphatic sign by which one could identify His disciples.

---

15. As covered in *TPotS*.

This identifying marker, the token that serves as evidence, is provided in John 13:35, "By this shall all men know that ye are my disciples, if ye have love one to another." Adhering to this or that belief or doctrine (even our cherished Sabbath and Holy Days) paled into insignificance in comparison to how we treat our fellow human beings.

I was finally aligning my life with this sign. I'd come full circle from, for example, the WCG-induced doubts of my former pastor and mentor in Switzerland about whether Albert Schweitzer, who didn't keep Saturday or the biblical holy days was a true Christian.[16] I was now looking for signs of the Holy Spirit, and finding them exclusively in works of love, not in adherence to any creed or set of beliefs. I wasn't personally turning away from my understanding of the rulership of the divine clock. I was still convinced that the pattern of worship it indicated was the one that I'd been following for over thirty years now. And yet I had become equally convinced that the divine pattern of worship was a cart that should follow the horse of love, not the other way around.

This insight supported what my relationship with my wife had revealed to me naturally over the last several years. Having a solid doctrinal basis for this was potentially a game changer for our relationship. It should have led to greater mutual understanding and respect. And it should have resulted in a positive breath of fresh air in our marriage.

Everybody's Got Something to Hide Except Me and My Monkey

Sadly, the strain in our relationship was increasing, and there was less and less holding us together. In that context, my new insights turned out to be yet another crack in the cement of what had brought us together in the first place, a common set of rigid beliefs. It seemed to highlight yet another flawed element in our foundation. From my perspective, the loosening of doctrinal rigidity was a freedom that took her further and further out of orbit from the things that I held dear. Ironically, my research into this topic—and the book I hoped would result—was one more piece of evidence to her that my work mattered more to me than she did.

---

16.   See *TPotS,* chap. 7, "You've Got to Hide Your Love Away."

The book was to be titled "The Curse of Eden," and it was to illustrate that the construct of female submission was rooted in sin and explain the dynamic that resulted. Even though these concepts did not help me improve my failing marriage, they did help me understand why it was failing. I could begin to grow beyond the toxic belief that the negative result of sin was an aspirational model. And this understanding led to more insights.

I came to understand that one of the intrinsic problems with sin is that it is an abdication of self-governance. This is evident in the charge to Adam and Eve's son Cain—and, by example, all mankind. God tells Cain that sin lies at his door and tells him to rule over it.[17] Many of us, as was the case with Eve, are content to hand over the reins of responsibility to someone we believe is stronger, especially someone we love or trust. The kind of love so frequently portrayed by classic Disney movies about princesses is really an abdication of personal responsibility in favor of wanting a knight in shining armor to rescue us, in this case, from sin.

As evidenced by the curse on Adam and how he responded, we are also generally foolish enough to assume responsibility for others that isn't rightfully ours. The rescue of damsels in distress leads to damsels being dependent on the rescuer. And it goes downhill from there.

By abdicating our responsibility to rule ourselves, or by being too willing to rule others, we are destined to become enslaved by sin. By extension, whoever is smart, powerful, or conniving enough can use our sin against us. This applies to all parties in a codependent relationship. And it aggregates into the system of systems that rules the planet, be it through governments, ideologies, religions, corporations and commerce, or any other means of people gaining control over other people. I began to see this as a core component of that which the Bible calls Babylon the Great.

These insights motivated me to invest time and energy into the manuscript for "The Curse of Eden." I outlined chapters that explored how this played out at various points in history and how it affects marriages today in the Christian world. However, this effort did not help me fully take personal responsibility for the phenomenon in my own life. Although my book had potential, it was a sprawling overreach that I had no business attempting at that time in my life.

---

17. Genesis 4:7: "If thou doest well, shalt thou not be accepted? And if thou doest not well, sin lieth at the door. And unto thee shall be his desire, and thou shalt rule over him."

This was sadly typical of how I had been living up to then, and how I would continue for some time. When God granted me insight that I should have put to use in saving my own marriage, I tried to use it to produce a work that might save others' marriages. Not surprisingly, without making any real progress on the book, my relationship with my wife continued to crumble around me.

Viewed positively, the study, the reflection, and the ongoing failure were helpful as a part of the slow and painful process of finally growing up and becoming an adult. This growth was immediately apparent in my career success and a slowly expanding clarity on certain key spiritual issues. I was gaining financial freedom and the confidence to redirect my attention toward what God was working out on earth today. God was about to send His Son back to earth, and He wanted me involved in the preparations. Like Jesus, I wanted to be engaged in the Father's business. While this was positive in some ways, in the short term it was fueling a return to an arrogance that I had been trying to shed.

Jesus had cut to the heart of the matter by telling the Pharisees, who might have held similar beliefs to mine, that Moses allowed divorce because of the hardness of their hearts. My heart was incapable of feeling or understanding what my wife was feeling. I was wrapped up in a self-centered world, desperately trying to be right and to do what was right. I failed to see that my marriage— and along with it, my relationship with a woman whom I loved and to whom I had dedicated my life—was hanging by a thread. My faith put me in a similar situation to my dad, who had grown up in Sweden and saw himself as fulfilling the classic breadwinner role modeled by his father. It was the "What more could a woman want?" approach to marriage.

I rationalized that my stance was unselfish and accommodating. We lived where my wife had chosen to live, in a beach area outside my financial comfort zone. I had funded her legal assistant training, which had led to a role she very much enjoyed as a judicial assistant working for a well-respected judge at the district courthouse in downtown Los Angeles. She was happily expanding her social network, including a connection with one of the Supreme Court justices of the state. She enjoyed her foray into hypnotherapy, which I had supported, though it initially had made me uncomfortable. She had new friends in that world as well, so on the surface things seemed fine.

Despite outward appearances, the framework of the marriage was shaky, and events were conspiring to bring down this house of cards. This introduces a chapter of my life of which I'm not proud. This part of my story is far from unique. Many a man has gotten into trouble balancing the struggle to provide for his family with a testosterone-driven desire to be a hero in the process. That qualifier is not intended as an excuse for my contribution to the cliché. They say the path to hell is paved with good intentions. My good intention was to catch up, financially, after years of putting God first, WCG style.

Steve, my close friend since my teenage years in Alaska, and his wife Lisa had been managing our rental property in Arizona, but they had bought a one-acre ranch on the far side of town and would not be able to continue. It was time to divest, and by orchestrating a sale of the house to our renter, we avoided broker's fees and maximized our profit. We were participating, to a small degree, in the most popular US pastime—wealth creation.

Because I had embarked upon a new career in the world of information technology, it seemed natural to apply what I was learning about software companies to an investment in them. So I began speculating in technology stocks, believing my insight gave me an edge over the average investor. I had jumped into the middle of the investor feeding frenzy known as the dot-com bubble. I opened an online stock account, and with the foolish belief that my recent success in the world of corporate technology was due to some superior intelligence on my part, began to trade heavily. I was, to use a metaphor supplied by a friend to illustrate the lure of the material world, a butterfly landing in honey.

It was easy to be successful at this on the right side of the bubble. Unfortunately, success reinforced my view that wisdom and ability was behind my success. So I opened a margin account to invest even more, using money borrowed against the stocks acquired with the money from the sale of the Arizona house. For better or worse, I had very little fear. The biggest problem with all of this was that, although my wife knew I was investing our money, she wasn't aware of the extent of it. As it turned out, I didn't really either. To put it mildly, I was getting a bit cocky over my newfound success.

We were now young, upwardly mobile professionals—"yuppies." Another acronym from that time that applied to us was DINKs—dual incomes, no kids. My six-figure salary from Deloitte was augmented by my wife's slow progress up the government pay scale. Since the money was flowing in, I dropped my resistance to her proposed home remodeling. My reluctance to her request had been that it would curtail investments in a market that was minting millionaires.

Although a remodel of our tiny, old kitchen would improve our living space and increase the value of the house, the potential return on investment didn't remotely compare to the potential upside of the stock market bubble. But since it might keep her happy and might turn a little profit in the process, I reluctantly agreed. Great plan, if only either of these "mights" had materialized.

A friend of my wife's recommended a professional contractor who had worked on the Bellagio Hotel in Las Vegas. While my wife was impressed by this story, to me it screamed "overpriced." I turned to Steve, who had lost his job after overextending himself on the ranch. Steve was a master carpenter, skilled in all areas of construction, and his bid to do the job was about half the other contractor's, making it a win-win arrangement.

But in order for Steve to come to California for this project I had to front him a loan to stave off foreclosure. My wife was quite upset with my decision to use Steve in the first place, so I didn't tell her a loan to Steve was part of the deal. This added another item to a growing list of financial decisions about which my wife was uninformed.

To complete the remodel, Steve moved in with us, which made my wife even less happy about my choice in contractors. As it turned out, there were indications that his financial problems may have been related to personal issues. While he was there, something happened between Steve and my wife. I really don't know if it was just her resentment at me for having my friend live with us, having chosen him over the contractor recommended by her friend, a dispute between the two of them, or something else. Whatever it was, about halfway through the project she began urging me to get him to finish the job and move out. Then she demanded he leave immediately and that I hire someone else to finish it.

I couldn't do this, because I had fronted him additional money when the project dragged on past another rent-due date on his ranch. Firing him before the job was finished meant saying goodbye to the money he already owed me— not to mention the cost of hiring someone else to complete the work. In addition to whatever was bothering my wife, I learned that his work had slowed down because he was working in our garage on a cabinet project for our neighbor, using my credit card for the materials. This fiasco was another big strike against me with my wife that couldn't have come at a worse time.

My investments had yielded a few winners, but after its peak in January 2000, the NASDAQ began a sickening plummet destined to continue for eighteen months. By July 2002, it would shed about 65 percent of its value. So while Steve was taking me for a ride, I was getting margin calls on my stock account and had to keep investing more in order not to lose everything.

3

You're Going to Lose That Girl

For religious Jews, to read the scriptures, and even to quote from them, is to be put in touch with the divine order of being. That is why in Judaism the study of the Hebrew Scriptures is worship. It is more important to study them than to obey them, it is said, because without study you will obey them in the wrong way.

W. D. DAVIES, FROM MY ODYSSEY IN NEW TESTAMENT INTERPRETATION

My belief that the stocks I had picked would ultimately regain their value was tempered with a growing awareness that the global financial system known as the free market was really just a big casino. Wealthy, powerful people behind the scenes—like "the house" in Vegas—structured the odds to work in their favor. I began to understand the old adage "If you don't know who the patsy is at the table, you're it." When the right amount of money is on the table, the big players shift their positions and cash in their chips and then take advantage of the scrambling reactions of small players, caught off guard by these sudden large movements. And I was scrambling.

I took the losses personally, not wanting "them" to get away with it. I fought back by doubling down—putting more and more of our available money into the market. I was trying to hold on to what I had left, in hopes of an upswing before they took all my money and shut me out of the game.

Honey Don't

Meanwhile, I was placing a better bet – on myself. A degree in business was critical to my future career, so I enrolled in the Keller Graduate School of Management in 2001. My wife countered by talking about her own desire to go back to school. This bothered me because I was investing in a masters of business administration specifically to enhance my ability to earn more money. The hypnotherapy program my wife had taken had been an expensive hobby. Now she was looking at programs that cost more than mine and seemed far less practical.

Up until now, her claim on her income as "hers," along with her control over it in a separate bank account was mitigated by the significant increase in my income in recent years. But the circumstances described above were changing all that. The tipping point in our relationship came when our investments were most upside down and margin calls were threatening to force me to put in more money than I could scrape together.

This downward spiral threatened to wipe out my stock account, putting our house at risk. It became harder and harder to hide this from my wife, even as I was increasingly ashamed that I had put us in financial danger. My feelings were conflicted, however, since I had brought most of the money into the family, and my initial investments of "my" money had doubled, tripled, and quadrupled what we had been able to save. Without my active investing, we wouldn't have had a stock portfolio or a house to lose. I was desperately trying to claw my way out of the hole I had dug with a mixture of shame and defiance, knowing that my decisions had been mine alone and that it had been a mistake to make them by myself.

Despite the stress of the continuing slide, I was having some success in minimizing the losses and staying invested in stocks that I felt had a good chance of turning around. But, just when I began to breathe a bit easier for the first time in well over a year, my wife upped the ante.

She now had her heart set on an "it" car that year—the newly redesigned 2000 Toyota MR2 Spyder. This was an expensive car, and this was no time to take on an additional expense. Our Mazda had plenty of mileage left on it, and it was paid off. I put this decision off with a variety of practical arguments, like taking her to look at the RAV4 mini-SUV instead, arguing that it was impractical to have two convertibles in the family.

She grew impatient and for the first time in our marriage demanded to know exactly what was going on with our finances. When I had created the spreadsheet to track our finances I had been eager to show off how well things were going and to get her excited about investing as opposed to spending. The projections I had created of what might happen if our investments performed well had motivated me, and I was hoping it might rub off on her. She had shown no interest then, and the last thing I wanted was for her to see how the current snapshot framed me as a reckless idiot.

For a while, I was able to obscure the truth, but as she pressured me, I resorted to outright lies about the extent of what I had invested in the market. However, this façade became ever more difficult to maintain, and my efforts to make the picture look better than it was just made it harder to tell her that she couldn't have the new car she wanted. Finally, she threatened to just go and buy the car.

Fearing that adding a car loan to our expenses would cause the whole house of cards I was managing to come tumbling down, I confessed that I had been lying to her about our finances. With her sitting stone-faced next to me in front of the computer, arms crossed, and the tension between us so thick you could cut it with a knife, I tried to walk her through the spreadsheets that documented our financial history since 1998.

My successful investments in the past made no impression. She refused to acknowledge that it was my aggressive efforts that had built our meager wealth in the first place, providing the funds I had continued to invest. She demanded that I immediately sell all of our stocks. I pleaded with her, explaining that it would be foolish to arbitrarily dump them but muddled through, partially complying with what amounted to the wrong request at the wrong time. Even though my investments ultimately made money for the family, I had lost her trust. Still, it wasn't yet clear to me that having lied to her was already the last straw—that Humpty Dumpty was broken, and couldn't be put back together again.

My wife decided to make it clear.

She had met a hypnotherapist who claimed to be a marriage and relationship counselor also.

Despite the one-time temporary success with golf, the idea of seeing a counselor separately, under hypnosis, seemed ludicrous to me. But having overruled her on the choice of a contractor, which had turned into the Steve debacle, I felt compelled to agree to her choice of therapist. So we began twice-weekly visits to an upstairs office in a small business park thirty minutes down the road. It cost $1,400 that we couldn't afford, due to the ongoing dot-com bubble burst, but it was a price I had to pay for lying to her.

The foyer was as Zen-like as he could muster in the cramped, generic office space. There was a cheap tabletop water fountain, ambient music, and an essential-oil-infused candle. The brown-leatherette patient's chair reclined like a kinder, gentler dentist's chair. Although I was comfortable enough in the chair, and the hypnotherapist was pleasant enough, it was an irritating arrangement. I was paying a pseudo-Freudian analyst to pretend to hypnotize me, to improve my relationship with my wife, who wasn't in on the discussion.

I say "pretend to hypnotize me" because he never actually succeeded. When I brought this up, his response was always, "It doesn't matter. You're in a relaxed state, which works just as well." Only I wasn't relaxed.

There was nothing relaxing about the cost, the waste of time, and the absurdity of it all. I would sometimes sit, counting the seconds on the wall clock, wishing that it would move faster. Each session was increasingly frustrating, as the amount of money that this charlatan was collecting grew, and I became disgusted with the farce. I was here because I had lied about my investments, yet his entire practice was a con game.

During what might have been my fifth or sixth session, he asked if I could recall the first time I felt anger. I couldn't evoke any early childhood feelings of anger, but after wasting one fourth of a $60 session saying "not yet," I decided to play along, pretending to feel some anger from a childhood memory. When

I pretended to connect with my anger from long ago, he asked, "Was it before or after you were born?"

That's when I connected with my anger.

I sat up, thanked him for his time and efforts, and stated that this was not working for me.

Then I left.

I told my wife I would not continue these ridiculous sessions. I had nothing against genuine marriage counseling, in which we would meet together with a trained counselor and address the real issues between us. This was not something she was willing to do. She was angry but seemed willing to let the matter drop. I breathed an unwarranted sigh of relief and began to believe that maybe the worst of the storm had blown over.

I had not given up on improving our marriage; it's just that my focus at the time was on our financial situation, filtered through a belief that by turning it around I would be able to save the marriage. With God's help, of course. I credited God for my success at Deloitte, which was critical to remediating the financial mess caused by investing in a declining market.

Arrow through Me

In keeping with its premier brand, Deloitte had offices in one of the finest pieces of real estate in Los Angeles. As I entered my second year there, I received my annual bonus along with a raise. With being enrolled in an MBA program, this meant that despite my current financial troubles a very bright future was just around the corner.

And being with Deloitte afforded me a variety of growth opportunities, from hands-on business technology consulting experience to a personality assessment as part of the management review process. The assessment analyzed motivation in three key areas: power, achievement, and relationships. My report showed an extremely low desire for power, which was not surprising. What did surprise was that while I held relationships to be most important, my above-average score in that area was eclipsed by my off-the-charts desire for achievement. This particular combination was problematic in several ways. For starters, my focus on achievement above that of relationships led others to question my motives, and my outright rejection of power made others uneasy entrusting me with it.

In an effort to change and grow, I attended a seminar by an expert in the field of the proper use of power. I learned that power doesn't necessarily corrupt; it just allows our tendencies a more free expression. Those who are not corrupt must learn to use power properly—which is often against their nature—or else yield inappropriately to those who are corrupt. My natural response was complete abdication, which benefitted no one.

My aversion to wielding power over others had been a contributing factor in my resignation from my position as a minister and administrator in the WCG. It had been more important to me to serve God from a spirit of wanting to help others. At the same time, achieving success was my primary motivation, which often got in the way of relationships with the people I sought to serve. How could I integrate these conflicting impulses? I wasn't sure, but I sensed that a significant change was on the horizon.

One fall morning, on my forty-minute drive to work, listening to one of the CDs in my growing collection, I noticed less traffic than usual. As I approached the parking lot, across the street and slightly below the top of Bunker Hill, it was almost deserted. As I got out of my car and crossed the street, the lack of traffic—both pedestrian and otherwise—brought the impressive installation where I worked into majestic relief.

Deloitte's LA offices are at 350 Grand Avenue, in the taller of two striking towers in California Plaza, completed in 1992. Perched on Bunker Hill, this award-winning complex houses under- and aboveground restaurants, extensive water fountain installations with a large reflective pool, and walkways. The base of the building features a brown granite exterior covering the first two stories, with a row of round windows below a row of rectangular ones nestled just under the third floor. From that base, a set of reflective blue-gray glass exterior panels stretch endlessly upward. When one climbs the steps leading up to the base and approaches the building, its sheer size hides the slightly smaller sister tower behind the curved front, which fades gracefully out to the straight angles of the two corners. All of this ascends majestically on high, almost, but not quite, placing the view of the top beyond the neck's ability to bend backward.

While the building is only the third highest in Los Angeles and the seventy-seventh highest in the US, its design and appeal are impressive. The

Deloitte & Touche logo is featured prominently, more than thirty floors up, in giant blue lettering. As Deloitte employees look up, the building appears to touch the bottom of the sky, like a modern Tower of Babel into which we could proudly walk, as long as we had the proper badge.

As I mounted the steps toward the front of the building, something didn't feel right. It was like an empty building in a ghost town, and when I arrived at the entrance, I found it locked. It was a Tuesday, and anyway, Labor Day had fallen on Monday the previous week. Puzzled, I headed back to my car, realizing that I was a media dropout who didn't follow minute-to-minute news, which often left me the only one who hadn't "gotten the memo" on any given current event. Perhaps a marathon or some other downtown happening had caused a traffic closure of the area. Back in my car, I decided to return home to work remotely on my laptop rather than driving out to the Deloitte satellite office near the airport.

It wasn't until after 9:30 a.m., Pacific time, as I was getting close to home, that it occurred to me to call my wife to find out if she was also affected, knowing that she worked not too far away at the federal courthouse. This was hours after all four planes had crashed and the twin towers (the ones in NY, not the ones in LA) had collapsed. I was probably the last American to learn about the events of September 11, 2001.

This was a major wake-up call for America. I'm sure every reader can remember exactly where they were and what they were doing when they learned about the terrorist attacks. Our nation and the world were transformed at that time. There are many theories about exactly what happened and why, as well as various interpretations of the meaning and effect on our future, prophetically or otherwise. Certainly, there were a number of warnings leading up to these events, going back to Columbine, and Timothy McVeigh in Oklahoma City. Even the Y2K hysteria and the dot-com bubble bursting seemed like dress rehearsals leading up to the destruction of these symbols of American economic might.

For me, 9/11 brought back the feelings of helplessness I had when encountering the out-of-control bus on Rosh Hashanah, the Day of Trumpets, in New York. I was pretty much over any personal need or desire to deliver a warning message to the world but was there prophetic significance to the collapse of the twin towers of the World Trade Center? Scriptures in Isaiah and

Revelation that discussed the fall of Babylon came to mind.[1] Revelation 18 describes the merchants of the earth as an integral part of Babylon, and among their merchandise are the bodies and souls of men.[2]

I had already noticed the prominence of wealth creation in the texts about Babylon the Great. But now the repetition in the phrase "Babylon the great is fallen, is fallen" jumped out at me. Eerily, it seemed to signify what America had just witnessed—the collapse, in rapid succession, of the two towers symbolic of world trade. Around this time, there were also several earthquakes in Los Angeles. I had been sitting on the eighteenth floor, late on a quiet afternoon, when I saw my building sway in relation to the other towers around us. The feeling was unnerving, as the comparative motion between the buildings was substantial, and though they were engineered to withstand these tremors, it seemed as though they could come collapsing down at any moment. All I could do was pray. And wonder, were we on the cusp of the long-awaited beginning of the tribulation that precedes the return of Christ? These questions would remain unanswered . . . for a while.

By that fall, our personal financial situation had rebounded. And yet these experiences and thoughts reinforced my growing desire to live my life in accordance with the magnified and honorable version of God's law, the law of love. This was particularly true of my approach to the Feast of Tabernacles.

---

1. Isaiah 21:9: "And, behold, here cometh a chariot of men, with a couple of horsemen. And he answered and said, Babylon is fallen, is fallen; and all the graven images of her gods he hath broken unto the ground." Revelation 18:1–3: "And after these things I saw another angel come down from heaven, having great power; and the earth was lightened with his glory. And he cried mightily with a strong voice, saying, Babylon the great is fallen, is fallen, and is become the habitation of devils, and the hold of every foul spirit, and a cage of every unclean and hateful bird. For all nations have drunk of the wine of the wrath of her fornication, and the kings of the earth have committed fornication with her, and the merchants of the earth are waxed rich through the abundance of her delicacies."

2. Revelation 18:10–13: "Standing afar off for the fear of her torment, saying, Alas, alas that great city Babylon, that mighty city! for in one hour is thy judgment come. And the merchants of the earth shall weep and mourn over her; for no man buyeth their merchandise any more: The merchandise of gold, and silver, and precious stones, and of pearls, and fine linen, and purple and silk, and scarlet, and all thyine wood, and all manner vessels of ivory, and all manner vessels of most precious wood, and of brass, and iron, and marble, And cinnamon, and odours, and ointments, and frankincense, and wine, and oil, and fine flour, and wheat, and beasts, and sheep, and horses, and chariots, and slaves, and souls of men."

At an early age, I learned that approaching the Feast selfishly, as a time to enjoy myself lavishly, left me empty. But when I had gone to the Feast with an attitude of serving a broader community, it was always spiritually rewarding. A focus on serving others was the surest way to serve God. I was now acutely aware that this needed to start at home with serving my wife. And I had a specific goal for the 2001 Feast of Tabernacles. I viewed it as an opportunity to reignite what my wife and I seemed to have lost. But this idea was not without challenges.

My wife wasn't attending any church, and we had both had our fill of ego-filled messages about doing God's Work from those who believed they were ministers in God's One True Church. David Hulme, in particular, kept coming as close as he could to implying that he was the one really following in HWA's footsteps without anyone being able to accuse him of having actually said it. Still, that's the group I was affiliated with. So when they announced a Feast site in Salzburg, it seemed perfect. Salzburg is one of the most romantic towns in Europe, and we'd likely be seeing people we knew from our time in Germany. To make sure the trip had adequate romantic cachet, I chose Paris as our arrival city in Europe.

Sadly, my creative efforts toward an ideal Feast/vacation compromise made neither of us happy. We arrived in Paris right before Yom Kippur, the day of fasting. We spent this always physically unpleasant day in a miserably jetlagged condition, holed up in a small hotel room near Paris. Then we traveled quite a ways to meet with some elderly members and a single woman who had stayed home rather than travel to their designated Feast site. I gave a makeshift sermon in French at their home, and we spent much of the day there in the interest of fellowship. My wife, who didn't speak any French, was probably reminded of her painful early experiences in Germany.

We then continued on to Austria, only to find no close friends from our time serving in the German-speaking region in attendance. There were a few I had known from my days in the Bonn office, but no one my wife could relate to. The weather was chilly with a fair amount of rain. My wife seemed to resent having to maintain a façade of interest in her former religion, and I feared this extended to her relationship with me as well. This was no longer how she wanted to spend her vacations. The time we spent together on the streets and in the cafés was tense and disappointing. My soggy hopes of recharging our marriage by going back to the roots of our relationship seemed to swirl down the drains of the streets of Salzburg.

Birthday

Returning to the US after the Feast, the treadmill of everyday life took over. In the wake of 9/11, the country was grieving, plotting revenge, and pursuing agendas to exploit the opportunity presented by the tragedy. I was expanding my success in business, and agonizing over all aspects of my personal life. Though I was going to considerable effort to save my marriage, my intellectual focus was channeled into my work on the ever-expanding, but ultimately doomed, manuscript for "The Curse of Eden." Documenting the challenges in attaining male/female relationships was a lonely echo chamber in which I imagined I was improving my relationship with my wife. Soon another six months went by, with me telling myself that things were still basically OK.

Along the way, I was continuing to make mistakes. My failing marriage had just begun to teach me that it was my own attitude and behavior, not the attitudes of those around me, which was damaging my relationships. An intellectually superior understanding of the message of the Bible was not going to fix that. The only fix for this condition was to expand my capacity to love. This, of course, was a matter of the heart, and easier said than done. But it was dawning on me, and it was this slow awakening that was critical in defining the next phase of my life.

In my marriage, my third strike and final wake-up call came on my wife's fortieth birthday. Our birthdays are one day apart, and three years earlier she had planned an elaborate party to celebrate my forty-year milestone. I, on the other hand, was like a deer in the headlights when it came to honoring my wife on her day. Did she want me to make a big deal about it or not? In the end, rather than communicating with her, I bungled it completely. In my indecision, I ended up giving her a trip to a spa, with an apology, the day after her birthday, which was my birthday. By this time, she was probably looking for a final excuse to leave. She claimed I had forgotten her birthday and moved out the day after mine.

I did my best to try to win her back. I wrote poems and had a friend help me set them to music. I worked feverishly to leverage the elaborate set of spreadsheets that tracked our entire net worth to represent an accurate picture of our finances, trying to explain every detail about the history that they contained and our now positive financial situation, hoping this would restore her faith in me.

And I sought professional help. The so-called marriage counseling with the hypnotherapist had been a negative experience, leaving us further apart than when we started. It had felt like a staged farce designed to bolster her claim that I was the problem. Now it was my turn to force her into counseling. I located two traditional marriage counselors, a man and a woman, and told her to choose one. She reluctantly chose the woman, and we began painful joint sessions to discuss our issues.

My positive efforts to rekindle her affection took place against a gut-wrenching backdrop. In our counseling sessions, she showed no interest in trying to salvage our relationship. Instead, she seemed intent on savaging me. She painted a vile, dark caricature of who and what she was married to. My deepest feelings, emotions, and beliefs, my emotional and spiritual identity forged in the turbulent events of my childhood, were built around the desire to never repeat the mistakes of my father. I couldn't help but defend myself, presenting my best side to the marriage counselor.

During the sessions and in my interactions with my wife and the counselor, I was a model of restraint and objectivity, channeling every ounce of my being into making sure that the evil creature she portrayed was at worst an exaggeration. While the counselor saw through my Teflon façade and held me accountable for the fire behind my wife's smoke signals, she could also see past my wife's anger and vitriol to her culpability. As she worked objectively to hold each of us accountable for our role in the failing marriage, my wife grew angrier. For her, it was all or nothing; either I take full responsibility for all the problems in our relationship, or she was done. As she bared her anger and bitterness toward me, something inside me was breaking. This couldn't be happening to me. I was devastated.

The rending asunder of the marriage covenant I had entered into with my wife and with God motivated me to draw closer to God. I could now see that God was not—despite my career success—blessing my efforts. Our rebounding financial security was no consolation for a failed marriage. As each effort to reignite my relationship with my wife failed, returning to my first love, spiritually, became my only hope.[3]

But where could I go next? What could I do to turn this hope into action? Whatever answer I might find was filtered through the only lens I had available, the general framework of belief that the Church of God movement had provided. But I was disillusioned with David Hulme's group.

He and his church was morphing into yet another example of the ego-led systems springing from the ashes of the WCG, fueled by the classic, scripturally faulty WCG tithing system. One aspect of Israel's wilderness years was that while Moses was on a mountain, communing with God and receiving the laws that were to provide a model society, the people built a golden calf to lead them back into Egypt. The appeal of Egypt was that they were free of the responsibility to think and act on their own. The irony began to dawn on me.

The Church of God system appeared to have more in common with the golden calf than with pointing us toward God and following him wherever he led. The leaders of these groups seemed intent on managing the space between God and us. This was no longer close enough for me. My focus was increasingly on Scriptures such as Micah 6:8: "He hath shewed thee, O man, what *is* good; and what doth the LORD require of thee, but to do justly, and to love mercy, and to walk humbly with thy God?" I wanted to practice true religion, as defined by James 1:27: "Pure religion and undefiled before God and the Father is this, to visit the fatherless and widows in their affliction, *and* to keep himself unspotted from the world."

Ever the self-critical one, ever quick to judge my own motives—even while considering such topics and in pursuit of such high ideals—I asked myself if I was really seeking God or just trying to make amends and cover up the areas of my life that were a mess. I wanted to strive for purity and not deceive myself. If my motives were not pure, there would be no real progress—just self-deception and shadowboxing.

I needed to think outside the box.

---

3. Revelation 2:4–5: "Nevertheless I have somewhat against thee, because thou hast left thy first love. Remember therefore from whence thou art fallen, and repent, and do the first works; or else I will come unto thee quickly, and will remove thy candlestick out of his place, except thou repent."

Mother Nature's Son

During the mid-to-late '80s, at the height of WCG's success, The WCG had developed a close connection to Thailand's well-loved royal family through the Ambassador International Cultural Foundation (AICF), a humanitarian outreach organization. Queen Sirikit, in particular, seemed to have had an affinity with HWA, and gifts and accolades had been exchanged over the years. Groups of Ambassador College students had spent a year in Thailand teaching English and assisting with other programs sponsored by the royal family. During that time, a school, the Waterfield Institute, had been established in Sri Lanka as well as programs assisting refugees in camps on the Thai–Burmese border.[4]

Leon Sexton, a fellow former-WCG minister, had represented AICF in Thailand and was connected with the king, queen, and other government officials involved with the royal family's projects to assist the country's most rural and underdeveloped communities. During the schism of the WCG Leon remained independent, while maintaining his personal connection to the royal family. The UCG allowed him to speak to their congregations while visiting in the US, enabling a flow of support. These funds were used to support programs in Southeast Asia, including Legacy, a school for Burmese refugees, which was also a training ground to support efforts at reaching people in Asia, WCG-style.

I was impressed by what I knew of Leon's dedication and willingness to strike out alone and without financial backing, to continue to serve those who looked to him for leadership. David Hulme had professed a desire to do this when he split off from the UCG, but Leon actually did it. My involvement with AICF, which for a time had been managed by David Hulme, had been limited, but I had always had a strong affinity with the approach. After two successive negative Feast of Tabernacles experiences with David Hulme's group, I decided to contact Leon. We quickly progressed from e-mails to phone discussions and discovered common ground. We agreed that I would travel to Thailand to assist with the Feast and to see what he and the Legacy school were accomplishing in Southeast Asia.

---

4. While these activities were subordinated to HWA's desire to fulfill the "Great Commission" (Matthew 24:14), which was paramount, the programs and services provided were designed to do well, and the students who participated generally did so with an attitude of genuine love for those they were serving.

It was a bittersweet experience to travel to a Feast site without my wife, but as usually happened at a Feast, I encountered old friends I hadn't seen in a while. One of these was a French classmate from Ambassador College who had been living in Germany for years and was going through a painful divorce. It was helpful to have someone with whom I could share some of the distress I felt at being separated from my wife. But despite, or perhaps because of, the pain I was feeling, I was more interested in finding a path forward than in licking my wounds. This approach was exactly what Leon was doing, forging ahead in serving God and his people.

Leon had taken several trips to India at the request of a native Indian, Michael Hubert, who had been ordained a deacon in the WCG.[5] When the WCG made tithing optional, support to third world countries such as India all but dried up.[6] The splintering of the WCG further ripped the struggling congregations apart, leaving Michael and his wife stranded and disillusioned with the corporate body of the church, despite still adhering to its essential teachings. This had happened within WCG circles all over the world, but the remoteness and economic circumstances of India exaggerated this effect.

Michael, with the support of his wife, had continued to do what a deacon does—provide service to those who needed it. Since there was no congregation for him to focus on, he began to serve those around him in his local community. The result was a mixture of humanitarian activities and teaching classic WCG theology. Leon supported Michael's efforts by visits to the region providing some limited financial support for a couple of small grassroots programs Michael had initiated in and around Chennai.

Leon had visited Chennai during the prior Feast of Tabernacles, assisting Michael and his wife in worshipping with and teaching a number of people who had no prior involvement with the WCG or any of its offshoots. Leon now needed someone to go to India to help conduct the Legacy-sponsored feast site in Chennai for this small but growing group. I was intrigued. My search for evidence of true religion, as defined by James 1:27, had led me to Thailand, where, in stark contrast to the stagnation I was seeing in other COG groups,

---

5.   A deacon in the WCG was ordained to an office that focused on physical service to the body of believers, in contrast to a minister, whose focus was spiritual service.

6.   See *TPotS*, chaps. 8–9.

I learned that God was blessing the efforts of a deacon in India focused on humbly serving those around him.

It seemed fitting that it had taken a deacon in India to put the attitude of foot washing into practice in a meaningful way.[7] I eagerly agreed to travel there to meet Michael and support his efforts. After a few hasty arrangements, I found myself on a plane to Chennai where I would spend the second half of the Feast. On the flight over, I meditated on the many and varied paths that had finally led me to visiting an area I had always associated with poverty and misery. Any prior thought of traveling there had been in the context of offering aid and sharing what I knew. It was a wonderfully humbling experience to be expectant of learning something I desperately wanted to understand—how to practice pure and undefiled religion.

When I arrived, I learned that, in addition to being supported by Leon Sexton's Legacy Institute, Michael Hubert was not ashamed to play the poverty card to seek help from a variety of COG groups to support his independent efforts. He was open and vocal about the needs in his region and his belief that the rest of the COG community had an opportunity to practice true Christian love by reaching out to their brothers in need. I was impressed with Michael, his approach, and the fact that it seemed to be working. The group in India was almost as large as the more established site in Thailand, and in contrast to that group, most of these people were attending their first ever Feast of Tabernacles. Among those who were not new, however, was a couple from Seal Beach, California, just minutes from where I lived in Long Beach. Kevin Fiske was a painting and carpentry contractor, and his wife, Sonali, was originally from Sri Lanka. We connected instantly, and all three of us commented on our amazement that we had never met before. We each belonged to different splinter groups whose minor doctrinal differences were used by the ministry to ensure loyalty to a specific group. Since I had left the UCG prior to moving to Long Beach, I had never attended their congregation just to the south of us. Instead,

---

7. Christ had taught His disciples to be willing to wash one another's feet and had made this a prerequisite for them to be considered part of Him. Foot washing, as modeled by Jesus, was practiced by the WCG and its offshoots at Passover. Prior to eating the unleavened bread and drinking the wine that were symbolic of the body and blood of the crucified Christ, members literally washed one another's feet, as a sign of humility and service to one another. This important component of our worship was in stark contrast to the attitude of superiority and privilege that the Government of God teaching seemed to confer upon the ministry.

I had been traveling forty miles north to Pasadena to meet with David Hulme's group. Given the tiny size of these groups to begin with, it would be comical if it weren't so tragic.

Over the course of five days spent in Chennai, Michael explained what he had been doing that had enabled him to pull together a Feast with these new people. He had started a charity called Shabnam Resources, the first word meaning something like "early rain" in a Himalayan tribal language. Under this umbrella he had initiated a number of miniprograms designed to help those less fortunate, of which there were many in Chennai, a city of ten million people, two million of which were homeless, including about four hundred thousand children.

On one day of the Feast, Michael, Kevin, Sonali, and I climbed into a rented, black, Western-style town car to visit one of these homeless areas and connect with some people Michael had met. We pulled into a narrow street inside a makeshift village and stepped directly into the sounds and smells of the lives of people living in homes consisting of boxes, crates, draped cloth, and blankets.

We were in the midst of a tent city within the city. What struck me first were the children I saw sitting with their mothers and fathers or playing in the dirt. The clothing they wore was colorful but dirty. The tents were small, and tightly crowded together. The tiny dwellings were in organized rows, stretching out beyond my line of sight. The odors, on the other hand, were chaotic. The pleasant smell of Indian cooking vied for my attention, along with the foul smells forcing their way into my awareness, as well as the dirt, the smoke, the noise, and the flies. The families we met somehow managed to make all of this seem normal. Some of their faces had smiles, whereas some had a gaunt, hardened look. What struck me most were the big, wide-open, white eyes looking up from within the dark faces. These eyes seemed to ask, "What are you doing here?

I felt like an intruder, until it seemed, the eyes started pulling me in.

Actually, what pulled me in was the tugging of little hands.

Everywhere, there were the hands of children reaching out.

I had heard of, but never experienced, such conditions, and the impact was overwhelming.

Michael was trying a number of ways to reach out to and serve some of the children in these situations. It was much easier to get assistance to these families by highlighting the specific plight of the children. And he made sure he had something meaningful to offer them that would resonate with his funding sources, meager as they were.

To illustrate his approach, he took us to an area just outside the tent city, where he and a couple of local college students he had enlisted tried to tutor homeless children. We had a box of apples, and were literally mobbed by bright-eyed and friendly children who wanted a piece of the fruit. It was a rudimentary program with about three volunteers who occasionally provided brief lessons in the area near where the homeless children lived. On the day I went with them, they had been chased away from the crumbling building outside of which they normally conducted lessons.

This was so unorganized that it could hardly be called a program, and there was more intent than achievement. Nonetheless, I was sold. I had to support these efforts. I asked Michael about his vision: How did he plan to make it more effective and produce better results? He explained that he wanted to build a small shelter so that the program would have a fixed location and time, not subject to changes in the weather. It would also enable the children to focus better on the lessons and to improve their attitude and morale, giving them the feeling that they were being treated with greater care and respect. This seemed a reasonable next step, so I asked Michael how much he would need to accomplish this. When he mentioned that it would cost about $200, it took but an instant to set the money aside mentally.

Penny Lane

In addition to the homeless children's program, Michael had initiated a project for the women in his neighborhood in Chennai. They designed and sewed cushion covers for sale, as part of a women's empowerment initiative. He was more interested in this program, as it would bring in cash, and he wanted me to find outlets to sell these in the West. I had used a similar approach to fund the summer camp I had established and directed in Germany. From 1990–1994 we taught teens how to handcraft large quantities of greeting cards, which were sold in bulk to banks and other organizations.

Michael gave me a few samples so that I could find outlets. I was impressed with the quality and design, and was enthusiastic about the possibility of marketing these in the West, especially if they were tied to a cause such as the one he was describing. Michael then mentioned that they would need some money to buy the materials for the covers and to jump-start a formal program.

On my last day in India, I made sure to squeeze in a trip to a touristy shopping area so that I could bring home some beautiful ornamental Indian items in my ongoing effort to try to win back my wife. At the exclusive shop that sold these items, I was able to pick up some samples of cushion-cover designs I knew would sell well in the US and Europe. Some of these I left for Michael to use as models, and a few of these beautiful cushion covers went home with me for my wife. I also gave Michael $200 from my dwindling festival tithe to begin the program.

As my jam-packed five days in India came to an end, Michael accompanied me in the taxi to the airport. Just outside airport security, I checked my wallet, then handed Michael an envelope I had prepared containing another $200. This was to cover the materials needed for the shelter for the educational program. Michael seemed surprised and delighted, and expressed his gratitude profusely. I asked him to report the results to me by e-mail. Then I boarded the plane, suffering a bit from the stomach troubles that always accompanied my visits anywhere that didn't adhere to Western standards. This had started at the end of my trip in Thailand and peaked during my first day or two in India. The trip had been so short that I had managed to gut my way through it (pun intended) without any major impact to my planned activities. Still, it made an already grueling fourteen-hour trip home, on airplanes and in airports, all the more memorable. It took two weeks after arriving home to flush all the effects out of my system, but this did not dampen the inspiration and motivation gained from this trip.

In reviewing a photograph taken on the Last Great Day of the Feast, I counted exactly forty people in attendance. This count was not just of interest to those inclined toward numerology (the number forty features prominently throughout the Bible) but rather because the majority of these people were new to the COG movement and had become interested because of the work Michael had been doing.[8] Kevin and Sonali were as eager as I was to get together and invited me over for dinner to talk about what we had experienced at the Feast in India. They were impressed that a US minister, especially one no longer in the full-time employ of any of the groups, was taking such an interest in a more humanitarian approach in a faraway country. They had long been advocating within the UCG for a return to the kind of outreach programs we had known in the WCG through AICF but felt the UCG was resistant. Sonali was especially excited, given her experience with the Waterfield Institute in Sri Lanka and its proximity to Chennai, geographically, culturally, and linguistically.

They volunteered to help initiate and manage the cushion-cover program in the US, and we discussed how to market and sell them. With Kevin and Sonali's help, this program was already poised for success. During this time, I had been trying to get together with my wife to share my gifts and my excitement about India with her. Kevin and Sonali seemed the kind of people she would really like. Perhaps the four of us would not only enjoy each other's company socially, but she might see that I was involved in something very positive—a natural step forward from where we had all come religiously and spiritually. I was still under the delusion that I might be able to reintegrate my wife into my connections with others from her former church fellowship.

She refused.

In the end, I couldn't even find an occasion to deliver my gifts to her. This was a devastating blow, and it weighed heavily on me. What kept me going as my marriage was falling apart was my engagement in India. It was fulfilling to work with a man who had integrated social work—with an emphasis on widows and orphans—into the pattern of worship with which I was familiar. Michael was using principles that would lead to peace and harmony, the Millennium, the "world tomorrow," as HWA put it, and I wanted to be involved.

The efforts in India were insignificant in scale but had a focus on what I believed to be at the heart of the Judeo-Christian message, that society should be restructured to the benefit of all, not just to that of the ruling few. In short, it was the fulfillment of the message of the Bible, the establishment of the Kingdom of God on earth. It was frustrating that my wife wasn't motivated

8. Appendix III excerpts Leon Sexton's *Legacy* newsletter report of events leading up to and during the 2002 Feast in India.

by this in the way I was, but she wasn't the only one unimpressed with my new direction.

David Hulme called me on the carpet to explain why I had attended an "unauthorized" Feast site. In my response to David, I reminded him that I was an ordained minister committed to serving the church. My ordination within the WCG had been to the rank of preaching elder. What point was there in me attending a Feast site where I wasn't allowed to perform the role God had ordained me to fulfill, which was to preach? This was a calculated statement, given that I believed David felt the same way about his ordination as evangelist. His feelings about his calling may have led to his decision to ultimately go against his UCG "unity statement" and start up a work of his own. These thoughts were behind the last sermon I delivered in David's church, titled "What Is the Work of God?"

The WCG had been built on the premise that HWA had a distinct calling to announce the imminent return of Christ, who would bring all nations into submission to the law of God and the way of peace, ruling the planet with a rod of iron. The Work of God, as a concept, had a larger-than-life meaning in the minds of the COG movement. David's group was one of several who felt it important to infer, if not insist, that they and they alone were doing the Work of God.

In *The People of the Sign* I shared how a student in the German region, an area where everyone referred to the regional director as "doing God's Work," had cracked an insightful joke by asking, "If Frank Schnee is 'doing God's Work' then what is *God* doing?" This joke no longer amused me now that seemingly anyone who had previously had a leadership role in the WCG was claiming their little splinter group to be the one now "doing the Work of God." Even more ludicrous than the claim itself were the increasingly meaningless distinctions between what exactly each one was doing differently to support such an audacious claim. My sermon used Scriptures to show that human beings were required to perform a variety of works, that there were works of the flesh and spirit, and that even Satan was doing a work. I suggested that God's Work was "bringing many sons to Glory," implying that much of what the COG movement claimed to be "the Work of God" was tangential at best.[9] The conclusion, and the point of the whole message, was that while we should all

---

9. Hebrews 2:9–11.

earnestly seek to support what God is doing, no one could or should lay claim to be doing God's Work.

I called for us to earnestly seek God's will rather than continue to assume blindly that what we were comfortable and familiar with was what God wanted us to do. I hoped to enable a discussion that would allow the church to align its efforts in support of God's purposes, instead of the goals of our leaders. I used the powerful lyrics from a song called "Fisherman's Daughter" by Daniel Lanois, to describe the result of claiming to be the One True Church:

> *I laid awake a whole night long, waiting for the sun to beat down on my head in this broken bed*
> *I laid awake and dreamt of ships passing through night, searching for shelter, stopping at no harbor*
> *I heard the screaming waters call sixty sailors' names*
> *Raging words, pounding on the sail like an angry whale.*
> *I felt the iron rudder skip, the smell of seeping oil, the heat of slipping rope. Failing hands, failing hope*
> *Every sailor asks . . . asks the question about the cargo he is carrying*
> *God's anger broke through the clouds and He spilt the cargo for all to see—*
> *The fault of the sailor, the fault of he who asks no questions, about the cargo he is carrying*

The combination of pointed Scriptures and potent lyrics highlighted how the split of the WCG had exposed the squabbling factions inside. I was nonetheless confident that in laying out the Scriptures—which to me were plain—I was initiating a dialogue. Perhaps we could begin to discuss how to enable the church to seek guidance directly from God more humbly. It was sincere, hopeful, and naïve.

Scripture ran counter to the dogmatic assumption within the WCG and its offshoots that whatever work the leadership was engaged in was the Work of God. My message called for a change in focus and perception, perhaps even in our identity. It was a controversial sermon, bordering on heresy for some. People listened. You could hear a pin drop in the room as I laid out my case. But that didn't mean anyone really heard.

The reaction of my audience in America contrasted starkly with the results on the ground in India. People there were embracing a message about divinely inspired social change, based on a foreign religion, in a culture very different from the Judeo-Christian world. For me, clarity on how the Churches of God had been off track was energizing. To understand how the COG movement was disconnected from God and was not following the cloud and pillar gave me hope that I might pick up its trail, and India was where my search for it had led me.

What had most captured my interest was the program that would help those children with whom I felt an affinity—the homeless children of Chennai. This resonated with my personal experience as a kidnapped international orphan, living with relatives, and later a ward of the state. I had been an outcast struggling with inner demons, and was ultimately rescued by the teachings of the WCG. My experiences developing youth programs and attempting to integrate them into the fabric of the WCG during the time of Tkach Senior's commission to "prepare the bride of Christ" seemed to have been a preparation for this opportunity. And it enabled me to diminish the cognitive dissonance created by my own failing marriage, as I imagined myself being prepared for a spiritual union.

From Me to You

My wife had moved out, leaving the house payment with me. I had to sell the house, but there was a lot of work left before I could do that. This work was painful to undertake in light of what it symbolized: one more nail in the coffin of our marriage.

At the same time, my relationship with my troubled younger sister was experiencing resurgence, perhaps because we suddenly had something in common. She had experienced a series of divorces and other broken relationships, and my failing marriage may have made me more accessible. In any event, she lived a few hours north, in San Jose, and worked as a landscaper in her own one-woman business. I invited her to come down and help me with the landscaping projects needed in order to sell the house. She arrived in a truck along with an old boyfriend from LA, even though she was living with another man in San

Jose. There was alcohol around, even though she was an AA member. She said her friend was the one drinking. I wasn't convinced.

Coincidentally, my niece was in town from Canada, which opened an opportunity for me to invite my wife on a three-way date to see the stage production of *The Lion King*. During the event, I turned my phone off, and I missed several calls from my sister. The voice-mail messages she left started out solicitous, then got panicky, then turned angry.

Either she or her ex-boyfriend had somehow tripped the alarm in our house. He had cut the wire to turn it off, and the security company had arrived. The neighbors couldn't vouch for her, so the police had been called. They uncovered that she was not supposed to be in Los Angeles, due to drug-related charges up north. Against all odds, this was all resolved with no major repercussions, but my sister insisted that I had orchestrated the event to get her busted.

So much for my brief period of being more accessible to my younger sister. While this was going on, I needed to restain the large deck on our roof. The deck was one of the most endearing and valuable features of the house; imagining a view of the beach, about two miles away and just out of sight from that deck had led us to buy the house. However, my inspection revealed a serious case of termites. This led to tearing down the whole deck and having the house tented and treated for termites. As I mentioned, this was emotionally stressful in addition to eating up my time and money while simultaneously reducing the overall expected resale value.

Somehow, I managed to get through these challenges and put the house my wife had forced me to buy upon threat of divorce on the market. On December 30, 2002, the sale was completed and half of the proceeds were deposited into my wife's account. My half was reinvested into a house in Pasadena. I invited a close friend to contribute and become a part owner. We rented out the third bedroom and had a bachelor pad that we hoped would also pay off as an investment.

Meanwhile, our painful marriage counseling sessions ended when the counselor began to indicate that some of what I was saying sounded reasonable and that my wife would have to try to meet me halfway. She accused me of hiding my true self from the counselor, and this attitude gave the counselor another opening to ask her to look at her own behavior. But my wife could not accept any part of the blame for where we were and refused to continue the counseling. Shortly thereafter, I received a letter from her lawyer.

I was being sued for divorce.[10]

This was a dagger through my heart. As we began the bitter discussions about legal separation and how to approach our material possessions and finances, I came to an even more painful realization. Like many others before me, I would need to retain a lawyer to assist me in defending myself from a woman with whom I had thought I would spend my life but who was now suing me to end our marriage on unfavorable terms.

In what you might call denial, but survival for me, I kept a glimmer of hope alive that I would somehow salvage my marriage. This helped me place one foot in front of the other in my career. And the excitement and hope I felt in my newfound belief that God wanted me to become more involved in India kept me spiritually motivated.

10. Two poems or song lyrics I wrote during this process are included as appendix IV. The first, "The Quest," portrays the beginning stages of insights I was gaining, along with my pain, while the second, "The Fight," illustrates the frustration and disillusionment that resulted from the ultimate failure of all efforts to reconcile.

4

Magical Mystery Tour

Alice: I simply must get through!
Doorknob: Sorry, you're much too big. Simply impassible.
Alice: You mean impossible?
Doorknob: No, impassible. Nothing's impossible.

– LEWIS CARROLL, FROM ALICE IN WONDERLAND

It was exciting to plan my return to India in response to Michael's request for assistance with Passover and the Days of Unleavened Bread. But part of me was holding back. He had asked me for a relatively large sum of money to build a baptismal area in the compound where he lived and worked, and where the feast was held. In response, I had repeatedly asked Michael him for a report on the construction of the shelter for the tutoring program.

At first, he ignored my requests. Then he sent a picture of a small blue tarp, attached to a wall and suspended over a sidewalk by two metal upright poles. The tarp looked like it might have been left over from the structure over the covered area where we had held services for the Feast. In any case, it seemed both a hasty response to satisfy me in order to get more money and woefully inadequate for the purpose.

At the same time, I was no longer comfortable providing financial support to David Hulme. Ten percent of my income, which I dedicated to support the spread of the gospel, was accumulating in the bank. As 2003 rolled around and it came time to book my flight, I agreed to send Michael the money he had asked for. This felt more like hope than faith, as indications of poor money management were a red flag, to say the least. But soon enough, Michael would have the chance to answer questions about the makeshift shelter.

The Long and Winding Road

After my plane touched down in Chennai en route to Michael's house, he informed me that a number of people wanted to be baptized. And he had my itinerary all mapped out to perform these baptisms. My first assignment was counseling four women in Chennai who had attended the Feast and, since then, the Sabbath services he had conducted. He hoped they could be baptized into our fellowship before the Passover.

As excited as I was by this news, I asked Michael about the $200 tarp. Somewhat offhandedly, he explained that it had been destroyed in a monsoon. However, my misgivings about his handling of those funds and his answer were washed away by the extent of the work on the baptismal area in his compound.

It was below ground, accessed through a large square opening in the cement, down a recessed staircase almost as steep as a ladder. The pool was filled via the collection of rainwater. It was an ingenious solution. It served dual duty as a reservoir to support the small compound, which included Michael's house and a small school building with a couple of classrooms under the large rooftop tent-covered meeting room. This was important for Sabbath services and the feasts, as well as during the frequent droughts in the area.

And there was another benefit. Several women who were making the cushion covers had previously spent a large portion of their day simply obtaining water for themselves and their families, which they had to carry from a distance. The reservoir freed up time for both their new spiritual pursuits and the project Michael had launched.

Work was also being completed on a substantial wall to provide privacy along one side of Michael's house. Since proselytizing was an illegal act in the state of Tamil Nadu, in which Chennai is located, this was an important and prudent addition. Michael explained that the money I had sent had been enough to build this wall also. My confidence in Michael's ability and in his approach to the challenges within his region was restored.

It had been a positive first day. Rather than fret about the waste of money on the shelter for the tutoring program and Michael's cavalier approach to it, I went to bed that night thanking God for the opportunities He had granted me. This trip was already exceeding my expectations.

The next day we had discussions (in English and in Tamil with Michael translating) with the four women who had requested baptism. Their knowledge and enthusiasm were impressive, and I had no concerns about their sincerity and commitment. After completing the counseling sessions, we headed outside to the baptismal pool.

The Churches of God practice baptism by immersion. The candidate must be completely submerged in the "watery grave." After baptism, the minister foreshadows resurrection by laying hands on the new convert, praying for the Holy Spirit to enter and dwell in the newly begotten child of God.[1]

My own baptism had been performed in a horse trough in Alaska in the minister's garage. Since then, I had performed a number of memorable baptisms. This one was in another league entirely. The steep descent on a narrow ladder into a dark underground cavern was a vivid visualization of this symbolic death. "Treacherous" is the word that best describes the backward descent through the relatively cramped opening. Not knowing the depth of water below added to the feeling of dread, as did the narrow slippery rungs, which seemed destined to cause a slip and serious injury. Adding to the atmosphere was the timing. It was the afternoon before one of the most solemn and significant evenings of the year, the Passover. The descent into the abyss for baptism was doubly nerve-racking when combined with its requisite reflection on Christ's broken body and shed blood, as symbolized by the unleavened bread and wine that baptized members took annually at this event. Although I was relatively young

---

1. WCG theology allowed nonministers to perform baptisms, but this was not a practice encouraged by the ministry. In WCG theology the new convert was "begotten," as stated above, i.e., impregnated with the new life by the Spirit.

and nimble, the four women who were joining me were not all equally so. A serious injury would put a damper on the pending events.

Despite my apprehension, I arrived safely at the bottom and found my footing. The water was relatively shallow, reaching to my waist, and the space was only about four feet square. Jayenthi was the first baptismal candidate, and she was an inch or two taller than I was. Now that we were both safely in the hole, the next challenge was finding a way to submerge her politely and gently, working around the ladder that jutted from one wall. Somehow, I managed to do so without her banging or scraping herself on the bottom of the ladder. She was the first, and the tallest, and having successfully accomplished full immersion with her, the next three were easier.

Once back up on the surface, the ladies dried off, changed, and assembled for the laying-on-of-hands ceremony. I placed my hands on the head of each person, one by one, while praying for God's Spirit to take up residence in these newly purified vessels. These ladies were now considered members of the body of Christ, and eligible to partake in the symbols of His broken body. Overall, this was the most memorable baptism I had ever been a part of.

It would not be the most memorable for long.

The next day we traveled by rented car to Tiruvannemalai, a farming village about four hours away. We planned to celebrate the First Day of Unleavened Bread with local farmers. The WCG taught observance of the Holy Days Moses taught, but with a focus on removing sin from our lives. Michael had connected with the farmers through an agricultural program he had sponsored.

The sights and smells that confronted us on this journey were quite different from anything I had ever encountered. Our visit to the homeless village in Chennai a few months earlier had been intense but was confined to a small geographical area. The road to Tiruvannemalai seemed an endless procession of travelers on foot, beggars, children, herded animals, and heaps of trash, burning or rotting by the side of the road.

The images from our air-conditioned windows were of people shuffling through squalor, with no understanding, much less hope, that it could be different. Here, the vision of how to effect change was completely obscured. The closest I had come to this was on my trip to Egypt, which had provided a glimpse of something similar but on a much smaller, less exhausting scale.

This was systemic, grinding poverty.

We passed through village after village of people trudging alongside the road, or sitting by it, watching the traffic. We traveled further and further away from the familiar, passing countless shrines, and idols, which underscored my existing impression that India was enslaved by false religion, which kept many of the people poor and ignorant. The memory of my near-death experience on the Nile had me paranoid about getting sick here; I dreaded having to exit the comfortable sedan to use the bathroom facilities.

Four-and-a-half winding, dirty hours of exposure to this finally brought us to the village where we were to celebrate the "Night to Be Much Observed." This was an especially peculiar WCG celebration that resulted from the difficulty in aligning the exact chronology of the Exodus in the Old Testament with the sacrifice of Christ in the New Testament.[2] Though I'd probably participated in this celebration thirty times before, this time it was the beginning of what would prove to be a significant milestone in my life.

We pulled into a semimodern, Western-style hotel, and Michael arranged with the concierge to rent a small suite for the evening. Food had been ordered, which we spread out across the large coffee table in front of the couch in the room. A couple of chairs were pulled up on the other side, and we had the setting for the meal. Two men joined us—one single, the other accompanied by his wife and two daughters. The food was a variety of tasty meat and vegetable dishes with rice and Indian bread. The daughters had learned some English phrases and poetry, which they recited for us. I was impressed by the closeness of the family and their sincere desire to share a special time together in the context of worshiping God according to His commandments. During dinner, I learned that although the two men wanted to be baptized, a serious drought

2. This celebration, unique to the WCG and the resulting COG splinter groups, is based on the understanding that Israel was commanded to stay up all night after partaking of the Passover and to leave in the morning. While they were observing this memorial, the firstborn of the Egyptians were dying in their sleep, as the death angel passed over the Israelites, who were safe behind doorposts painted with lamb's blood. The Israelites were further commanded to observe the event throughout their generations. Their day began at sunset and ended the next day at sunset. With Christ being crucified on the afternoon leading up to the Passover, the WCG observed both the Passover at the onset of the fourteenth of Nisan, per the Hebrew calendar, as well as the next evening, called the Night to Be Much Observed. The WCG viewed this as the celebration of Israel's departure from Egypt with a high hand. They were first spared from death, due to the blood on their doors, and were then sent out with gifts and treasure, by the broken, grief-stricken Egyptians who had not been protected. See Exodus 14; Numbers 33.

had made it difficult to find a suitable location. The closest option was a public swimming area—more than an hour away.

So the next morning we headed down another long road, this one a bit straighter, better paved, and less dusty overall than the one that had brought us this far. It was not well trafficked, though, and didn't seem to be heading anywhere in particular, just further away. After an hour or so on this road, I spotted a huge, yellow, plastic sculpture with a colorful head, off to the right. It was a twenty-foot high cobra god guarding the entrance to our destination—a public aquatic park. As we passed under the hood of the cobra god, we encountered a number of other smaller shrines and religious statues, featuring a strange and fascinating mix of animals, humans, and religious imagery. This combination garden and swimming park featured a number of pools and garden areas, which, due to the drought, more closely approximated an exotic swamp. A very unpleasant one.

Yellow Submarine

As we pulled up to the entrance, a pervasive stench seemed to emanate from the mouth of the great hooded cobra god. And as if its noxious breath were not enough, it bared its fangs in our direction. As we entered the park, the sun beat down oppressively, and I realized that it wasn't actually the breath of the cobra god, but the land under its dominion, that generated the foul odor.

Because of the drought, this normally pond- and lake-covered area had experienced a tremendous amount of evaporation. Reduced water levels had exposed large tracts of mud to the air and sun. The vegetation in this normally verdant park was dying, in the fetid remainders of previously larger and deeper bodies of water, and was rotted in the muck at the bottom of the stagnant and shrinking swamp that resulted. An eerie stillness pervaded the area, which seemed devoid of any animals, along with the powerful reek that was causing visitors to steer clear. It was as if Satan, the great deceiver who used false religions to oppress and enslave, had created a strange and foreboding pantheistic park, ripe with potential for disease and misery.

Winding our way through the park, we eventually got to the public outdoor swimming pool, roughly Olympic in size, and with a diving platform at the far end. The size was the only thing Olympic about this pool. It was made of untreated cement, and the internal sides were covered with algae. My mind began working overtime.

The survival chances of any Westerner foolish enough to crawl into that water, much less one as prone to illness as myself, did not seem particularly good. The algae were evidence of a lack of chlorine or any other kind of purification, and who knows what microbes dwelled in the murky pool. They were likely to be as exotic, and toxic, as what had hit me in the bowels of the ship on the Nile. A snake handler might have considered the cobra god park to be the mother of all opportunities to prove his faith, but I was under no such illusion. God had no obligation to protect me from serious and even terminal illness. Friends and classmates who had volunteered for WCG and AICF programs in Thailand and Jordan had contracted intestinal issues that had plagued them for years. Ministerial trainees in Africa had contracted malaria or other permanent, debilitating health problems. During my time in Germany, I had been grateful to serve God in a region free from such environments and experiences.

Some evil disease was surely lurking in that pool and if I were foolish enough to get in it, God might just be willing to let it attach itself to me. This was not a lack of faith; it was pragmatism. It was a realistic assessment of the potential price of being faithful—counting the cost.[3] I would not be the first servant of God to suffer severe tests and trials—even death—in a faithful, but perhaps foolishly applied, pursuit of "God's will."

My decades-long struggle with a chronic, crippling disease, and my years of diligent effort and focus on sorting through medical advice, literature, and self-help options available was fresh in my mind. Having slowly, with God's help, climbed out of the dark pit of serious health problems I was anything but eager to embrace that kind of pain again. My experience in Egypt was also fresh

---

3. Luke 14:27–33: "And whosoever doth not bear his cross, and come after me, cannot be my disciple. For which of you, intending to build a tower, sitteth not down first, and counteth the cost, whether he have sufficient to finish it? Lest haply, after he hath laid the foundation, and is not able to finish it, all that behold it begin to mock him, Saying, This man began to build, and was not able to finish. Or what king, going to make war against another king, sitteth not down first, and consulteth whether he be able with ten thousand to meet him that cometh against him with twenty thousand? Or else, while the other is yet a great way off, he sendeth an ambassage, and desireth conditions of peace. So likewise, whosoever he be of you that forsaketh not all that he hath, he cannot be my disciple."

on my mind. Nor would getting sick again help me to assist Michael with these programs in India. No lesser a personage than Christ Himself had warned us against tempting God in this way.

In other words, there was no angle that I could find to make what I was about to do seem like a wise choice.

Yet my Jonah days were over. I had to go where God led. That was the point of my trip to Thailand, which had resulted, now, in this second trip to India. A compromise might do. I didn't have to be in the water with the candidate; I could sit on the side and lay on hands from there.

Michael shook his head in that uniquely Indian way, looking somewhat like a friendly bobblehead doll that might be saying yes or no. With a wide, toothy grin, reminiscent of the Cheshire cat, he explained that the men believed that I needed to get into the water with them to perform the baptism. If I was to follow the pillar and cloud, my only choice was to baptize these men in the manner they expected, as they looked to me for guidance, in faith, as a man of God.

As all this was going through my head, I noticed a guard by the open-air entrance, eying us carefully. Michael had informed me earlier that there was a law against proselytizing, and explained that we would have to be discreet. The only white man within miles was conspicuously standing in swimming trunks. In order to come anywhere close to discreet I had to swim.

The best way, it was determined, to accomplish a baptism under these circumstances was to climb up on the diving platform together and perform the baptism by holding hands and jumping in together.

As far as baptisms went, this one was definitely outside the box.

The first candidate and I clambered up on the platform, and joining my right and his left hand above our heads in a triumphant, statuesque pose, we jumped in together, side by side.

This was not too wise, in terms of preventing potential infection.

The water shot up my nose, and possibly elsewhere. Spluttering, we swam for the side. The pool had a large deep end, so even though we were at the midpoint along the length, we clung to the slimy edge, as the water was still too deep to stand.

We decided the second candidate should just climb in from the side. So we swam out a ways, where I performed what was intended to look like a "playful dunk" to the curious guard, and after a couple of perfunctory laps to make it look real we decided that the three of us could now get out of the pool.

As we toweled off in the hot sun, Michael took a few pictures to commemorate, and we determined our work there was done. The baptism count for the trip was now up to six. Soon we were back in the car, slowly winding our way through the drying, pungent swampland, past the cobra god, and back onto the open road.

Ten minutes later, the car broke down.

Don't Pass Me By

My recollection of my emotions during my time spent at the side of the road after this most memorable baptism is of a growing feeling of dread. I was further off the grid and out of my comfort zone than I had ever been, and the oppressive heat seemed an emanation of the cobra god's power, from which we had apparently not quite escaped. Fresh from a fourteen-hour trip to India and reeling from the thirteen-hour time difference, I felt particularly vulnerable to whatever exotic diseases most certainly had accompanied me out of the cobra god swamp. Standing in the hot sun, next to a broken-down car, on a long, lonely stretch of broken pavement, somewhere, far, far away from wherever I should have been, I was now certain I would succumb to its imminent attack.

The driver caught a ride after some ten minutes of hitchhiking, and after what seemed like far more than a couple of hours, he returned in another car. We then switched places with him taking up the roadside vigil while we rode back to Tiruvannemalai. We were unloaded at a small town square with a mini-temple, which was bigger than a breadbox but smaller than a typical Starbucks. We took up residence to the side of it on a three-foot-high mound of what was either dirty sand or sandy dirt, presumably intended for construction of one sort or another. From our low perch, I watched as local worshippers paid homage to Ganesha (the elephant god of Hinduism) with prayers and incense. They returned my curious and somewhat furtive glances as they went about their religious business.

Soon, several extended family members of the two who had been newly baptized met us, and there was some food shared. It grew darker and cooler, which was more pleasant not only to me, but unfortunately also to various flying insects. Bites from the mosquitoes and their even more annoying smaller- and faster-winged allies added thoughts of malaria to my growing paranoid list of fates that might befall me before this adventure was over.

After some time, the villagers, escorted by Michael, left to catch the last bus home, since, as farmers they lived a ways outside of the town proper. I sat on the dusty, dirty pile for another hour or so, as the slow stream of Ganesha's faithful seemed to grow steadier. I hadn't really understood what we were waiting for, what our options were, or why we weren't more aggressively pursuing them. I had been inexorably sucked into the shuffling life that I had observed on my way to Tiruvannemalai the day before, from the relative comfort of our now-deceased, air-conditioned sedan. I had sought to avoid contact with the elements of this country that could do me in, but my flimsy protective barriers had all been ripped away.

During all my previous travels outside the heart of the first world— whether as a tourist in Egypt or on assignments in countries like Hungary, Estonia, and Russia—I had been in control of where I was with some ability to communicate in one of the languages I had learned.

This was different.

I had cast myself into a global mosh pit, and unfamiliar hands were carrying me around. I felt helpless and was completely dependent on Michael. My questions about him resurfaced as he let me know that he preferred I stayed there while he left to arrange a solution to our car trouble. I was no stranger to operating in a survival mode, whether navigating foreign countries or living in a tent in Alaska. However, at all times I had been certain to know where, if you will, the emergency exits were located, how to use the oxygen mask overhead, and the value of the life jacket under my seat. Now, I was essentially lost and alone in a town I could barely pronounce, with signs I couldn't understand.

As it got darker it grew colder, and the bugs grew more numerous and aggressive. My jeans, damp from the swimming suit under my pants, had dried, but my shirt was not warm enough for the increasingly cool breeze. I was dirty from sitting on dirt and from shifting around from the mound, to Ganesha's shrine, to the steps of a nearby building nearby, and back to the mound. I was also increasingly impatient. With so much experience at problem solving, submitting to a complete lack of control was psychologically draining.

Mitigating my frustration somewhat was a sense that this was the part of the experience that God most wanted me to learn from.

Just when the situation was becoming intolerable, Michael reappeared, explaining that he'd found a garage that was going to fix the car. A taxi shuttled us over to the part of town where the car had been towed. I was hopeful we'd soon be heading back toward something a bit closer to civilization. Upon climbing out onto a semicovered, oil-stained slab of cement, this hope quickly faded. "We need a part that the garage doesn't have," Michael explained, as our driver again headed off into the night. I had little faith that he would find the part at this hour and quickly resigned myself to spending the night on the cold, hard, dirty cement.

It was now after midnight, and Michael and I each found a piece of dirty cardboard. Placing the cardboard, least-soiled side up, on the least-oily portion of cement, I laid my weary body down just inside the outer edge of the extended roof. The temperature was moderate there, out of the breeze, but the mosquitoes were even more ferocious in the still warmth of the outdoor area. With visions of malaria dancing in my head, I managed to doze off.

A startling circus-like din brought me rudely back to my current reality.

By some bizarre and sinister coincidence, this was the night of a festival in which the people of the town and the surrounding areas arose before dawn to march around a nearby mountain in the light of the full moon. The whole region was afoot, and pilgrims grasping candles, with children and animals following behind, all marched down the street right in front of my improvised mat. They, and others on the street behind the garage, were all chanting, honking horns, and shaking and ringing whatever religious instruments they had with them. There were probably ten thousand people or more, on the move for several hours.

Michael explained to me what the festival was, but I was not interested. My interpretation of such things was still colored by WCG-derived ideas about the pagan origins of religious worship. Given that this mode of thinking was applied liberally even to those who professed a Christian faith, you can imagine my perspective on what I had been experiencing over the previous thirty-six hours. My WCG-influenced theology labeled all of this under the broad heading of satanic deception. I viewed the poverty and relative ignorance of the people around me in the country as a symptom of being enslaved by a false religion, which kept them from connecting with the true God.

The hard cement and biting bugs were bad enough, but the cacophony around me made it utterly impossible to fall back asleep. And it had gotten colder, so I tried to rest inside the car for a while. But there I couldn't lie flat, and somehow the mosquitoes seemed to both detect the warmth and exploit a secret entryway. When I moved back, the pavement seemed harder, the air colder, and the mosquitoes more aggressive, as a never-ending night became more oppressive.

I was there to support Michael, but it had come about due to my relentless drive to both follow God and proclaim Him to others. I had felt He was bringing me into contact with others with whom He was working. In WCG terminology, these were minds specifically selected and opened by Him, just waiting for a minister to teach them.

So why was it always such an uphill battle? Was it satanic opposition? My own weakness?

I would eventually discover the significance of what was happening around me. But even then, an inkling of something much bigger was beginning to dawn on me. It was the beginning of the end of my own closed-mindedness. My focus was on believing God had brought me there to help others, but as my own discomfort, exhaustion, and other self-centered concerns took center stage, I realized that the trip might have more to do with God specifically working with me than whatever I might accomplish for God. Over the previous few years, I had overcome beliefs that had limited me in my career and kept me from achieving financial independence. Finally, it was time to examine some of my core religious beliefs.

In the areas of life that are more spiritual in nature—my marriage relationship and religion, for example—some of my beliefs were still working against what God was trying to reveal to me. Like Jonah, I had previously resisted following God's lead. This was the time and place He had chosen to regurgitate me from the belly of the giant fish that had swallowed me.

Speaking of time, it doesn't actually stop, even when it seems to. The agonizingly long and memorably bad night eventually morphed into a long, dull, tired morning. By about 10:00 a.m., the part had been found and fitted. We climbed into the car and began the long journey back to Chennai.

Good Morning, Good Morning

Or maybe the right part hadn't been found. Or perhaps it wasn't properly fitted. Or maybe that wasn't the part that had been defective.

A trip that should have been about four hours took about seven, due to a loss of power and resulting frequent stops. Along the way, we had to get food from street vendors, including tea from cracked cups that did not seem properly washed. By now, with everything I had been through—the two immersions into water of decreasing quality, the exhaustion, the dirt, the food, the bugs—it was unavoidable. I was going to become ill, so I ate and drank whatever was served up.

Finally, around five o'clock that afternoon, we approached Chennai, that vast sprawling city of ten million people, with its four hundred thousand homeless, in the midst of a rush hour of gargantuan magnitude. The various and widely divergent modes of transportation all seemed equipped with noisemakers of fearsome effectiveness and were all operated by drivers of limitless energy and impatience. This fueled the growth of a migraine due to loss of sleep, which had begun upon our departure from Tiruvannamalai.

The driver's herky-jerky finessing of our limping car through Chennai didn't do my screaming head any favors. Under these circumstances, the dirty pothole-filled side street that led to Michael's house seemed an oasis. It was the first sign of anything familiar since the odyssey had begun.

At the previous Feast, I had used my second tithe funds to book an upscale, Western hotel room. This time, to make more funds available for Michael's projects, I was staying in the Hubert's exterior studio. I walked up the outside staircase at the back of the Hubert residence without glancing at the compound it overlooked, which Michael had built to support his programs and serve others.

Opening the door to my clean, sparse, and very hot room, I reached for the switch of the window-mounted air-conditioning unit. I surveyed the seven-by eleven-foot expanse before turning toward the small bathroom area. I opened the door and, squeezing past the tiny sink, bent down to reach through a dog-door-sized opening and turn the outdoor-style faucet handle to slowly fill the small bucket in the far corner with water. A minute later, I had enough to fill the tiny hot-water heater mounted above the sink and turn it on. I returned the bucket to its place, filled it again in preparation for a visit to the toilet in the other corner, and waited for the water to heat enough to make my sponge bath more satisfying. Soon I was wiping off the accumulation of grime with a washcloth, careful to keep my arms and legs close to me to avoid bumping up against the half-wall–half-curtain at my back

Returning to the main room, I faced the small bookshelf and table next to the small bed, which was a mattress on a raised, plywood surface. Firm mattresses had always eased my formerly chronic back pain, and having spent much of my life living out of a suitcase, in small places that included ten months in a tent in Alaska, this was a perfectly comfortable arrangement. The air was admittedly on the hot and stuffy side, since Michael had asked that I use both the water and the air-conditioning sparingly, but after Tiruvannemalai this humble space was my private Taj Mahal.

However, my relief at being back was more of a Band-Aid than a cure. Despite my current state of near exhaustion, it was the first Day of Unleavened Bread. I was scheduled to deliver a sermon in just a few hours. I had to keep putting one foot in front of the other.

I managed about ninety minutes of sleep before Michael woke me up to head to the meeting hall to deliver the sermon to the ten people who had assembled for the service, including the four newly baptized women. Everyone was excited by what was happening, and the message was well received. This went a long way to ease my nervousness about the remainder of my stay. Still, I was intent on making sure dinner was light and quick, so I could retreat upstairs to relax, enjoy some privacy, and get a good night's sleep.

Michael, however, wanted to discuss the next activity on the itinerary he had mapped out for me. We were to leave in the morning to visit a small group of people in a little town called Gudiyatham, some four hours away. Michael was working with a group of HIV sufferers in what he called an "AIDS village," and he had volunteered me, as a minister, to meet with them.

I sat speechless for a moment, and finally said, "Wow," quickly adding, "I really need to get some sleep, and after all that's happened in the last couple of days, I'm hoping I'll wake up feeling up to the challenge of heading back out into rural India."

Having escaped from the discussion without reacting negatively and without committing to go, I retreated up the outside staircase to my room and lay down on the small, hard mattress. Somewhat guiltily, I got up to turn on the air conditioner, knowing that Michael and his wife, Terrencia, did not have air-conditioning inside the house. Even as tired as I was, after Michael's news I needed to cool the room down a bit in order to fall asleep.

My mind raced ahead faster than the room was cooling. While pondering whether to accompany Michael to the AIDS village, an unwelcome but familiar pain began growing in my stomach. Hoping it was just nervous emotion, I turned off the air-conditioning and managed to doze off.

At some dark and unknown hour, I was awakened by stomach cramps which evoked flashbacks of my scare in Egypt. After a quick visit to the far end of the room, I was relieved in more ways than one. This was not as bad as that. Then another wave of cramps hit me, worse than what I had just experienced. Though I wasn't having delirious worries about dying, I began riding wave after wave of wanting to. I tossed and turned through the dawn hours until Michael invited me down for breakfast before departing for Gudiyatham.

The only thing I wanted less than breakfast was to travel to Gudiyatham. I was not visiting an AIDS village in backwater India. My room may not have had a five-star rating, but it had a toilet and sink. It was a relief to have a valid excuse not to go.

I let Michael know that, although it was a nonlethal dose, the cobra god's venom had nonetheless penetrated my system. "Regretfully," I said, which was only partially true, "we have to postpone the trip." He took it in stride and agreed to bring me some bottled water and a couple of mangoes. This gave me the time I needed to take stock.

I had expected this trip to be spiritually important. Michael's aggressive schedule of activities and the resulting baptisms had validated that expectation. But the situation had spiraled out of control. This was much more than I had bargained for. I needed to regain my equilibrium.

WCG theology was the mirror image of Messianic Judaism. We worked backward through Christianity to connect with the forward-looking promises of the Old Testament. We diligently and sincerely sought to obey the law while following the guidance of the spirit, in faith. We were the Woman of Revelation 12—the only church that kept the law and also had the Testimony of Jesus Christ.

So why had the WCG been ripped asunder, and why was it continuing to splinter? What was the missing ingredient? Were we not the authorized living branch, the rod of Aaron?[4] Did aspects of our theology and accepted understanding keep us from achieving the kind of regeneration we had hoped for?

Experience, including my severe health trials, had taught me (as with the Apostle Paul) that spiritual insight usually comes during times of weakness. God might be trying to show me something, and I dove into the Bible in anticipation of getting answers.

Moses's efforts to lead the children of Israel from Egypt to the Promised Land had been on my mind, so I began reading the accounts of that familiar story. Their forty years of circuitous wanderings in the desert seemed increasingly relevant to my experience, and as Michael returned with the water and mangoes, I read chapter after chapter in my efforts to draw closer to the source of the cloud and pillar they had followed. It quickly became apparent that it involved pulling up one's tent and moving to a new location, spiritually speaking. This was important.

Much of the authority that WCG members had accorded to HWA came from repeated comparisons to Moses. One example was the oft-repeated admonishment to "hold up the hands of God's Apostle," using the analogy of holding up the hands of Moses.[5] This implied, actually, that the WCG fulfilled both the governmental role of Moses and the spiritual role of Aaron. HWA was the "pastor-general" and the rest of the ministers were spiritual Levites.

If you state something often and emphatically enough, people can come to believe it unquestioningly. This particular belief was driven home with pile-driver force and systematic regularity. Gerald Waterhouse, a well-known and

---

4. Numbers 17:6–8: "And Moses spake unto the children of Israel, and every one of their princes gave him a rod apiece, for each prince one, according to their fathers' houses, even twelve rods: and the rod of Aaron was among their rods. And Moses laid up the rods before the Lord in the tabernacle of witness. And it came to pass, that on the morrow Moses went into the tabernacle of witness; and, behold, the rod of Aaron for the house of Levi was budded, and brought forth buds, and bloomed blossoms, and yielded almonds."

5. Exodus 17:9–12: "And Moses said unto Joshua, Choose us out men, and go out, fight with Amalek: tomorrow I will stand on the top of the hill with the rod of God in mine hand. So Joshua did as Moses had said to him, and fought with Amalek: and Moses, Aaron, and Hur went up to the top of the hill. And it came to pass, when Moses held up his hand, that Israel prevailed: and when he let down his hand, Amalek prevailed. But Moses hands were heavy; and they took a stone, and put it under him, and he sat thereon; and Aaron and Hur stayed up his hands, the one on the one side, and the other on the other side; and his hands were steady until the going down of the sun."

generally respected WCG evangelist, for example, had made numerous world tours, speaking to virtually every member, with the goal of pointing the brethren to headquarters. This meant, he explained, that God had established His government in His church and that HWA was God's Apostle, the authorized earthly representative of that government. Moreover, God was actively engaged in and backed up the thinking and decisions of HWA and the ministerial hierarchy of the WCG.

We tied this to the seat of Moses referred to by Christ in a discussion with the Pharisees.[6] The Pharisees were a religious and political movement, a brotherhood of individuals opposed to the priestly authority, appealing instead to a learned understanding of and teaching on the law.[7] On the surface, Jesus's reference to the Pharisees' occupation of Moses's seat seems to endorse them in that role. Without going into the textural arguments—for example, considering the possibility of a Hebrew version of Matthew, and/or other scholarly approaches—this is not logical.

The verse actually says that both the Pharisees and the scribes sat in this seat. The *Encyclopedia Britannica* provides a brief description of the two groups: "In the 1st century, scribes and Pharisees were two largely distinct groups, though presumably some scribes were Pharisees. Scribes had knowledge of the law and could draft legal documents (contracts for marriage, divorce, loans, inheritance, mortgages, the sale of land, and the like). Every village had at least one scribe. Pharisees were members of a party that believed in resurrection and in following legal traditions that were ascribed not to the Bible but to 'the traditions of the fathers.' Like the scribes, they were also well-known legal experts: hence the partial overlap of membership of the two groups."[8]

These teachers bickered notoriously over many points of the law. If both sat in Moses's seat, which version should you follow? Did God expect anyone to obey conflicting commands issued by squabbling factions? And, regarding the Pharisees, for example, Christ said, "Let them alone: they be blind leaders of the

6. Matthew 23:1–3: "Then spake Jesus to the multitude, and to his disciples, Saying The scribes and the Pharisees sit in Moses' seat: All therefore whatsoever they bid you observe, that observe and do; but do not ye after their works: for they say, and do not."
7. *Jewish Encyclopedia,* s.v. "Pharieees," by Kaufmann Kohler, accessed September 26, 2017, http://jewishencyclopedia.com/articles/12087-pharisees.
8. *Encyclopaedia Britannica Online,* s.v. "Jesus," by Jaroslav Jan Pelikan and E.P. Sanders, last updated July 5, 2017, https://www.britannica.com/biography/Jesus.

blind. And if the blind lead the blind, both shall fall into the ditch."[9] Clearly, Christ was telling people not to accept the authority of blind guides leading them into a ditch.

In my opinion, Christ was referring to both the scribes and Pharisees as usurpers who *claimed* a seat they had no right to sit in, while He was nonetheless advising His followers to carefully consider what these teachers of the law (the Scriptures) were saying. He rounds the advice out with a warning about their general hypocrisy, so that rather than simply obeying the teachings of these squatters, His followers were empowered to form an opinion based on the Scriptures. Only if the teaching was faithful to the Scriptures should it be followed.

The irony of appeals made to the authority of "blind leaders of the blind" was generally lost on those within the WCG, because WCG leadership compared itself to Moses and Aaron, not the Pharisees. Truth be told, however, we should have given more attention to Christ's statements about the Pharisees, especially to how he referred to the ritualistic washing of hands.

Tell Me Why

Daniel Boyarin's recent book *The Jewish Gospels* has deepened my understanding of what Christ said about hand washing. In a section entitled "Jesus Kept Kosher," Boyarin explains that Jesus uses the law to show that the Pharisees—though they were experts in the law—didn't understand it. They missed key distinctions in the law itself and jumped to wrong conclusions about its spiritual application. His examples support the view that rather than abolishing the law, Jesus magnified it and made it honorable.[10]

The main spiritual lesson is contained in a phrase in Mark 7:3. The text conveys that the Pharisees "do not eat unless they wash the hands by means of a fist." Washing the hands with a fist describes the practice of pouring a small amount of water into the strategically formed hole of a loose fist to wet both the outside of the hand and the inside. This is a powerful illustration.

Since water was scarce and this ritual was performed often, the Pharisees had perfected this technique and apparently used it with a flourish to affect

9. Matthew 15:14.
10. See Isaiah 42:21.

the impression of righteousness or superiority. Christ brilliantly deploys the expression "with a fist" to imply that they used the law as an act of aggression. Matthew 23 features Christ's withering attack on the Pharisees in which He declares multiple "woes" against them. In verse 13, He declares, "But woe unto you, scribes and Pharisees, hypocrites! For ye shut up the kingdom of heaven against men: for ye neither go in yourselves, neither suffer ye them that are entering to go in." The inference is that the Pharisees used the law against other people, including "washing with a fist" to display a superiority that actually drove others away from God.

There is no better illustration of the distinction that was beginning to dawn on me about my beliefs. We in the WCG may have been technically correct in our interpretation of Mark 7, but, speaking from my own experience, we tended to carry ourselves with a degree of smugness. Unlike the Pharisees, we accepted Christ, but like the Pharisees, we prided ourselves on our obedience to the law.

With my understanding and acceptance of the diversity of the world around me growing, attitudes prevalent within the COG movement were becoming less acceptable. And this awareness shed light on my approach to relationships. I was becoming aware that in my most important relationship—my marriage—I had washed my hands with a fist.

Despite my best efforts and intentions toward humility, my adherence to standards and laws that went unheeded by the bulk of those around me led to tension in my relationships with them. My focus had enabled a heroic transformation from a troubled juvenile delinquent into a young man striving to become a model citizen of heaven. A resulting mini–identity crisis had been resolved by accepting the truism that you can be so concerned about being called self-righteous that you never approach righteousness. And in classic college sophomore irony, I had fasted each week in order to understand Job and overcome the sin of self-righteousness, just in case I was suffering from it. [11]

Believing that we had God's favor as a result of living in obedience to Him made it hard not to view others as inferior. And if they bristled at our attitudes toward them, it was due to their basic unrighteousness—because unrighteousness resents righteousness like darkness hates the light.[12]

---

11. See *TPotS*, chaps. 5–6.
12. John 3:20: "For every one that doeth evil hateth the light, neither cometh to the light, lest his deeds should be reproved."

In this, we were very much like the blind Pharisees. It was virtually impossible for anyone else to shed light on where we were wrong. Would even Christ Himself be able to get through to us?

Do I overstate the case by asking if even Christ could get through to us? Perhaps, but consider this: we had arrived at a set of self-referential, circular beliefs. Our adherence to the Sabbath and Holy Days was proof that we were God's people. Keep them, and we were kept by Him. This logical loop was then hermetically sealed in that anyone from the outside seeking to contradict us was deemed a deceiver seeking to subvert our faith.

Our self-referential beliefs were easy to maintain, despite serious errors in our framework, because WCG leaders, from HWA on down, refused to give credence to accepted biblical scholarship while using pseudoscholarship to claim adherence to the text. Linguistic, historical, and textual analysis might largely be recognized in other circles, but we relied on a near-mystical belief in our leaders' connection to God. To be a member in good standing you had to accept their authority and trust their rendering of biblical meaning. They sat in Moses's seat. In all this, WCG leaders were like the Pharisees, who presumed to sit in Moses's seat. And Christ did not get through to the Pharisees.

These insights gave new weight to an earlier suspicion, that the collapse of the WCG was the only way for light to enter into our hermetically sealed hall of mirrors, in which our own inaccurate views of reality were constantly reinforced. This trip was proving to be a more powerful reality check than I had bargained for. The similarities and differences between the signs of the two covenants might yield greater clarity.

From my perspective, a massive twist of cosmic irony ensued when Christianity rejected the Sabbath in an overreaction to the Jews having rejected Christ. It caused Christianity to reject the only sign Christ formally gave about Himself, the sign of Jonah.[13] Their rejection of the three days and three nights—the one and only sign of who Christ was—came in the form of a Friday afternoon crucifixion and a Sunday morning resurrection, covering merely one full day, two partial days, and two nights. Perhaps Western Christianity was

---

13. Matthew 12:38–40: "Then certain of the scribes and of the Pharisees answered, saying, Master, we would see a sign from thee. But he answered and said unto them, An evil and adulterous generation seeketh after a sign; and there shall no sign be given to it, but the sign of the prophet Jonas: For as Jonas was three days and three nights in the whale's belly; so shall the Son of man be three days and three nights in the heart of the earth."

not much different from what I had seen from my car window on the road to Tiruvannemalai—corrupt edifices built on flawed understanding and millions bowing down to the idols enshrined by our institutions and our egos.

This thorny topic of the three days and three nights is related to the idea of a calendar established at the beginning of creation, "And God said, Let there be lights in the firmament of the heaven to divide the day from the night; and let them be for signs, and for seasons, and for days, and years."[14] The heavenly bodies serve as a planetary clock and calendar, and as signs. This idea is not exclusive to the Bible. Traces of this can be seen in the Egyptian pyramids, which as mentioned may have been astronomical instruments, and the Mayan calendar, which used the zodiac to cover a vast period of time, a gigantic astrological epochal cycle, which famously ended in 2012.[15]

The biblical calculations of the calendar are rather complicated, and so there is much opportunity for widely diverse interpretations. The WCG was united under HWA's dogmatic determination on issues related to the calendar— not only the observance of a weekly Sabbath but also of the annual Sabbaths, along with their prophetic significance. These were signs, identifiers of a divine relationship in which we were "sanctified" or set apart as special. Christ had both fulfilled these days at His coming and opened up their special prophetic significance, revealing details about His return.

Through our special relationship, we were the only group on earth that knew what Christ had really done and was about to do.

Yet I had struggled for years with how our emphasis on this sign led to a separation between us and other Christians. My conclusion had been that these Sabbaths constituted a private sign. In other words, even though the Sabbaths were historically applied to a group of tribes with common heritage—a "nation," if you will—the sign was between God and them, for their benefit, not as a sign to others. The Sabbath keepers were to know who they were, but that knowledge was not for outside consumption.

Even the seemingly critical one and only sign given by Christ can be seen in this light. Perhaps that is why He couched it in the terms He did: that He was only issuing it because of the demands of an evil and adulterous generation. And

---

14.   Genesis 1:14.
15.   December 21, 2012 marked the end of the long-count Mayan calendar, a 5,126-year cycle.

perhaps that is the reason the sign hasn't seemed to identify anyone definitively. Many, if not most, areas of obedience were intended by God to be personal matters and only caused contention and damaged relationships when we tried to make them a badge of righteousness.

When outsiders, quite naturally, reacted negatively to our emphasis on our righteousness, it reinforced our belief that most people were "not called." Our arrogance was visible, causing most to conclude that our belief in being "God's people" was just delusion. They couldn't understand what we understood. The sign of the Sabbath was not intended to solve this particular challenge. Thinking it would was another example of washing our hands with a fist.

While Christ acknowledges that the world has a bias against those who are different, He admonishes—even commands us—to pull off a miracle nonetheless. Christ's disciples must reflect a profound, godly love for our brothers and sisters. The miracle that Christ expected us to pull off was the sign of the covenant He brought. It is love. What I hadn't realized with this degree of clarity before was how important Christ's statement was, when He said, "By this all will know that you are My disciples, if you have love for one another."[16]

This was the visible sign of His covenant. The sign He gave about the three days and nights was about Him—to those who, in faith, would recognize Him. In the same way the Sabbath identified God to Israel. But now God didn't want to be the only one to recognize His People, as was the case with Israel when they kept the Sabbath. Those under the Christian covenant were to be objectively recognized by outside observers. And the way you would become known as a disciple of Christ would be by being seen as having love.

Only those objectively loving their fellow humans could be considered People of the Sign. These people, and no others, would constitute the One True Church. In contrast, those who adhered to tenets of COG theology believed that others would somehow recognize us through our observance of the sign of the Mosaic covenant, the Sabbaths, our obedience to the Ten Commandments, and other teachings in the Bible. If they didn't recognize that we were of God, we could write them off as being blind.

We couldn't have had it more backward. Such attitudes constituted a form of blindness on our part. Creating such divisions between us and others ensured we could not fulfill the sign of Christ's covenant.

---

16. John 13:35.

The magnitude of the dead end at which I found myself was becoming more apparent. My entire adult religious experience had been within a group that thrived on establishing clear distinctions between who was and who was not following God. We were applying the law in a way that Jesus condemned, using the symbolism of "washing hands with a fist," judging people on whether they agreed with our dogmatic interpretation of biblical doctrine.

This attitude labeled anyone who questioned us and our beliefs as being cut off from God. Whether they understood the Bible correctly or not, their approach was generally more loving than ours. So regardless of whose understanding of the Bible was more accurate, they were the ones obeying the law of loving one another, while we were not. And yet we judged them as not being of Christ.

My experiences within groups characterized by such judgmental attitudes had pushed me to pursue true religion. This quest had led me to India and to a more Christlike relationship with my fellow man. The importance of this new direction was growing more apparent with every day I was spending there. The spiritual antidote to HWA's interpretation of our favorite touchstone Scriptures was a comprehensive understanding and application of his late wife Loma's favorite Bible passage, "Behold, how good and how pleasant it is for brethren to dwell together in unity!"[17]

My personal connection to Saturday as the Sabbath day, which we described as the "test commandment," was as strong as ever, but it wasn't my place to administer this test to others. And if I did wish to look for criteria to assess whether someone would be willing to follow Christ, then love was the criteria to use. If we wanted to be considered true Christians, objectively, we had to present love to others in a recognizable form. We had to represent it.

This may be an oversimplification, but it summarizes an overriding principle. Anything else is spiritual self-delusion.

I consoled myself by knowing that HWA had advocated a similar oversimplification during his last years. He repeatedly explained that the two trees in the Garden of Eden represented the "'give' versus 'get' ways of life." Hard-liners had derided this as watering down the truth, even though it came from the one they had accepted as an apostle of Christ for our day. No babies were being thrown out with any bathwater.

17. Psalm 133:1.

Rocky Raccoon

My first four days in India had been a triumphal celebration, a basking in the glow of confirmation for having followed God's guidance. My determination to manifest my belief in love to humanity by following God wherever He led, and serving whoever He led me to, had led me to this tiny tabernacle, Michael's little apartment. After throwing caution to the wind, I had succumbed to some exotic bug likely ingested in the fetid public pool inside the domain of the great cobra god. Despite what I now personally knew about the horrors of the impoverished side of India, Michael was asking me to travel even further from anything safe and familiar, like Alice down a rabbit hole—to visit an AIDS village. After my encounter with the cobra god swamp, pulling back seemed more like wisdom than fear.

The Days of Unleavened Bread are a time of introspection and growth, even if one is not holed up in a tiny upstairs room in India with limited air-conditioning and little water, hot or otherwise. I was feverish, but the waves of cramps diminished as I slowed down my food intake to mangoes and water only—no bread, leavened or otherwise. This allowed me enough mental clarity to get serious about resolving the question of wisdom vs. idealism. In other words, should I agree to visit the AIDS village?

Despite my growing awareness that Christ directed us to focus on love of others, when Michael came in to discuss our morning departure, I thought, *Sure, no problem. Once the scientific expedition brings back ice crystals from the hot place, proving it has, in fact, frozen over, I'll be more than happy to visit an AIDS-infested area of this continent of misery.* My actual response was a bit more gracious. "I'm in no condition to travel just now, so we will have to pray, wait, and see." When he left, I crawled back into bed in my hot, little room.

I was on the edge of the gangplank of faith, at the end of which there seemed to be nothing but a fall into shark-infested water. I felt exposed and needed guidance. I opened my Bible again, and between water, mangoes, and the restroom, I read.

The answers to my questions centered on the similarities and differences between Moses and Christ. For the WCG, Moses was a type of Christ, and a critical component of our understanding rested on the fact that Moses was not allowed to enter the Promised Land, as covered in Numbers 20:12, "And the

LORD spake unto Moses and Aaron, Because ye believed me not, to sanctify me in the eyes of the children of Israel, therefore ye shall not bring this congregation into the land which I have given them." Most Christians say this was because he got angry with the children of Israel or because he struck the rock to which God had instructed him to speak. Essentially, they boil it down to Moses and Aaron being unfaithful.

The text leads one to conclude that Moses acted as though he and Aaron were the ones bringing the water out of the rock, failing to make an appropriate distinction between themselves and God. This is not to say that Moses, elsewhere called the meekest man on earth, did not understand the distinction.[18] Later Moses explains that it had more to do with Israel's disbelief, which is certainly in keeping with Moses as a forerunner of Christ—taking responsibility for the sins of the people. But my study shed new light on the WCG movement's "Armstrong problem," in which we turned HWA into our modern-day Moses.

HWA crossed the line in ways that Moses didn't. Adopting the title of Apostle and comparing himself to Moses are two major examples of this, not to mention that doing so was ample evidence he did not possess Moses's meekness. He openly admitted to "cockiness" in his autobiography. More important is the perception of others. Everyone from HWA on down— including those who suggested the title of Apostle to him—assigned to him (and, to an only slightly lesser degree, to themselves) an inordinate proximity to God. When the faithful realized that the proximity was overstated, to put it mildly, their faith in the leadership was shaken. This scenario played out repeatedly in the WCG and the resulting splintering Churches of God in a number of ways, all variations on the same theme.

I then read the story of the passing of leadership to Joshua and the tragedy of Israel botching their opportunity to become a spiritual nation upon inheriting the Promised Land. As Israel finished the settlement phase and began to struggle with what it meant to be an independent people in charge of their own destiny, we come to the saga of Saul. It is one of the most fascinating and tragic of all the biblical and historical events.

I had often read the discouraging story of how Israel was unable to fulfill God's wish that they turn the Promised Land into a utopia, as a model for the

---

18. Numbers 12:3: "Now the man Moses was very meek, above all the men which were upon the face of the earth."

rest of the world. All Israel needed was faith; that is, for a majority of the people to follow their exemplary founding fathers Moses, Caleb, and Joshua. Then they could have become the model nation God wanted them to be.

The WCG wanted the direct guidance and support Israel had tossed aside. Most members believed that HWA would lead us into the Promised Land. We were excited at how HWA had appeared to fulfill the Great Commission by taking the gospel to world leaders as a witness. Israel had failed to look past Moses and Aaron, and our acceptance of HWA as a Moses-like figure, God's Apostle, was a modern-day example of the same problem.

When our belief that HWA would be alive at Christ's return was shattered by his death, we had quickly rebounded because most initially believed that the commission of his successor, Joseph Tkach, fulfilled the role of Joshua. He would prepare the WCG to meet the Groom—leading us up to the return of Christ and into the Promised Land, His kingdom. We were all going to be kings and priests and under Christ would turn the entire world into a utopia, directly governed by Jesus Christ and flowing with milk and honey.

Our dedication and faith, not to mention the wealth of our tithe used at the Feast of Tabernacles, provided an annual, believable, real-world foretaste of this future promise. This had all crumbled, forcing us to realize our answers had left us with huge unanswered questions. I continued to read with interest, because the answers seemed just beyond the horizon, almost within reach.

Tomorrow Never Knows

Everybody wants to rule the world.

— *Tears for Fears, from* Songs from the Big Chair

The question that suddenly occupied my thinking was whether the Government of God doctrine in the WCG had sprung from a divine source or from the imagination of men. Flipping back to Genesis, I confirmed a hunch based on my recollection of "The Curse of Eden" manuscript I had recently abandoned. Sure enough, the first time the Bible references any kind of rulership among humans was when God told Eve, "Thy desire shall be to thy husband, and he shall rule over thee."[1]

Revolution 9

Although it sounds like God subordinated Eve, He was merely stating the natural outcome of choices made by both Adam and Eve. Adam now carried a

---

1.   Genesis 3:16.

burden of responsibility for Eve in a world that would resist his every effort. He would bear the consequences of his inevitable failure to rule with justice and integrity. This two-way curse resulted from Adam and Eve having a damaged relationship with God and with each other.

God created man and woman in His image and gave both dominion over the entire earth and all that was in it.[2] They were sovereign before Him, over all that God had placed under their dominion. Sin, in this view, is an abdication our God-given right to rule ourselves—the trading-in of our sovereignty for varying degrees of slavery.

To illustrate this dynamic, imagine a straight line with two extremes on either end: on the left side you have slavery, which is to be owned and controlled, and on the right side you have sovereignty, which is to be above and unencumbered by those things that enslave others. Being created in the image of God, as spiritual beings, we are given sovereignty—free will—the freedom to choose. This is one of the greatest gifts God has given to us. But our choices are too often abdication in disguise— we give up our sovereignty and begin an inevitable slide into slavery.

Many Scriptures tell the individual under such authority how to handle having fallen into slavery, including a command to submit to those in authority. This is balanced out by Christ's condemnation of those on the other end of that relationship, who in accepting a role of authority over others tend toward varying degrees of oppression and various forms of codependent dysfunction. This condemnation includes those who assume religious authority, those who tend to "wash their hands with a fist."

The construct of the Government of God within the family institutionalized this curse. When God informed Eve that because of her sin her husband would rule over her, it was not the establishment of a preferred form of government. The situation that was created by this was not one that was spiritually superior or one that even worked particularly well. Rather, this was a precursor to His message to the prophet Samuel about Israel's folly in wanting a king. He was

---

2. Genesis 1:26–27: "And God said, Let us make man in our image, after our likeness: and let them have dominion over the fish of the sea, and over the fowl of the air, and over the cattle, and over all the earth, and over every creeping thing that creepeth upon the earth. So God created man in his own image, in the image of God created he him; male and female created he them."

acknowledging Eve's choice while warning of the bigger problems that would result from it.

Sin enslaves us all. Our relationships suffer as we abdicate and fail our way into dysfunction, with some accepting authority over others. Even Moses, who was exemplary in service, saw his leadership doomed ultimately to failure. A variety of Scriptures support this perspective. Humans are not capable of ruling without sinning. Nor can we assume "Christ in us" enables us to assume such a role, because Christ Himself rejected it. Why would He agree to fulfill such a role "through" weaker and more imperfect human beings? Being a helper of joy is not the same as assuming a role of authority.[3]

God does not wish to implement a structure of institutional authority, with some ruling over others.

It is sin that erects such structures. Our life in Christ delivers us from sin, and as a result, we can be freed from bondage to others. The more we willingly and perfectly submit to God, the less need there is for any authority at the human level. We are brothers and must understand that all forms of pyramid rulership are inferior to equality, which is needed to live in love and harmony with each other.

Clearly, the COG's view of governmental authority was a type of bondage and was not of God. Anyone who accepts a role of rulership over others will eventually have to repent of having done so, because it is born of sin. It is not what God intended. It is a result of and a cause of further sin.

This does not mean that administrative structures are to be avoided. They are a necessity in organizing how we can best serve each other and deliver the most effective and helpful solutions for all involved. But traditional rulership, within authority structures that sanction enforced obedience as opposed to mutual submission, is a type of slavery of the ruled, resulting from their sin. The tragic irony is that rulers are often bigger sinners than the ruled, in all manner of ways, including oppressing those under their authority.

HWA and those who modeled themselves after him were guilty of encouraging idolatry, the system of the golden calf. It is impossible for someone in this role not to interfere with the direct relationship that each of us is supposed to develop with God. Intentionally or unintentionally, the head of

3. II Corinthians 1:24: "Not for that we have dominion over your faith, but are helpers of your joy: for by faith ye stand."

such an organization inserts himself between God and other people. This is an inevitable result.

When we look to individuals to rule us, we reduce and erode our faith and trust in God. It becomes a repetition of the sin of Adam and the curse that is its result. This insight gutted the doctrine of a supposed Government of God being in force in the church. Instead, God intended for each person to govern himself through faith in God and the inner working of the Holy Spirit.

This may seem impractical. We have no evidence of God's intent ever having been implemented in a systematic way on the planet. But that's the point. Since Adam and the curse, it has been impossible. But the Bible does provides some interesting glimpses into this, such as Proverbs 6:6–8, "Go to the ant, thou sluggard; consider her ways, and be wise: which having no guide, overseer, or ruler, provideth her meat in the summer, and gathereth her food in the harvest."

All this may seem fanatical to some, who may invoke the Borg (of *Star Trek* lore) to decry any utopian vision that would use the ants as an example, but it seemed to me to be in line with other prophecies. Consider how the lion lying down with the lamb requires a radical alteration to the instinctual behavior of species. Such radical alteration of instinctual behavior summarizes the nature of the utopia God ordained for humans after the return of Jesus Christ, to rule the world for a thousand years of peace and prosperity.

Imagine if all mankind collectively determined to cooperate rather than to compete. John Lennon may not have gotten the specifics right, as he asked us to imagine no possessions, no religion, and nothing worth dying for, but the sentiment was correct. Imagine if there was no need for anyone to rule over anyone else. Imagine if self-governance were the rule, not the exception.

Having seen in Scripture that rulership was a curse that resulted from our abdication of our sovereignty helped me view the entire Bible from a fresh perspective. It also illuminated why the One True Church, with its Apostle of God for today, had fragmented into many churches with various and sundry "mini-me apostles"—as church members continued the pattern of failing to mature.

HWA and his deputies laid claim to the seat of Moses, just as the Pharisees had done. In the case of HWA and the WCG ministry, I can attest to a high degree of sincerity in trying to point people to God in faith, just as Moses had done. But in the process, the administrative system was based on men invested with authority to rule over other men, and then going about exercising it and enforcing their own rules in every imaginable area of life. The model used as an example was the one introduced by the priest of Midian, a pyramid structure of "captains of ten, fifties, hundreds and thousands."[4]

To summarize this lengthy section, Moses was known as the most humble man who ever lived. Yet even the humblest man, when leading a people willing to abdicate their sovereignty as Israel did at the golden calf, would not be able to succeed in leading them to God. Meanwhile, those under such a system are enslaved, in a new way, a codependent way. Religion becomes corrupted by the sin and mutual enslavement that results when individuals yield responsibility to those in leadership positions within the system of systems. They naturally abdicate their responsibility to relate directly to God,

The temple had an outer court for the Gentiles and an inner court for the Israelites. Once inside the actual temple, a veil covered the entrance to the most holy sanctuary, where the high priest entered once a year with the sprinkling of blood. In the New Testament, and under the Christian covenant, in effect through the death of Christ, this system became obsolete. This is symbolized by the veil in the temple being torn in two at Christ's death, which symbolized a momentous change from severely restricted access to direct access to God.[5]

No more was a human high priest, or a human priesthood, needed. From then on, Christ, the Son of God, was our high priest. Christ's sacrifice completely changed the nature of our access to God in a variety of fundamental and astonishing ways.

Now, sick and in India during the Days of Unleavened Bread (symbolic for getting rid of the leaven that causes our humble selves to inflate), I got clarity; the WCG was a system designed to lead people out of slavery to false doctrine but substituted slavery to a human organization.

We had misappropriated divine authority.

This insight settled concerns and doubts related to claims by HWA and the WCG.

The WCG had taught hundreds of thousands in its congregations, and hundreds of millions through its print, radio, and television ministry, to get

---

4.   Exodus 18.
5.   Mark 15:38.

serious about God and the Bible. The WCG had convinced a sizable portion of those reached that God had a plan that He was working out today. But it had never been the One True Church administering the Government of God. Never had disobedience to its claims of divine authority had implications to anyone's eternal salvation. Once this concern was put to rest, other insights flowed.

In Greek, for example, the word "temple" is from *naos,* used to designate the holy of holies when the Hebrew Scriptures were translated into Greek. A modern rendering of the Hebrew expression would be "most holy" and the sense of the word is that of "sanctuary." With that in mind, certain New Testament passages take on enhanced meaning. Read the following, for example, knowing that in each case, temple is *naos,* meaning, the "most holy sanctuary": "Know ye not that ye are the temple of God, and that the Spirit of God dwelleth in you? If any man defile the temple of God, him shall God destroy; for the temple of God is holy, which temple ye are.[6]

He not only allowed us to come into His presence in the most holy sanctuary, He put His presence within us. Every Christian who has His Spirit is a sanctuary (*naos*) of God. To allow the teachings of others to enslave us and to have them rule over us is to defile that sanctuary, by limiting the access of God's Spirit, by allowing a human to claim to be a priest, to stand in the opening to the most holy sanctuary.

Before we go further with this, a word about Moses. Christ never, not once, says anything negative about Moses. I was not willing to turn my back on Moses. That Moses blamed the people had less to do with his own foibles and everything to do with a prophecy about how Israel would treat Christ.

Lady Madonna

Christ is the groom, coming to claim his bride. The Old Testament records the betrothal between God and Israel, and in the New Testament, God sent His Son to woo and marry His betrothed, the nation of Israel. Instead, at the altar Pontius Pilate offered up Christ or Barabbas and the people chose Barabbas, condemning Christ, their fiancé, to death. In killing the groom, the bride annulled the Old Testament marriage covenant between God and herself.

---

6.   I Corinthians 3:16–17.

This allowed God to open up the marriage covenant to all humankind, not just the "chosen people." The marriage covenant provides a sanctified union in which God can impregnate, using His Spirit. Christians are thus conceived, as sons of God—or, "born again," in conventional evangelical terminology. While pondering this marriage symbolism, it occurred to me that the structure of the temple, where Israel came to commune with God, was symbolic of the female sexual anatomy.

The temple—complete with its outer and inner courts and the most holy sanctuary—enabled the people to symbolically participate in a close, personal relationship with God. Like it or not, the veil in the temple was also symbolic. It served the function of the hymen, in place in women prior to full sexual intercourse. The Mosaic law even had provisions to verify that it was still intact at marriage.[7] These "tokens" of marriage were the documentation that validated the legitimacy of a marriage. The need to provide these tokens of marriage elevated the role of the hymen in preventing consummation of the intimate relationship, until, as God ordained, this takes place within the covenant of marriage. And it provided proof that upheld the sanctity of a marriage that had been entered into between two people in good faith.

This is partly due to the Old Testament view of what constituted a marriage. Full sexual intercourse constituted a binding marriage relationship. It wasn't the ceremony, vows, prayers, rings, or anything else that determined whether a man and woman were bound together in wedlock. Since the tokens were the woman's, I'll write this from the female perspective: the first time a

---

7.   Deuteronomy 22:13–21: "If any man take a wife, and go in unto her, and hate her, And give occasions of speech against her, and bring up an evil name upon her, and say, I took this woman, and when I came to her, I found her not a maid: Then shall the father of the damsel, and her mother, take and bring forth the tokens of the damsel's virginity unto the elders of the city in the gate: And the damsel's father shall say unto the elders, I gave my daughter unto this man to wife, and he hateth her; And, lo, he hath given occasions of speech against her, saying, I found not thy daughter a maid; and yet these are the tokens of my daughter's virginity. And they shall spread the cloth before the elders of the city. And the elders of that city shall take that man and chastise him; And they shall amerce him in an hundred shekels of silver, and give them unto the father of the damsel, because he hath brought up an evil name upon a virgin of Israel: and she shall be his wife; he may not put her away all his days. But if this thing be true, and the tokens of virginity be not found for the damsel: Then they shall bring out the damsel to the door of her father's house, and the men of her city shall stone her with stones that she die: because she hath wrought folly in Israel, to play the whore in her father's house: so shalt thou put evil away from among you."

woman had sex, she was married to that man, unless the woman's father was opposed to the union.

The veil was in place until such time as she (Israel) was ready to enter into the marriage relationship with God, which was to be consummated at the arrival of the groom—the Son of Man, the second Adam, Jesus Christ. Note, however, that the marriage had to be without fraud, and thus there had to be acceptance of the bride, Israel. I've struggled to understand how this fits together, and through a variety of circumstances and interactions with other believers, in pondering this issue, here is a summary of the conclusion I came to.

The rejection of the groom (Christ) by the bride (Israel) and the subsequent death of the groom, made it possible to consummate the marriage with a spiritual Israel, all humankind. God does not abandon Israel, as she is included in the relationship of God and His bride, consummated by the tearing of the veil. In reality, God is neither male nor female, but in this analogy, He is male, and the symbolism of the veil and entering in, is decidedly female. Israel and humankind—collectively and individually—are in the feminine, receptive role, and we need to invite the indwelling of the Holy Spirit into our own most holy sanctuary—our bodies and our inner *naos*, our heart of hearts.

The apostle Peter explained that Paul often wrote of things difficult to understand. I believe that God wants us to enhance and expand our understanding, our maturity, our vision, and our acceptance of the unbelievable majesty, and ultimately, the unknowable nature of the essence of God, even as we seek to understand more and more about God and our relationship to Him. The tearing of the veil, the resurrected Christ presenting Himself to God, and the circumcision of the heart of the lovers of God make it possible to know God more intimately than ever. It brings to mind the Hebrew word translated "know," which includes the connotation of sexual relations. The dowry needed, to show appreciation for this relationship with God, is to love one another, to be People of the Sign.

With the tearing of the veil, the people of God had no more need of intermediaries. They now had direct access, and priests were obsolete. Ministerial claims of divine authority to rule over church members (the "bride of Christ"), in the WCG and elsewhere, have serious implications. You might compare the whole construct, now that Christ has come and the veil has been torn, to a strange spiritual harem, with the priests as the eunuchs. (In this context, the teaching that the priesthood must be celibate is a tragic irony.)

Doctrinal houses of cards support such constructs. Flimsy arguments seek to establish that the ministry has the right and responsibility to rule over others. This was characterized as the "Government of God" in the WCG. But none of this was God's original intent or desire. Inherent in the WCG focus on government was an emphasis on the idea of rulership. It was emphasized in marriage, in the church, and in our relationship with God. But none of this was God's original intent or desire and Jesus's "from the beginning it was not so" statement about divorce illustrates why that is important.[8] A focus on authority, even God's, resulted in less opportunity to focus on love, which is true north.

My work on "The Curse of Eden" manuscript had led to a conclusion that was opposite of the WCG view that each man was the Government of God representative within his family, over his wife. When Paul wrote, "For the husband is the head of the wife, even as Christ is the head of the church: and he is the saviour of the body," he was actually proclaiming the opposite of what the WCG taught.[9] Christ submitted Himself to His bride, not the other way around. Paul was overturning an age-old sexist approach in which a weaker wife had submitted to a stronger husband. Clearly, the Christian approach was new and revolutionary in this regard.

The symbolism of the marriage of Christ and Israel is interesting in this light. Given the cycle of slavery and freedom, it was logical to have a priesthood—a system of rulership over the bride-to-be—until such time as the sin could be blotted out and the relationship restored. Spiritual beings who are truly sovereign are symbolized by the preclothing Adam and Eve who could be happily naked and innocent before God.

Adam failed to help the woman that God had given him, choosing instead to follow her into sin. His own sacrifice could no longer help her, as he was now in the same boat as she. No matter how hard he worked—and since the earth was cursed he would be working hard—he would not have what it took to restore a proper relationship. His sacrifice would be extreme, despite and because of ruling over her in a dysfunctional relationship. And yet his efforts would always be insufficient to restore the relationship to its intended state.

---

8.   Ibid.
9.   Ephesians 5:23.

Christ, however, both paved and illuminated the way: a sacrifice that would be transformative, rather than enervating. Through the sacrifice of Christ, a path to restoration is made possible. We have the understanding and the power to create relationships that are closer to the pristine state of love and true equality. But to do so, we have to banish the negative concepts of the curse, not let them influence our thinking and draw us into dysfunction.

Official WCG theology recognized that the priesthood, as such, had been abolished and that we are all equal before God. We just didn't practice it in the WCG for two reasons. One was the desire of the membership to return to Egyptian-style slavery, to abdicate adult personal responsibility, to be stuck in a childlike state of naïve trust. The second was that some, given the chance, were both willing to take the responsibility that others were abdicating and arrogant enough to believe they were closer to God or more capable than others were. So despite efforts to orient people toward a tighter orbit around God, the gravity within the system pulled us away.

As I was studying and reflecting upon these matters, Michael Hubert was pressuring me to go with him to the AIDS village. He had booked another car and told me that it was expected, that they had been waiting for me for months.

With the insights I had gained from three days of intense study, God had me right where He wanted me. He had granted me enhanced spiritual understanding, largely because of my finally being willing to follow Him where He wanted to lead. The decades-long abdication of personal responsibility, in favor of slavery to a fraudulent system of government, had ended.

I was physically weakened from three days of intestinal flu without solid food, which meant I was ready for the next leg of my spiritual journey. Although it felt certain that a visit to an AIDS village would only make matters worse for me, physically speaking, this was the shore upon which the great fish had vomited me up. It was time to gird up my loins and follow God.[10]

---

10. Job 38:3: "Gird up now thy loins like a man; for I will demand of thee, and answer thou me."

I Feel Fine

The AIDS village was near Gudiyatham, a town with a population of about two hundred thousand, more than four hours from Chennai. We headed out early on the morning of the Last Day of Unleavened Bread. This was no triumphant journey; I was lying down in the back while Michael and the driver were up front. My stomach was somewhat stable, given that it contained only mangoes and water. This didn't mean I wasn't nervous about the situation, and when I did manage to sit up, it wasn't to enjoy the scenery. It was to keep an eye out for signs of Western-style facilities.

On the way, Michael explained that in Indian society the concept of "untouchables" is still deeply embedded, even if it is not politically correct to practice it openly, AIDS sufferers were outcasts, often along with their entire families. Their children were deprived of education because of fear the disease would spread among other children through close social contact.

A respected civil engineer, M. S. Rajendran, had contracted AIDS five years earlier and passed it to his wife and unborn son. The negative treatment he received from family and society, not to mention the guilt he felt at having infected his family, drove Rajendran to work tirelessly to establish an economic foundation to build enclaves for those such as himself and his family. He had established five centers providing housing and medical help, support from caregivers, and moral support to victims and their families. Here, those who were HIV-positive could try to build a life apart from the society that had cast them out.[11]

Uninfected children did not live there but were allowed to visit. Michael had visited with these people to explain about God and His power to heal. He had built up their anticipation of an American minister who could visit them. He wanted me to bring them words of encouragement. Learning this shifted my focus away from the ongoing cramping to a knot in my stomach of a different kind. What would I tell these poor, helpless people? What was their expectation of me as a minister of God?

I was out of my league.

---

11. Appendix V is an excerpt from Leon Sexton's *Legacy* newsletter describing his earlier visit to this village.

I was a firm believer in God's power and willingness to save and heal and my recent experiences were inspiring, but I had no delusions of grandeur; I harbored no secret fantasy I might suddenly become the conduit of a miraculous mass healing. And in case I was tempted to allow my ego to migrate in that direction because of miraculous divine intervention and instantaneous healing in my own life, God had ironically, comically, and perhaps strategically sent me to the AIDS village hunched over in the back of the car, praying I could make it through the day.

As we drew closer, my thoughts darkened even more in anticipation of the horror of what awaited me at a backwater village of terminally ill Indian untouchables. My typical response to any expectation of divine healing in those asking me for anointing was to pray that God's will be done, in the knowledge that we are all perfected through our trials, leading to an ultimate "spiritual" healing in the resurrection. Physical healing might come now, but most trained in the WCG (despite stories of miraculous healings in the early days) knew it was increasingly rare and thus highly unlikely. This didn't seem to be the right message, yet the mass removal of HIV that would be needed to give these people back the lives they had lost did not seem to me to be in the cards. Were they hoping it was?

Upon arrival, we drove into the driveway of what looked like a large and comparatively fancy estate. The first impression lifted my spirits. The facility, or hostel, was a gated community with a two-story main building, paved driveway, pleasant vegetation off to the side, and a generally well-kept appearance. The day was sunny but not overbearingly hot. Overall, this looked more like a garden than a place of death. In short, it was not at all what I had expected, and I began to breathe more easily.

We had been delayed due to road conditions and traffic, so we were hastily greeted and ushered inside the compound. From there, I was led upstairs where the twenty or so citizens of the little community were waiting, seated on the floor. The faces were tired and sad, some visibly thinned by the disease, others seemingly healthy, but all eyes dull with psychic pain. My spirits, which had been lifted upon viewing the clean and well-maintained grounds and facility, began to drop again as I looked into their faces. There was a palpable depression in the room.

I joined them on the floor, and noted how their expectation was covered by a blanket of failing hope. Whatever relief I had felt vanished, as my dread at having to speak to this group teamed up with my already-angry stomach, hitting me with a series of painful cramps. The pain, discomfort, and general uneasiness sapped me of whatever positive energy I was trying to muster, and probably reflected in my own expression.

But it was too late to turn back now. With Michael as my translator, I began to address the group.

I spoke to them about God and His desire that all should live full lives and experience good health. But I explained that circumstances and the folly of humanity often led to a world where misery could take root. This can affect the lives of the innocent and guilty alike.

Although I didn't share with them my own weakened state, I certainly conveyed a sense of empathy as I spoke of our condition of slavery to sin and the despair that all humankind experiences. I spoke to the sadness of their situation but also of their condition as an opportunity to understand the true reality of life apart from God. I assured them that all this was in order for God to have them turn more fully to Him, to experience the fullness of life in alignment with God.

I spoke of God's desire to heal, to become our doctor, to lead us out of ways and attitudes associated with darkness and misery. His goal was to turn our desire back to the path that leads to light and happiness. I assured all present that it was God's desire that all of them seek Him for assistance to walk this path more fully.

I also explained that in order for us to feel and understand God's desire for connection, He had sent His own Son to us. He had allowed His Son to experience the very same suffering that we all are subject to. Accepting the sacrifice of His Son was a path to the acceptance of God, and that through the example and assistance of His Son, a healing of our state of abandonment could be achieved.

I concluded with assurances to them that God would be with them on their journey.

I thanked them for their invitation, and their graciousness at letting me speak to them.

I expressed my desire to meet with them again on my next visit to the area.

When I stopped, the eyes seemed to be brighter; the faces seemed to project lightness, if not light. This may have been enhanced by the change in the angle of the sun coming in from the large broad opening in the wall behind the group. Nonetheless, the atmosphere of the room had changed from one of heaviness to one of hope. There was an increase in the energy level. I was encouraged, relieved, and because of the five days of illness and virtual fasting, exhausted.

My mind turned to the ride home and a desire to make a quick getaway.

Wait

I think the group may have sensed my mental withdrawal, as an awkward silence reigned until broken by discussion in Tamil between Michael and Rajendran. Then Michael said, "They would like you to talk to them about baptism."

I was taken aback. I had just baptized four women in Chennai who had been under Michael's tutelage for some time. Then I had baptized two men under the hood of the cobra, as it were, who had less experience but had nonetheless kept the Days of Unleavened Bread. They had evidenced an understanding of the overall plan of God and had, in my mind, shown the type of dedication needed to meet the baptismal criteria established by John and Peter—bringing fruit of repentance.[12]

I asked Michael if he had explained the need for the current audience to follow God's law. "Yes," he said, "but you should review the matter with them."

I turned to Acts 5:32 to show the group that God gives His Spirit to those who obey him; I also turned to Micah and James to outline the basic principles of a Christian life before talking about specific commandments. This took about fifteen minutes, during which I was becoming physically uncomfortable in my position on the wooden floor. Five days of almost no food had left my normally small posterior skinnier than normal; the way I was sitting had caused my legs to fall asleep, and I was beginning to feel faint.

So I again thanked them and encouraged them to stay in touch with Michael, who could instruct them in greater detail about the godly life, one aligned with His plan and purpose. A somewhat lively Q & A session followed.

---

12. Matthew 3:7–8; Acts 2:38.

Though most of it wasn't translated, I saw engagement and passion. There was also some confusion and agitation, especially in Rajendran, related to my overt reluctance to take this any further.

"They are ready to be baptized," Michael explained.

I was not convinced, but that was not the only reason I was still hesitant.

As embarrassing as it is to admit, after the clarity gained in my personal study and prayerful reflection over the previous three days and nights, I was concerned about my safety. Despite the surprisingly high standard of cleanliness of the relatively modern facilities, I was hyperconscious of what it might mean to get into who-knows-what kind of water with a succession of AIDS-infected people living off the grid in a backwater area of India. In my near exhaustion, even coming here had been a further step into a physical and psychological zone of discomfort. I was already sick, and had no interest in proceeding any further in that direction.

So I told Michael that I felt he should work with the group, and we could discuss baptism in more detail when I or another minister returned for a future visit. I was ready to head back to safety. My body language probably communicated that I was mentally already halfway to the door.

At this, Rajendran—who understood English well, and could express himself in it when needed—blurted out, "These people will be dead before they get another visit from a minister."

These words struck a nerve. I had been focused on determining:

- Do these people know what their leader is asking on their behalf?
- Is Rajendran sincere?
- Are these people pawns in a game of connecting to Western financial assistance?
- Do these AIDS sufferers view baptism as a supernatural cure for AIDS, or as an outward expression of a lifelong commitment to follow the example of Jesus Christ?
- Are they even aware of an expectation of lifestyle changes?

But Rajendran's protest instantly raised my awareness of the immediate plight of these people. I pushed aside my nagging questions and personal discomfort and decided to discuss the purpose and intent of baptism. In the process, I would try to get a read on the individual faces, which to me, as a foreigner, seemed almost indistinguishable, one from another. I needed to see them as individuals and try to discern who was listening and grasping the meaning and who was not.

I walked through the example of John the Baptist, who had declined to baptize those who did not bring forth the fruit of repentance. I decided to tackle the topic of healing and the need for spiritual healing across the planet. God and Christ were more interested in healing hearts and minds than bodies because without the former the need for the latter would continue unabated.

Given the added time to translate what was being said, this discussion added another twenty minutes to the overall meeting, which was now well on its way to Gerald Waterhouse–like proportions.[13] Most seemed fully engaged, although a couple of listeners struggled to stay awake in the warm upstairs room in the heat of the afternoon. I concluded my remarks and then asked Michael to ask those still interested in baptism to raise their hands.

The hands began to rise, and after a few seconds, almost everyone had a hand in the air.

Michael and I discussed the situation and agreed that brief individual counseling sessions would be appropriate. Each person who had expressed an interest was asked to wait their turn. I then led the first candidate back to an adjacent bedroom and gingerly sat on the edge of a bed.

With the candidate seated on the floor and Michael as an interpreter, I tried to determine their understanding of baptism. I explained that it was for the remission of sins and an outward sign of an inward submission to God. I counseled them about the sacrifice of Jesus, the Anointed One, which made it possible to be pure and righteous before God. I explained that baptism was public acceptance of a private offer from Jesus Christ to dwell within us through the Holy Spirit, to guide us and give us the strength to forge a new path.

I explained that true healing is spiritual. If God were gracious and He determined it to be in their best interest to heal physically, it would come from the inside out. Nonetheless, I cautioned that Jesus had suffered terribly and that we were required to pick up our own cross and follow Him.

---

13. A WCG evangelist who made numerous world tours, famously delivering sermons lasting more than four hours.

I asked them one by one: to repeat back some of the key points, to speak up if they had any questions, and to state if they were willing to accept Jesus as their personal savior.

Twelve of them responded affirmatively; Rajendran was number thirteen.

It had been five days since I had eaten a full meal, and I was near exhaustion. My stomach was still reeling from the cobra god's curse; the long trip, the duration of this visit, the heat, and the stress of being in an AIDS village in a remote area of India were all taking their toll. I took a deep breath, and tried to brace myself for what I knew was next.

I was going to have to get into whatever water they had available for the baptism.

I exited the bedroom, walking through the upstairs meeting hall where the people were sitting and waiting for the baptism to commence. I thought about how asking these condemned sufferers if they were willing to pick up their cross had seemed harsh.

Was I being expected to lead by example?

Was I being asked to sacrifice myself, in order to give hope and a new spiritual life to people looking for a way to commute their death sentence?

Having highlighted the need to take up Christ's cross, I found it weighed heavily on me. Was this what God had in store for me, now that He had finally convinced me to follow Him wholeheartedly?

It seemed like a walk down death row, in which the inmates would be freed at the end, with me taking their place.

The sound of my own footsteps, in my Western shoes, accompanied by the soft shuffling of bare feet on the stone behind me, filled my ears. The procession was slow, and we packed ever closer together, like sardines, as we descended. Michael's back was but inches in front of me, as he led the way back down to the main floor. He had spent the better part of a hot day traveling, and his sweat-soaked shirt was so close to my face I could almost taste it.

Down, down, down the narrow staircase we went. We arrived at the bottom; I was sandwiched between Rajendran in front, then Michael, with the group at my back. Instead of taking a left to the main entrance, we exited a side door into a courtyard.

It was 3:05 p.m., and the sun hung low and bright—just above eye level. I was temporarily blinded by its brightness. When Michael moved forward, I felt its warmth on my face, chest, and shoulders. I heard the sound of birds. As my eyesight returned to normal, I noted several large trees, a grassy area, and flowers. The pleasant nature of the surroundings contrasted with the knot in my stomach that was generated from my belief that after this day my future would be irreparably changed. I could almost taste the dread welling up inside, but I forced myself to move forward.

Then I saw it.

It was centered on a raised cement platform that was about a foot high and about eight-feet square. It was nestled under shade trees, looking like an above-ground cement hot tub.

It was a baptismal pool.

As we approached it, I found it was about four-feet deep. It was newly built and filled with the clearest, purest water I had ever seen, glistening blue and white in the sunlight.

Shame washed over me, as the negative thinking that had blinded me fell away. My guilt turned just as quickly to humility, and then praise at the realization that God, in His greatness, had filled these people with the faith needed to prepare for this day, as evidenced by this stunning cement pool. A surge of joy and energy followed, my response to God's blessing being poured out upon us all.

I began the process of, one by one, baptizing the people who had built this little baptismal pool in anticipation of an elder arriving to baptize them. As each one joined me in the pool, I could see that some were not visibly affected by the virus at all. Others were extremely thin, struggling to climb over the edge, with large eye sockets that framed eyes revealing pain and sorrow.

After I dunked each one in the water, they stepped out of the pool and waited with a towel for the others. When all thirteen had been baptized, we again ascended the stairs to the second floor of the hospice, returning to the room where we had conducted the Bible study. There, one by one, I performed the laying-on-of-hands ceremony, asking God to pour his Holy Spirit into each new convert. They kneeled or sat in front of me as I kneeled and rested my hands on their head. Michael translated.

I did my best to couch the prayer in terms that would be both encouraging and educational. Each prayer probably only lasted two or three minutes, but this meant holding my arms and hands outstretched for a half hour. In my weakened condition, my shoulders were sore and my arms felt like lead weights. When we were done, we asked a group blessing for God's protection, guidance, growth, and shepherding. I was now truly exhausted and let Michael know we needed to hit the road. As exciting as the day had been, it was almost too overwhelming to take in. I don't recall my thoughts on the way home. I do recall feeling numb and drained. We arrived in Chennai in the dark, and I crawled upstairs and collapsed in my little bed.

Little Child

Upon awakening, I reflected on my previous day's experience. I recalled stories from the early days of the WCG in which evangelists had gone on tours across the US and elsewhere, baptizing people into God's One True Church, led by His Apostle out in California. This had enabled the corporate entity to grow larger and more powerful. This was like a surreal echo of that era, due partially to the exotic locations we had visited, but mostly the intriguing insights gained along the way. In this post-WCG era, the gravity that had held God's One True Church together had been removed. The people held in its orbit had separated and scattered, and I was making my way through the debris, leveraging its legacy and spiritual understanding, but with the freedom and the uncertainty of not being bound by a corporate structure.

Building a religious organization was the last thing I wanted to do, especially after realizing that the entire Government of God construct was of men, not of God. Yet an organized approach and some form of structure would be needed to serve people effectively. Now that I was feeling better, it was time to initiate discussions with Michael on how these nineteen newly baptized members of the body of Christ could best be served.

My belief, validated in an exciting way by these baptisms, was that if we simply focused on what God wanted us to, we would be in alignment with His Work of bringing many sons into glory.[14] The enthusiasm, sincerity, and speed with which these new converts had embraced what must have seemed strange Western ideas validated this belief. This fueled an eagerness to continue

---

14. Hebrews 2:10.

to explore this path and to focus on activities that exemplified humility and service to those in need.

Two Scriptures described this: Micah 6:8, "He hath shewed thee, O man, what is good; and what doth the Lord require of thee, but to do justly, and to love mercy, and to walk humbly with thy God?" and James 1:27, "Pure religion and undefiled before God and the Father is this, To visit the fatherless and widows in their affliction, and to keep himself unspotted from the world."

Having gotten clarity of purpose, I realized it was time to establish programs to minister to physical needs that would deliver lasting benefits to the recipients. In pursuit of this goal, I was working on entrepreneurial ideas to use US dollars to fund Michael's programs to serve others. This would provide both a reason and resources to return for future trips to pursue both humanitarian and spiritual goals.

It was natural to draw from my experience with the WCG's astounding success, as well as my recent professional experience. I wanted to leverage both in helping Michael expand the tiny program that connected university students with homeless children. This was the embryo of an educational big brother– big sister program, which could be funded by individuals and organizations. Funding needs would be small by Western standards.

For $25 per month, a student could spend a couple of evenings per week tutoring several children, and the same amount would support a child's participation. Corporate sponsors could provide branded items such as backpacks or T-shirts. Connecting the tutor with the child would deliver the most valuable component, the personal attention and encouragement needed for the child to stay in school. Tutors would gain a valuable reference for future employment. The program would begin at the first-grade level, with the goal of providing enough tutoring to enable children to progress with their peers. Donated schoolbooks, uniforms, and shoes would encourage students to meet quarterly milestones. Those who met the minimum graduation standards at the end of each year would be able to continue for another year.

Although this planning was in its infancy, we had a business model that could be successful. The next step was to work with Michael to detail an initial project plan of what he needed to accomplish. This included developing tutor and child candidate profiles, with interview questions and agreements to be signed. It also included identifying which universities might grant credit or offer support to students to participate, provide potential locations, and accept the children, in support of such a program.

My first assignment was to establish a foundation in the United States. I made a list of individuals who might join us. Once we had an entity established, we would seek corporate support and go on a campaign to enlist the first set of sponsors who would provide the monthly payments for the tutors and students.

In all my excited thinking about the tutoring program, the cushion covers were all but forgotten. Michael, ever the master of timing, had about two hundred silk cushion covers ready for me as we were preparing to leave for the airport. He insisted I take them with me to kick-start the program. This was good news. I stuffed what I could into my packed luggage and filled most of a carry-on bag.

When Michael dropped me off at the airport for the thirteen-hour trip back home to California, I suddenly became concerned about taking these goods out of the country. I needn't have worried; the abnormally large quantity of cushion covers wasn't noticed, and soon I was winging my way to the US via Germany. In hindsight, what I should have worried about was how these cushion covers had materialized so quickly and unexpectedly.

But for now, my heart soared and my mind raced along with the plane that was taking me home. Looking out the window in the bright sunlight as I headed west, I marveled at the contrast with my night flight from Maui seven years earlier, after having resigned from the ministry of the WCG. God had answered my prayers for guidance beyond my wildest dreams.

I had emerged from my Jonah years with my faith intact. Nine days earlier, on my way over from the US, I had had no idea what awaited me. Nineteen baptisms, encompassing a group of women in the city, farmers in a village, and the bulk of a small community of outcasts had been wholly unexpected. Despite my initial skepticism, they all were people drawn to God, convicted of the need to follow His Word, and eager to participate in His plan for them. My own understanding had also grown immensely. I had cast off any remaining attachment to the idea of a divinely authorized hierarchical government. In casting off the idea, I was freed from the mutually dysfunctional problems of the responsibility of being a ruler and of the abdication of the ruled.

Surprisingly, the most exciting part was that I really had no idea or expectation about God's plan for these people. It was God's doing, not my own nor anyone else's, that had brought this about. I had merely followed Michael's lead, as he focused on finding and helping people in need. He was following where God directed, with no plan or forethought of his own.

The results created opportunities to establish plans and programs I could sink my personal and professional teeth into. And given the disparity in standards of living between the US and India, it would be feasible to develop programs that would make a real difference in the lives of the people involved and become the basis for expansion of the small groups of believers into their surrounding communities. These programs had altruism in their DNA. They existed to fill humanitarian needs and so were naturally aligned with the spiritual principles recorded in God's Word.

Michael's training as a deacon and his concern for these groups had ensured that the need was the focus, not the desire of any individual, or organization, to develop a following. And God was blessing the efforts to serve by sending His Holy Spirit into the lives of those with whom we were coming in contact. There was just one problem with all this motivation, energy, and excitement. I was coming home to a bachelor pad and to painful divorce proceedings.

The divorce, though not yet final, had finally begun to sink in. My failed marriage was a nagging reminder of an underlying disconnect that I had yet to resolve. My work on "The Curse of Eden" had provided some initial ideological resolution on the challenges of male–female relations, but that had only led to changes in thinking. Changes in behavior were required to reverse the curse. My initial fledgling attempts to change the way I approached my role had not borne fruit in my marriage, but they did enable me to understand some broader spiritual issues. I had ample time to reflect on these on the twenty-plus-hour trip back to Los Angeles International Airport.

I Will

The pursuit of selflessness was a path to the heart of Christianity, and I was now devoting my life to plunging forward into that heart, with no holding back. God had brought me to a stage where I could fully embrace role models like Albert Schweitzer and Mother Theresa based on their fulfillment of the sign Christ gave and independent of their particular theology or their performance against my standard of doctrine. Even adherence to the divine clock (i.e., Sabbath and Holy Days) was secondary to the light that shined forth from the people who followed them. Christ outlined this, for those with eyes to see, in His famous Sermon on the Mount.

He first states, "Ye are the light of the world," which should grab the attention of those readers who remember what I've highlighted about the opening verses of the Bible. And in case there is any doubt about the intended visibility and prominence of this new heavenly light, he adds, "A city that is set on a hill cannot be hid." He wraps up this particular example with a statement that fits hand in glove with my claim that John 13:35 elevates His followers' loving behavior to the level of a token, a sign of the covenant, "Let your light so shine before men, that they may see your good works, and glorify your Father which is in heaven."[15] Disciples of Christ provide the evidence, the tokens of their faithful marriage to Him, by pouring themselves out to help those who need it most.

The somewhat esoteric knowledge about the sign He gave regarding who He was—the duration of His time in the grave—was less relevant than the sign of who His disciples were, those who loved each other, which is the sign that explains why He had willingly spent that time in the grave. And the light generated by followers of the true sign of the Christian covenant overcomes any darkness resulting from incorrect doctrine because "love covers a multitude of sins."[16] My respect for these icons of faith grew with my understanding though I had neither desire nor intent to spend my days personally ministering to the most miserable of the disadvantaged. It was more appealing to launch programs that would help them improve their situation.

In reference to my own suffering, it took about two weeks to recover after returning home. But this was a minor annoyance compared to the passion with which I threw myself into my career, while also commencing work on the platform from which to serve in India. A first order of business was to get in touch with my friends Sonali and Kevin, the ex-WCG couple down the street from me whom I had met at the Feast in India the previous fall. They were eager to learn about everything that had happened, and I excitedly shared the unexpected and exciting events I had experienced. We decided to each focus

---

15. Matthew 5:14 and 16.
16. Proverbs 10:12; I Peter 4:8.

on a different aspect of the work that Michael was doing, under the banner of Shabnam Resources, in India.

Sonali was excited about the cushion covers and had Kevin's full support. They would manage the cushion-cover project, and I would focus on the tutoring program. Sonali was networked with various groups and had experience selling similar items at local markets. She was optimistic that the women's empowerment concept behind the cushion covers was an appealing story that would lead to sales.

Unfortunately, when we began looking more closely at the two hundred cushion covers I had rapidly shoved into my bags before leaving for the airport, we were disappointed and concerned. Although a few of them, the ones Michael had showed me, were of decent quality and had interesting designs, the bulk of them were of shoddy materials, poor workmanship, and unappealing designs. They would be difficult to sell, regardless of the humanitarian aspect.

The rather astounding disparity in quality, I assumed, was likely a result of an overly zealous mass-production effort on behalf of Michael and the women who wanted to get the program started. Still, I determined to find out how and why it had happened. Without quality control, the program would never succeed.

Despite the poor quality, we had some initial success, largely due to our enthusiasm, a lot of hard work, and discounting the covers. It was a bit embarrassing, though, since they were so shoddy and plain that the people who bought them would probably never actually use them. The $10 purchase price was basically a donation to a worthy cause. But we didn't lose hope since the initial samples were well made and beautiful.

With Kevin and Sonali managing sales, my involvement in the cushion-cover project was limited to helping with marketing materials and ideas. This let me focus on my expanding vision for the educational program for homeless children. I reached out to my international network; I and the seven others willing to become founding members each contributed a token $250 to confirm our commitment and provide funds to initiate the establishment of the foundation. Among them was a classmate from Ambassador College who had recently taken a job helping the Omidyar Foundation find ideas in which to invest. Pierre Omidyar was the founder of eBay and was making his peace with being a billionaire by helping fund start-ups in the nonprofit sector. Another was a man who attended the UCG and had been approached separately through Michael's e-mail fundraising campaigns. He was interested in supporting one of Michael's farm projects and was planning to attend the Feast of Tabernacles in Chennai.

Although my experiences in India were important from a spiritual perspective, success in my career had made it easy to move forward quickly. I now worked for Deloitte & Touche, one of the premier accounting and management-consulting firms on the planet. And it was time to make use of the Deloitte network.

I reached out to partners in the nonprofit area of Deloitte Consulting who gave me guidance on what to do and what not to do, and helped me initiate the paperwork to establish a 501(c)(3) charitable organization. They also told me about a competition with large cash prizes for nonprofits that incorporated free market and business principles. I also began a series of articles targeting the WCG groups, in the hopes of interesting members to get involved in this unique new venture. The first of these was published in the May 31, 2003 *Journal of the Churches of God* and covered Michael Hubert, the past Feast of Tabernacles, and the programs we were working on. The story left readers with a sense of more to come. My recent trip was only hinted at in the article, and I knew the exciting events in the next installment would grab people's attention.

One person was already paying attention: David Hulme, the president and increasingly autocratic head of the church I still attended. As I remember it, he pulled me aside one day at church to ask why I had attended Holy Day services elsewhere, which led to what I thought was a cordial discussion about India. "As an ordained minister," I explained, "my calling and duty is to minister to people. Since you no longer provide me the opportunity within your organization, I've found outlets overseas." I then shared the news of how the groups in India were growing and of the nineteen recent baptisms.

His response to the baptisms caught me off guard. He explained it was his duty to inform me that he had discussed my situation with his ministerial services team, and they had decided to revoke their recognition of my ministerial credentials. I wasn't shocked, but it was still unexpected. Yet, always quick on my feet and a bit predisposed to challenge authority, I calmly replied, "Whether your group recognizes them or not doesn't affect God's opinion on the matter."

David seemed to nod, almost imperceptibly. He had never been a bridge burner. "I understand your perspective," he said, "and while I might tend to agree with you personally, my responsibility is to the church. I can't authorize ministers to run around doing their own thing. I have to protect those who are weak."

I extended an olive branch: "You have a responsibility to run your organization the way that you believe is best. If I were in your shoes, I might be forced to make the same kind of decision." But this was a backhanded agreement. The truth was that I had moved outside of any hierarchical authority structure and wouldn't be wearing his shoes under any circumstances. I had come to see such "protection" as a type of unauthorized dominion. But I was freed of needing the approval of his organization or those within it.

So I followed up, adding, "At the same time, you now have a bigger problem."

"What's that?" he asked.

"A member you don't recognize as a minister who thinks he still is one," I replied.

The conversation was coming to a head, but his response was more positive than I expected.

"As long as you're not openly causing division; we'll just have to monitor the situation over time."

After that, I continued to attend services with his group, but not without increasing tension with some of the people I had considered my friends. I had always spoken my mind, and as I drifted further away from where the rest of the membership was, my alternative perspectives on just about any topic were increasingly annoying to them.

One of my friends there was Edwin Stepp. At AC, Edwin had assumed my role as David Hulme's administrative assistant when I graduated. Unlike me, Edwin had continued to work for David after his graduation. During the split between the WCG and the UCG, he had embarked on a career in marketing and advertising.

At some point, David had rehired him. They continued to be close, while Edwin and I shared a mutual respect, as well as enjoying each other's company. Our wives had also been friendly, at least prior to my wife's departure.

One Sabbath at church, I was talking with Edwin about India and my perspective that there were ways to reach and serve people that were different from the corporate and hierarchical approaches with which we were familiar. A suddenly angry Edwin let me know that, given my disagreement, it would be best if I stopped attending. Apparently, he and others were looking for reasons for David to disfellowship me. In the late summer of 2003, it was time for me to move on again.

Attending with David Hulme's group had been a logical choice that felt safe and comfortable for a while. It had been several years since I had felt this strongly that I was right with God, out on the edge, where He was working. Now, where I attended church was no longer of much importance to me.

It Won't Be Long

In every truth there is something more than we would have expected, in the love that we receive there is always an element that surprises us.

– *Pope Benedict XVI*, Charity in Truth: Caritas in Veritate

In the early stages of my professional experience as a management consultant, I was impressed by the success of the celebrated names in capitalism. I was enamored by the business savvy of colleagues and customers both inside and outside Deloitte, and what the business school taught. It was surprising that I had been able to achieve a measure of success within a premier consulting brand like Deloitte without having formally learned what my competition within the firm had studied.[1]

By 2003, however, my MBA coursework was helping me understand how to maximize shareholder value. Marketing, statistics, finance, and management by objectives—every class in my MBA program was filled with things I should have known already but didn't. Since I was up to my neck in the practical application of what we were studying, the material was relevant, fascinating,

---

1.   Being hired by Deloitte without an MBA was a rare occurrence.

and easy to process and retain. My practice area within Deloitte was strategy and operations, and my coursework was immediately applicable to the business challenges of my clients.

I was learning about the frameworks that govern how our society and economy work, and the principles and tools used to build profitable companies. From my vantage point, within a top-rated accounting and management-consulting firm, it was easy to grasp both the material and its implications. But as with every other area of my life, I saw many things differently. I filtered the economic and business science through the Golden Rule: "Do unto others as you would have them do unto you." This contrasted fundamentally with using "maximize shareholder value" as a prime directive.

The Fool on the Hill

This was but one reason my honeymoon period with Deloitte was ending. The economy had yet to recover from the dot-com crash, and people were being let go. My successful engagements with Wells Fargo Bank were winding down, and my main sponsor within Deloitte had shifted his focus away from the real estate systems that had become my specialty. Without a sponsor to connect me to the clients of the firm, it was impossible for me to develop the new business I needed to generate billable hours for myself and others. I resented that Deloitte made this *my* problem, by evaluating me based on my billable hours, when it was the fault of partners failing to sell enough work to keep us busy.

So-called free markets weren't supposed to work this way.

Involvement in the stock market, business school, Deloitte, and consulting clients across industries helped me understand both how the system of systems was supposed to work and how it actually did work. A few wealthy folks were majority owners of powerful entities designed to make money. These were hierarchical structures like the pyramids I had seen in Egypt. The owners harvested through transactions at the bottom. In some cases, these were crops planted by the pyramid; in others, harvesting was done in other people's fields. Wage slaves did the actual work of planting and harvesting.

As these pyramids—these living organisms, these collectives—grew, savvy managers shifted attention away from small transactions at the bottom to internal manipulation to represent the value differently, enabling large increases in money to flow in from the capital markets. Accounting firms such as Deloitte audited and represented the value of the pyramid to the investment community. Shrewd tactics, enticing financial markets to provide more capital, could magnify the capabilities of the pyramid. The larger the pyramid, the more important such maneuvering became, and the ability to fabricate short-term wealth in this manner opened up opportunities for executives to siphon off large portions of it.

The reward potential is enormous for the priests and pharaohs of the pyramids, who create downward pressure on the wages and benefits of the workers, who become increasingly expendable and replaceable. Sadly, their dependence on the increasingly dominant pharaohs and taskmasters grows. Continuing the analogy, the modern slaves put to the task of building these corporate pyramids are soon forced to build brick without straw, while executives count on massive bonuses if things go well. In a disaster, executives have golden parachutes, but employees are either strapped to their seats or kicked out of the crashing plane without so much as an umbrella.

In a bankruptcy, for example, employee pensions are often wiped out to provide ready cash in a restructuring. Names such as WorldCom and Enron were coming into the popular consciousness, both of which had spectacularly imploded, vaporizing enormous amounts of wealth. The root cause of their implosion was greed, but it was the phenomenon of focusing on gimmicks or fraud and money generated by the capital markets that made this possible. A primary method of enablement, in the case of these two companies, was the use of accounting gimmicks related to real estate assets.

In other words, the owners are aligned against the free flow of information which enables free markets. Their focus is in controlling and manipulating the flow of information. Exotic accounting of real estate was a sophisticated shell game perfected by a combination of consultants, tax advisors, accountants, auditors, and the executive management at these two companies. Deloitte wasn't the industry leader in such chicanery, but it was one of the so-called "big five" accounting firms at the time.[2] And I was a recognized industry expert in real estate systems. Now, I have to be very careful about what I say next, and how I

---

2.   The others were PricewaterhouseCoopers, Ernst & Young, KPMG, and Arthur Andersen LLP, the auditor of WorldCom and Enron.

say it, because Deloitte and other companies I mention have enormous resources that can be brought to bear against anyone they consider a threat. What I will say is that Deloitte had several bases covered for clients who wished to hide or misrepresent expenses and income, capital versus operational budgets, within or between divisions and entities. Specific strategies were deployed within the likes of WorldCom and Enron which helped inflate their valuations to fraudulent and disastrous levels. And I was becoming more and more aware of exactly what these were and how they worked.

The Enron and WorldCom scandals drove our primary competitor, the legendary and respected Arthur Andersen, into insolvency and disintegration. Although these corporate disasters were spectacular, they were isolated, and the economy as a whole remained strong. This meant that, like rats from the proverbial sinking ship, many of the partners and principles of Arthur Andersen were able to scramble aboard other ships in nearby waters, salvaging their careers. When Arthur Andersen collapsed, the "big five" was one member short. I jokingly referred to the remaining firms as the "final four." This was intended to highlight that we were all engaged in similar kinds of activities.

Deloitte was cautious about picking up too many of those scrambling for a new home, but one, a former executive with Sun Microsystems, joined us after a brief stay with Arthur Andersen. This man became an important mentor to me at Deloitte, and I mention it here not to in any way disparage him, but rather to attest that the methodologies and approaches used at both companies were very similar. Many books and documentaries provide evidence that the big consulting and auditing firms were complicit in the bubbles and the illicit activities that occurred in many large corporations. The 2006 documentary *The Smartest Guys in the Room*, based on the book by the same name, is one of my favorites. In less than two hours you will not only learn about Enron but will also receive an education on the nearly unbelievable scope and impact of profit-driven misconduct. A more recent example is the 2015 movie (based on the 2010 book) *The Big Short*.

My point is that I now had clear and specific insight into the tools and tricks that upper management and their advisors used to "maximize shareholder value." During the time I was working at Deloitte and obtaining my MBA, I became aware of the possibility of such impropriety. It didn't take long before I saw this in action at Deloitte. The firm was helping a large wireless company with the rationalization of its lease portfolio. The lease portfolio covered all of their cell tower sites, and very large sums of money were involved. My role was not on the rationalization project directly; I was a value-add expert in real estate management processes and software whose task was to find out how expenses had gotten out of line and recommend process changes and an appropriate system that would prevent this from recurring.

The client company was not very interested because it was just packaging the company for sale, so I was deployed in a minimal way to see if I could create a business case around process improvement and automation that would pay for itself. In designing an interview plan for the executives responsible, I discovered an odd metric. A stock analyst had compared the cost of real estate per customer across wireless companies to highlight that this company had four times the real estate costs of its competitors. This unusual metric became a focal point in asking why this company had managed its real estate so badly.

Tracking costs at their source, and reporting accurately on them across the company, is the antidote to bad business behavior. The implementation of processes and systems to do this for real estate functions was my specialty. During the interview process, I sought to understand why this company didn't do this, and the consistent response was "our Company doesn't care about real estate costs."

I was puzzled. Why would upper management not care about this large component of their cost? Business School 101 taught the exact opposite: you get what you measure. In fact, they did care because they had now hired a very expensive firm to get these costs under control.

Then it dawned on me. Business School 201 is that culture comes from the top. I thought about the cultures of Enron and WorldCom. I reflected on what was happening within my own industry, the accounting and consulting industry, which enabled such things to happen. "Poor management" of real estate costs just happened to enable the shifting of a large amount of expenses from one part of a company to another. And more importantly, poor management practices enabled top executives to deploy plausible deniability.

I speculated that the wireless unit was probably already saddled with higher-than-average costs, but the parent business had covered these costs elsewhere before spinning it off. The resulting shift in investor perceptions about the value of the wireless business generated huge bonuses and stock appreciation.

Now it seemed the same game was being played a second time, in preparing the wireless company for sale. A successful sale at a higher valuation would net the orchestrators of the sale millions of dollars in bonuses. And the buyers would end up holding the bag on a company that was worth less than assumed.

And yet even as my awareness of the shenanigans in my industry and the industries of our clients was growing, my career was taking an upturn. Because of my work at Wells Fargo, I had aligned myself with Deloitte's SAP practice. SAP is a German software company specializing in enterprise resource planning (ERP) systems, the massive software packages that manage accounting and many other functions of the world's biggest companies. At the time, SAP was the fourth largest software company on the planet, behind Microsoft, Oracle, and Symantec, and implementation costs of $100 million were common. In the wake of the big accounting scandals, new accounting regulation known as Sarbanes-Oxley was designed to hold executive management accountable, which SAP was trying to leverage to force integration of real estate information with the ERP system.

I became a go-to person for many of the firm's largest clients and SAP extended me an invitation to travel to Germany to present at their European-partner day in Heidelberg. It was exciting to go back to Germany on a business trip, and unlike my earlier experience with the Corporate Real Estate Portfolio Alliance, this time I knew my stuff.

I had already been asking myself why SAP was largely unsuccessful at deploying its real estate module in the United States, when in Europe it was often part of its standard configuration and deployment. While some companies made a conscious choice not to track real estate costs, thereby enabling internal accounting improprieties, I also uncovered a key regulatory difference. In Germany, large financial institutions were able to invest in real estate as a business, meaning they could own real estate for profit. Banking and accounting regulations in the US prohibited this.

Having been designed and built in Germany, the SAP module for real estate was designed to function more like a property management system than a lease administration or space planning system. Without getting too technical, there was more benefit in implementing and using the complicated, expensive, and relatively bureaucratic system to cover this function in Europe than in the US, where the added complexity, expense, and tedious management of such a system weren't required from a financial planning, management, or audit perspective.

I had considerable public speaking experience, familiarity with German and European culture, and the ability to use bilingual humor. My sophisticated international audience could appreciate this but wasn't expecting it. As a result, my cavalier style, joined with the respected brand of Deloitte and an insightful message tailored to their business, helped make my message a big hit.

The conference turned into a whirlwind of celebration, at the sessions during the day and on the town in the evenings. In the beer halls of the enchanting tourist and college town of Heidelberg, I made many connections. The cherry on top of this came when SAP extended me an informal invitation to return to speak at their global-partner day in Berlin.

Don't Bother Me

This brings us back to my dilemma at the telecom company. I was fairly confident that my hunch about accounting games was accurate, and I tried to dig deeper into past and present cost allocation. It was important to me to try to blow the whistle on what may very well have been fraud. However, it did not take me long to realize that I had no evidence that would stand up in court, and I wasn't going to be getting access to any.

And I would be pitted against people vastly richer and more powerful than myself; I would be truly all alone in whatever battle I decided to wage. Neither my client nor Deloitte would want this to be made public. Any digging around at my level (which was not very high in the pyramid) would set off alarm bells before I got very far.

I've described corporations as pyramids, but they are also like living entities and I found myself at odds with their internal immune systems. My general belief system set me at odds with a world I perceived to be at odds with God. Christians are sent into the world but are not of the world.[3] Corporations have the profit motive baked into their DNA, and they exist only to make money for their owners. These entities are like cold-blooded dinosaurs, having to devour to survive and thrive in a competitive beast-eat-beast system of systems.

---

3.   John 14:17; 17:14–16; and 18:36.

Becoming deeply involved in the material world, studying its business practices, and moving up the ranks of its corporations was not without internal conflict.

Reflecting on the example of Daniel at the court of King Nebuchadnezzar resolved this internal conflict. My current path was helping me to learn specifically what worked, what didn't, and why, from within the system known as Babylon. The return of Christ was still imminent, and my calling was to assist with the establishment of the Kingdom of God on earth. When Christ returned, I would be better equipped to help set up a new economy, one that would match the millennial goal of having the wolf lie down with the lamb.

The thing for a Christian to do was to be a "fifth column," a force for good behind enemy lines—to work to change the greedy cutthroat culture from within. It was my belief that ultimately the power of good is always able to overcome the power of evil, if and when it is God's time to do so. As long as He was continuing to grant me success and favor, I would not change my course. But how would I resolve my current dilemma? I was part of something I considered evil and even illegal.

The answer was actually quite simple. I told my superiors that my initial discovery work would not lead to an engagement and got myself removed from the project. The senior manager who had just joined Deloitte from Arthur Andersen helped me with this transition. He was from a wealthy European family and, although short in stature, was charismatic and connected. He and I hit it off instantly, and I had a new sponsor who was being groomed to become a partner. The firm had asked me to work on a major pursuit in Texas with Nokia. Even though the business was not awarded to Deloitte, we worked together on the proposal and in the process developed a positive working relationship.

Seeing evidence of corruption at higher levels encouraged me even more to channel energy from my career successes into the spiritual path I had discovered in India. This also papered over the angst I felt in living apart from an estranged wife who had filed for divorce. I still felt that if I balanced my focus on my relationship with God and my pursuit of business success, I might go through a dark period in my marriage, but God would be able to turn my wife's heart around. The areas of my life that were working seemed to validate this idea.

For example, through the sale of our Long Beach house and the arrangement I had with the investment house in Pasadena, I climbed out of the hole I had dug for myself in the stock market. And during positive stock fluctuations, I sold some of our holdings, providing a cash buffer. I was no longer worried on a daily basis about what the market was going to do, and whether I was going to get a call from my broker demanding I invest thousands of dollars we didn't have or face the entire portfolio being liquidated. Once I could demonstrate to her that our financial worries were solved, she might forgive me for having lied to her about it.

My wife had a different approach to resolving our differences. My lawyer informed me that her lawyer had demanded our financial records. I dutifully packed up all of our bank and stock account statements, real estate documents, 401(k) and other investment records, and dumped two banker's boxes full of records at her lawyer's offices.

These records documented the trail of money from our jobs, through houses, stocks, and funds being moved back and forth from various accounts in pursuit of low interest rates. As real estate values had risen, I had opened equity lines on top of loans and invested in the market. I also tapped into zero interest credit offers and juggled money back and forth between them to avoid the high rates that kick in when promotional periods end. My efforts to manage our financial assets aggressively had created a complicated and mercurial flow of money and a messy trail that was nearly impossible to follow. The effort I had put into this had paid off financially, but all the gyrations did not look good in an environment of mistrust and suspicion.

While my wife's lawyer was sifting through our records, my dad was getting remarried. His twenty-five-year marriage to my stepmother had ended when she died suddenly of a brain aneurysm, just as my mother had.[4] Dad didn't waste any time getting engaged to a woman he had known in the WCG in Alaska whose husband had died of cancer. Dad reached out to me to see if I would perform the wedding, which I did in an intimate ceremony at my older sister's house in Canada. This was a boost to the family relationship, and Dad and his new wife supported my efforts in India, having signed up as the seventh founding member of the foundation-to-be.

During our time in Canada, Dad and I talked about real estate. I was eager to continue shifting our remaining assets out of the stock market into real estate and began working with him to accomplish this. He had been living in Washington state and had built two fourplex apartment buildings and bought a

---

4.   See *TPotS*, chap. 3, "She Came in Through the Bathroom Window" and "Misery."

couple of small houses to rent out. We formed a partnership to invest in single-family homes, which he and his new wife would rent out and manage.

As the time came to depart for the Feast of Tabernacles in 2003, the stock market had largely recovered, which enabled me to shift money from the stock market into two houses I added to what we hoped would be a growing portfolio. My strategy of riding out the stock market roller coaster had turned a near disaster into a happy ending. I had more than quadrupled the money my wife and I had managed to save together.

All of this left me hopeful that I could reverse the pending divorce. However, just before the Feast of Tabernacles, the legal proceedings took a turn toward nasty. Influenced by the fact that I had hidden the state of our finances; my wife, through her lawyer, was attempting to prove that I was hiding money or assets. Part of me didn't believe that she believed it. My step-uncle, who prepared our taxes, had always been on friendlier terms with my wife than with me. She said he told her I was hiding money, so I called him on it.

"Where did you get that idea?" I asked.

"You're a smart guy," he said, "and I have no doubt you have put money aside."

"You've had full access to any and all our financial statements. Your outrageous claim is not only unethical, it's ruining any chances we have of reconciliation."

"You're just like your dad," he angrily replied, having previously shared that he felt Dad had mistreated his nieces and nephew after the death of his sister.

I ignored the bait and said, "If you have any evidence, then show it to me; otherwise you need to formally retract your accusation."

He blurted something unprintable into the phone and hung up.

Here, There, and Everywhere

I eagerly boarded the plane for India again, hoping to leave the nagging oppression of my pending divorce behind. To have my wife accuse me of stealing from her hurt me deeply. And the pain was made worse by the idea that God hates divorce, which was deeply ingrained in my psyche. Deep down, I felt my wife knew I had not done what she was accusing me of. This partially dispelled the cloud of doubt spewing forth from my now nearly severed marriage covenant. My general outlook was confident that this was all part of God's plan, and my trips to India were a powerful reinforcement. There was an enormous sense of spiritual excitement and divine adventure that came from being directly involved in what God wanted for my life. I was eager to get back out on the edge of the gangplank, where the Spirit was at work and faith was evidence of things not yet seen.

Through my work at Deloitte, I had connected with Rajasri Systems, a small offshore-development company. The president of the company wanted me to come see him on my trip to Chennai. I planned to discuss with him a website we would use to connect the sponsors with the tutors and children they were sponsoring, featuring profiles, pictures, and samples of the work and progress of the students. I was getting more and more excited about the possibility of launching a full-fledged foundation that could help accelerate activities in India.

My travel included a one-night stay in Japan, but I seriously underestimated the travel time to and from the airport. Without enough time for a decent night's sleep, I arrived exhausted to the familiar little room attached to the main building of Michael's compound. There was no time to recover from jet lag, as Michael had every minute booked.

First was a visit to Gudiyatham, the AIDS village. This was on the Day of Atonement, Yom Kippur—a day of fasting, twenty-four hours without food or water. The upside of making such a long trip during a fast was that I wouldn't be eating or drinking anything that would make me sick. I had asked to save the expense of a rented car, so we rose early and boarded a train.

From the station, Rajendran walked us through the small town to pray with a single mother and her two children. We then scrambled to arrive, exhausted, at the location of a worship service for the baptized members. Twenty faces, most of them familiar, met us, but being late, we had no time for greetings, and the atmosphere was muted. The somber atmosphere was likely due to the fasting, and the thematic nature of the day, which highlighted the plight of those who were HIV positive in India. After the service Rajendran explained that one person had moved away, but there had been no deaths from among those in his community. However, one man was thinner and more fragile than before, as the HIV virus had had its way with him. A highlight of the service was the presentation of a gift of high-quality Bibles translated into Tamil, one for each of the baptized members.

However, the matter of the shoddy cushion covers had me viewing events in India with suspicion. Rajendran, for example, seemed distracted and disengaged from the religious aspect of the Day of Atonement, despite it being one of the most holy days of the year. On the way home from Gudiyatham, Michael and I discussed the situation. Rajendran, he explained, was a busy man, with many responsibilities.

Back in Chennai, I learned that the member of my foundation-to-be who had planned to attend the Feast in India had cancelled his trip at the last minute. He had sent his travel money to Michael to buy goats for the folks in the HIV community. There was an ingenious dual purpose; the milk would help sustain them physically, while caring for the animal would help sustain them emotionally. So we were a man down in terms of establishing the tutoring program, but an American college student, Ryan Foster, more than made up for this loss.

Ryan had taken a year off from his studies to serve a second term as a faculty member at Leon Sexton's Legacy Institute in Thailand. Ryan was sent by Leon to assist with the schedule of services and activities. The days between Atonement and the Feast were devoted to discussions on the diverse projects under the umbrella of Shabnam Resources, Michael's charity organization.

It was time to have an accounting of cushion-cover sales, in more ways than one. Despite the atrocious quality of the product, we had sold seventy-five covers, for a total of $695. Under the circumstances, this was a big success, but what I learned about the program was disturbing. According to Michael, Jayenthi, one of the recently baptized women, had used the money I had provided to purchase inferior manufactured cushion covers. I had been tricked into pawning off cheap, mass-produced cushion covers by means of staged photos that misrepresented their origin.

The Women's Initiative for Financial Independence in India had deceived its unsuspecting participants and the consumers. But I needed assurances from Michael that such deception must not be allowed to occur again. My attempts to solicit agreement from Michael were met with excuses for himself and the people he worked with. Westerners simply couldn't understand life in India. I had never been in Michael or Jayenthi's situation and didn't want to judge them. Nor did I wish to get involved in the details of what had transpired between them or where the communication breakdown had occurred. I backed off. Rather than force a groveling apology, I thought there were many positive things to focus on. The next three days were a case in point.

Wednesday we met with Rali Panchanatham of Rajasri Systems to commission the development of a website to support the homeless children's program. In the afternoon, we followed up with the registration of the domain for TeachAKid.org and drafted a scope document for Rajasri to use to get started on the development of the site and the initial content. Thursday was spent planning for translation at multiple Passover Feast sites. We also made the decision to send a young woman to Leon's Legacy institute in Thailand.[5] This led to a rush to arrange for the visa and additional expenses. We met with her on Friday regarding conditions for her acceptance to Legacy and had follow-up discussions on how to proceed with the cushion-covers program. This led right up to the long-awaited opening ceremony for the 2003 Feast of Tabernacles in Chennai.

The time spent in positive planning for the future erased the negativity I had been feeling about past mistakes. Michael had implemented changes to enhance and upgrade the entire experience: improved ventilation, decorations, and catered group meals. By the opening service on that Friday evening, we could tell that this Feast was going to be special. More importantly, several of the newly baptized people were integrated into the plan and would help with the execution. Ryan Foster joined a couple of the newly baptized men being scheduled for sermons or sermonettes, expanding participation and variety in the spiritual messages as well.

I was disappointed to learn that the folks from Gudiyatham would not attend. But it seemed unwise to mix these groups at this time. Michael and I were scheduled to travel there during the latter half of the Feast, leaving Ryan and other assistants to carry on in Chennai. Even without them, we had sixty people on the opening day, a significant increase over the forty that had attended the year before. And signs of a healthy congregation were in evidence. These included broad smiles, active attentiveness, and participation in the form of questions during the messages being delivered. All this, despite the heat. I recognized the

---

5.   Beulah Indhu, a young volunteer in the tutoring program who had been baptized the previous spring.

women whom I had baptized, some of whom were accompanied by children or other relatives and friends, and the two men from Tiruvannemalai, and also noticed a number of other new faces from that farming region.

Over the course of the next five days, Saturday through Wednesday, there were several sermons and sermonettes, as well as the blessing of little children, a ceremony to present the cushion money to the women's group, a presentation on their program, and the collection of an offering.[6] There were also evening and family activities, with entertainment and dancing, all of which the children participated in. Community relationships were being built within this diverse group of sixty-some people.

With the Feast in Chennai going so well and with the momentum for creating a humanitarian foundation as opposed to a defunct, obsolete, and onerous tithing system, I began to fret about leaving the group in order to meet with the group in Gudiyatham. The Chennai group and the farmer families from Tiruvannemalai were forming a vibrant, Spirit-led community. It was extremely rewarding to contribute to this overwhelmingly positive atmosphere, and I wanted to stay.

But the bigger reason I didn't want to go to Gudiyatham was my doubt about my adequacy and the message I had prepared for them. What triggered the doubt was a local newspaper article I read, by chance, about a family in the region. The father had lost his job and had taken the lives of his wife and children, then committed suicide. The article discussed the social pressure and feelings of disgrace that led to this situation. Though the source of this father's disgrace was different, the article mentioned HIV carriers in India as another group at risk, socially, to such pressures. HIV carriers tended not to die of AIDS. The majority of them took their lives long before the disease could accomplish that. This was one of the reasons Rajendran had worked so tirelessly and had such government support for the establishment of communities for these outcasts.

My sermon had been prepared prior to leaving the US, with Chennai in mind, and it had resonated with this excited, positive, energetic group. How would it come across to an audience of exiled HIV outcasts, living under a palpable death sentence? As I reviewed my notes in the car, en route to the second half of the Feast in Gudiyatham, the message and the Scriptures I had

---

6. WCG tradition held an annual ceremony to pray for God's blessing upon any children who had not received such a blessing previously, based on Matthew 19:13–15.

chosen seemed all wrong. The one giving me the most heartache was "I have set before you life and death . . . choose life, so that you and your children may live."[7] As I considered the potential impact of these words, I recalled the depressed state I had seen them in during my spring visit. Rajendran's words were coming back to haunt me: "These people will be dead before they get another visit from a minister." The challenge to "choose life" might seem more like a cruel taunt than a hopeful message.

As I pondered my options, throwing out my notes and winging it seemed like a recipe for disaster. If this was the message God had inspired me to prepare, I would trust Him to deliver what He wanted these people to hear. I had cast myself into the global mosh pit of love and humanitarianism. All I could do was follow the lead of the Spirit. With these thoughts swirling around in my head, I discussed my concerns about Rajendran's sincerity with Michael. We agreed to judge Rajendran's sincerity by the fruit in evidence in the group of newly baptized brothers and sisters. [8] And since we were now approaching our hotel near Gudiyatham, we would soon have our answer.

I Want to Tell You

The next morning, Thursday, day six of the 2003 Feast of Tabernacles, we entered the compound operated and maintained by the HIV cooperative at about 9:30 a.m. There were several smiling faces there to greet us. We were welcomed, offered refreshment, and then taken around back, past the baptismal pool that had caused me to repent of my doubts about these people on my previous visit. As we turned the corner to the open garden area, overlooking a field, in the back, I saw a large peach-colored-cloth covering, with a design of fruits and flowers, tied to two large trees and held up on two other sides by poles with stakes.

These amazing believers had constructed an outdoor tent to celebrate the Feast of Tabernacles. The cloth covering integrated a vine as a wall, in front of which tables and chairs were arranged, providing a natural backdrop for the

---

7.　Deuteronomy 30:19 (NIV).
8.　We discussed fruit for repentance earlier, but Jesus also applied this principle broadly in Matthew 7.

speaker. There were chairs, filled with twenty-five to thirty people, arranged in a semicircle, facing me, and behind them were trees from which the cloth was suspended.

My past Feast experiences had been at hotels and convention centers, and I had always enjoyed the luxury and feelings of privilege. But my new brothers and sisters from this far-off culture had simply and elegantly followed the command to erect a tabernacle to celebrate the Feast. As Michael introduced me, I was reflecting on how this seemed the most scripturally accurate example of a celebration of the Feast of Tabernacles that I had ever been a part of. This was clearly the fruit of sincerity and obedience to God.

I was immediately filled with a positive spirit, as I sensed the quiet spirituality of the participants who so eagerly awaited our arrival. This time there were children present who had been granted permission to visit their parents for the Feast. It was hard to judge to what extent just having the families together was affecting the mood, but it was so positive, so uplifting, that it seemed impossible that this was the same group of people I had visited and baptized just six months earlier and had met with a week earlier.

We exchanged bowed handshakes, smiles, and translated greetings. Here, at their home location, their demeanor was different from the Day of Atonement. Here everyone seemed happy and vibrant. After a short period of positive and inspiring fellowship, we sat down to conduct the service. I noticed that the members each had their own new Bible, distributed a week earlier at the Atonement meeting.

Since all the Bibles were identical, Michael could refer them to specific page numbers, avoiding delays caused by people unfamiliar with the names and order of the books. This was a big plus in a service already slowed down by the translation. It also enabled us to continue having volunteers read the text in their language, instead of Michael doing so each time.

The translation of the Bible into Tamil, I'm told, takes advantage of the particularly beautiful and poetic nature of classic Tamil. This meant, however, that it was often difficult for the uninitiated to read. Similar to our reading the King James Bible, with its use of "thee" and "thou" and outdated idioms and expressions, which can be challenging, the classic Tamil is apparently even more difficult for the reader. However, hearing it read is very satisfying to the listener.

Michael opened with a sermonette in Tamil. Some of the Scripture readers stumbled a bit as they read their passages. But it did not dampen their enthusiasm to participate, and both the parents and children paid close attention to Michael.

When my turn came, I spoke with the excitement I felt at being able to be part of God's outreach to instruct people in a new way of life. I spoke about a biblical pattern of worship, which revealed and enlightened us on how God is bringing "many sons unto Glory."[9] The power of Christ and the Spirit living in them would transform their lives. The fruit would be the hope and the faith to establish straight paths for their feet, paths leading to eternal life, in joy and spiritual abundance.

It seemed to go over well, in that it held the interest of the entire audience. I was relieved to get through it and see them all awake and seemingly eager to hear more. At that point, we took a break to prepare for lunch.

Lunch was like a big family picnic. There were a variety of seating areas— on the low cement wall encircling one of the very large trees; the chairs used for the service hastily reconfigured in a circle; the area around the baptismal pool—all of these made makeshift picnic tables. The kids had a blast, and the adults were beaming.

When we finished the meal, it was time for the blessing of little children. There were approximately fifteen children, some nearly teenagers. Normally this service is performed for young children the minister can pick up and hold, but sometimes parents who are new to the church want this ceremony performed for their older children, too. In sizing up the situation, I decided to ask a common blessing on all the children, instead of fifteen individual prayers, each needing to be translated.

So I referred to the Scriptures where Christ had asked a blessing on children who were brought to Him in order to explain how and why we performed this ceremony. In praying for children, it's customary to ask for protection. This took on new meaning, as some of them had the HIV virus and all were at least exposed to it. It was not hard to pray in an especially heartfelt and fervent manner. As I began to ask God to protect and guide these children, yet another equally important concern quickly came to my awareness.

As I prayed for guidance and wisdom for the parents to teach the children in love, I realized I had to ask our heavenly Father for the parent's strength and

---

9.   Hebrews 2:10.

healing, for their children's sake. Not only did the parents need God's help in their new walk, they needed help to stay alive long enough to raise and nurture their children. Thoughts of my own childhood entered in at this point. Feelings from long ago, while singing "Hey Jude" at the top of my lungs on a Swedish hillside, filled my heart as I prayed for these children who were so at risk of experiencing the same sense of loss, only worse.[10]

I wanted these children to have what had been denied me.

They deserved loving parents who would be around to care for them, to protect them, to provide for them, physically, emotionally, and spiritually. But they were at risk of being abandoned by the ones who loved them—and at risk of being exposed to the stark reality that no one else would love them the way their own parents would. In praying aloud, it was all I could do not to choke up.

In asking God to shower mercy and healing on the parents, I held no false hope. Only God can know how and when He will decide to heal and extend life, or to let nature take its course. So I made sure to ask, in my prayer, that if it were to be God's will that any of these parents not live to see their children reach adulthood, that God would take care of them, watch over them, and adopt them as His own. I also asked that He would teach these people to love and care for each other, to build a strong community so that if one parent, or one child, were in need of help, there would be others close by to offer the help that was needed.

The prayer went on longer than any public prayer I had ever prayed before or since. I could tell, also, that many of the parents and children were visibly moved at the outpouring of love and concern that I had felt rushing through me. I felt connected to God, on behalf of these people who had never heard such a prayer, who had never heard anyone in a spiritual role such as the one I represented to them request such things on their behalf. It is hard to be objective when describing an event in which I was the focal point, but it seemed to me that the sincerity and power of the event was manifest. There was silence, there were tears, there were smiles, and there were numerous hugs and handshakes at the end of the ceremony.

The next day we had another morning service, in which Rajendran was to deliver the sermonette, but I don't recall him being present to do so. What I do remember vividly is that the group was even more attentive and interested

---

10. See *TPotS*, chap. 1.

than they had been the day before. There also seemed to be a slight increase in attendance, and all of the children had expectant, happy faces.

Early in this message, as it came time to read the first Scripture, I was pleasantly surprised to see one of the children raise her hand to read. I called on her, and she rose to read, with visible joy and pride on her face that she was allowed to participate in the service. From that moment on, it was difficult for the parents to get a chance, as all the children wanted to read. The blessing of the children had made an impact on them. They felt a part of and were involved in their parents' new faith.

The message that I was delivering outlined the Holy Days revealed to Israel, explaining their meaning in a Christian context. I covered how each one pointed to the various ways in which God and Christ were teaching and training humanity to accept the revelation and plan of God, leading up to the return of Christ to earth to deliver a thousand-year utopia. These eager new believers were reading in their own language and hanging on every word that poured forth from the Bible.

The mood was joyful and exuberant, not dark. Verses from the four-thousand-year-old book of Deuteronomy sprang as though resurrected from the pages. Consider Deuteronomy 30:4: "If any of thine be driven out unto the outmost parts of heaven, from thence will the Lord thy God gather thee, and from thence will he fetch thee."

These were powerful words of encouragement for those who had (some were of a Christian background) or had not (most were of a Hindu background) previously learned about God rescuing Israel from captivity and slavery in a foreign land. These people were dispossessed outcasts, lower than the untouchable caste, driven out, as it were, unto the outmost parts. You could tell that these words spoke directly to them, as they intently considered the contents of these strange verses from the God of Israel, declaring that He would gather them unto Himself.

Verse 5: "And the LORD thy God will bring thee into the land which thy fathers possessed, and thou shalt possess it; and he will do thee good, and multiply thee above thy fathers." This was the promise of a new dwelling place, and the transformation of their compound underscored the feeling that it would be fulfilled. The construction of the baptismal pool had led to the tent, and the picnic and the families, and the meal, and the prayers and the love descending on these people, as they gathered under the shade of the Lord.

And verse 6: "And the LORD thy God will circumcise thine heart, and the heart of thy seed, to love the LORD thy God with all thine heart, and with all thy soul, that thou mayest live."

We spent a few minutes discussing the intervention of God in their lives directly—His way of working with them, changing their outlook, changing their thinking, changing how they would feel about their situation and their prospects. And the offer and hope of life. That God's wish and desire for them would be to walk in the newness of life.

Thank You Girl

Then we arrived at the part of the message I had agonized over in the car, wondering how a group of people infected with a fatal virus would receive it. With some trepidation, I asked them to read verses 11–14. As I read along silently in English while one of the children read in Tamil, I was astounded at the context of the verse about "life and death" that had given me such heartburn: "For this commandment which I command thee this day, it is not hidden from thee, neither is it far off. It is not in heaven, that thou shouldest say, Who shall go up for us to heaven, and bring it unto us, that we may hear it, and do it? Neither is it beyond the sea, that thou shouldest say, Who shall go over the sea for us, and bring it unto us, that we may hear it, and do it? But the word is very nigh unto thee, in thy mouth, and in thy heart, that thou mayest do it."

It struck me that I had traveled beyond the sea and halfway around the world to find people in a situation where such ancient words of hope would be meaningful and relevant. But here we were. And no, this was not difficult for them, even if culturally foreign. They grasped, understood, and—more importantly—believed these words. They were calling upon God. They were accepting and honoring His offer, right here and right now, with all their hearts.

They were choosing to believe God.

They were willing to obey God.

And the blessings were immediate.

Their outlook had dramatically changed. They were not in fear of death. They were confident that God would be guiding them to a new life. They were ready to stand up and follow the pillar and the cloud, right here, right now, wherever it might lead.

Far from being a gloomy affair, with concerns about death hanging in the air, the Feast in Gudiyatham had become a vibrant celebration of life. I actually perceived a glow beginning to emanate from the faces of the crowd. I sensed the Spirit shining through these people, and their joy, hope, expectation, and faith seemed to be growing with every verse that they read.

Another child read verse 19: "I call heaven and earth to record this day against you, that I have set before you life and death, blessing and cursing: therefore choose life that both thou and thy seed may live."

The mood was transcendent in every face, in every expression, in every eye fixed on the Bible in their hand, on me, or on Michael, who was translating; I could see these people expressing a strong, confident, faithful desire to choose life. Any considerations that might otherwise drive sick, impoverished, helpless, and hopeless outcasts to despair and thoughts of suicide were banished far, far away from that place and time.

I was stunned. It was dawning on me that God had led me to a place I never would have chosen to visit, had I even known it existed, to select and speak words I never would have selected rationally. And yet, somehow, a powerful, perfectly tailored, Spirit-filled message of hope and salvation was being hand delivered. To be used in this way, despite my personal problems, faults, and flaws, was overwhelming. I felt incapacitated, unable to move or even speak. Several times I had to take a brief breath, clear my mind of all thought, and simply proceed with the message on the paper in front of me, which seemed to be coming not from me, though I had typed it, but from another realm.

But there was one moment remaining in this sermon that was to stand out above all others and become permanently etched into my memory. As we proceeded through this section of Scripture, we reached the one that tied it directly to the Feast of Tabernacles. When I called out Deuteronomy 31:10–13, a young girl, probably about eleven years old, raised her hand.

She spoke with a voice as clear as a bell and with exceptional pronunciation and flow. Though I spoke no Tamil, I could tell that this girl had no problem reading the text. The other children, and even the adults, had struggled with the archaic, poetic text of the classic translation. Yet this girl read easily, with a beautiful cadence, enunciating the words, driving the following message home:

And Moses commanded them, saying, At the end of every seven years, in the solemnity of the year of release, in the feast of tabernacles, When all Israel is come to appear before the LORD thy God in the place which he shall choose, thou shalt read this law before all Israel in their hearing. Gather the people together, men and women, and children, and thy stranger that is within thy gates, that they may hear, and that they may learn, and fear the LORD your God, and observe to do all the words of this law: And that their children, which have not known any thing, may hear, and learn to fear the LORD your God, as long as ye live in the land whither ye go over Jordan to possess it.

The powerful realization hit that somehow this Scripture had been and was being fulfilled here, in this place, with and by these people. This, again, was overwhelming. God also seemed to be speaking directly to me. He seemed to be both chiding and inspiring me for having doubted that I would experience Him in action. The blessings streaming forth as a result of simply being willing to follow Him were real.

But even more poignant was what this sweet, beautiful child's voice was reading. She was reading about gathering children and strangers to the Feast. The WCG and its offshoots had always identified with this symbolism. It describes how the children of Israel who had "not known any thing" would hear and "learn to fear the LORD," who would lead them from captivity, poverty, and despair into a glorious Promised Land flowing with milk and honey.

And these verses were being read by dispossessed children who had been all but orphaned. Disease and the actions of the state had forced a separation from their parents. Their experience paralleled my own. I had felt victimized by the way my life played out in comparison to my peers in the West, and these children were in circumstances far worse than mine had ever been. I had been eleven when I attended my first Feast of Tabernacles, as a lost little boy in a foreign country many years ago. We had essentially the same emotional challenge at the heart of our struggle:

Who loves you? Who will care for you? Who will teach and guide you? Who will show you how to get through life? Who will ultimately lead you in a positive way, a way that will bring peace and happiness, versus disease, poverty, and despair?

It would be God.

As we wrapped up the Feast and the Last Great Day, which featured another morning sermon, there were a number of inspiring discussions with the group, and other shared experiences over the course of this second stay in Gudiyatham. I spent more time with Rajendran, discussing his life, his vision for the people and the program, and just generally, for the first time, developing a bit of a relationship with him.

Certainly, the experiences of the last few days had allayed any concerns and fears about whether God was involved here or whether the situation was infected by man-made efforts at building edifices to human ego in the way I had seen other efforts in the COG world become corrupted. Seeing Rajendran in his office, seeing how his heart was consumed with the work he had responsibility for—not just for this compound but for several other such compounds in India —I developed a much less judgmental and critical perspective. He was as committed and genuine about these efforts as I had become about the need to build the TeachAKid program, to provide a work of love, and a source of finances as a physical foundation for the spiritual blessings that were so much in evidence here.

As we returned to Chennai, I was meditating about what we had experienced, and I realized I needed to continue with my planned series of articles in the *Journal*. I began to make some notes and asked Michael the name of the girl who had so delightfully and eloquently read the Scriptures on learning about God and moving forward triumphantly to possess the Promised Land. Michael explained that it was a two-part name, meaning "fruit" or "flower" and "language."

Although it's difficult to translate a name, I played with the name in my head.

"Fruit Speaks?" I asked.

Before Michael could answer, I recalled our conversation just before getting out of the car; we had agreed to judge the matter of Gudiyatham by its fruit.

The token God had granted me was overpowering and unmistakable.

The message could not have been any clearer, even if the fruit and flower designs woven into the tapestry used to form the tabernacle under which we had met had begun singing praise to the Glory of God.

What You're Doing

Prior to my first trip to India, my life had been very different. My reason for going had been my disillusionment with the WCG/COG movement, particularly David Hulme and his group. Thirteen months later, I was no longer attending his church. My wife had filed for divorce, and I was living in a house with two other single guys. Even so, my financial situation was improving, along with my career. I had joined the "millionaires club" after selling an engagement worth more than $1 million. Now I managed a delivery team with over $2 million in personal and $8 million in team sales to my credit, even as we were gearing up to sell additional services related to the five-year road map I had created.

But this growing success and the experience I was gaining professionally was nothing compared to the motivation and energy I was feeling spiritually. The power of having seen the Spirit of God in action in the lives of people in India baptized for less than a year was amazing. God was not only alive and well, but also willing to bless and honor anyone willing to follow Him. As inspiring and exciting as all these experiences and related insights were, they also represented an enormous challenge. How should I respond to these events?

God had led me to the other side of the planet to introduce me to people seeking His guidance. What was my personal responsibility to such remote persons who had wanted a minister to come teach and baptize them? And in what context would I carry it out? Having taken the reader on a meandering journey through my personal experiences and my shifting perspectives on my religious heritage (across two volumes), it's time to summarize a few key lessons learned along the way. This list is not exhaustive; it simply highlights my position, at that time, on the official teachings of the COG movement. It also hints at what might come next.

- God never intended for humans to rule over each other. The WCG/COG model focused members on human rulers. Christ brought freedom.

- The Holy Spirit teaches us, not a group of privileged overseers pretending to "minister." A ministering servant is a helper of joy—not a title of authority.

- People's direct access to God is hindered, not helped, by a hierarchical structure of ministerial authority derived from a Government of God teaching. Any desire to collect and own servants of God under an organizational banner is spiritual poison.

- The biblical tithing system was based on the increase from an asset base. Requiring multiple tithes on gross income is a destructive teaching.

- Men do not occupy a position of divine authority above that of women. Love and mutual submission is God's intent.

- The ability to understand spiritual truth is granted to all, based on our choices that either make us more open (humble) or resistant (prideful) to God.

- Good works and gifts of love—not belief statements—are the sign of a true Christian. What we do is much more important than what we profess.

- God would use anyone interested in preparing for the return of His Son to earth, regardless of the truth, error, or even the existence of the COG movement.

I was more motivated than ever by a sense of obligation to this last bullet point—to teach people to be about their Father's business. And I felt the best way to teach and train people how to do this was still through the pattern of worship which included the Sabbath and Holy Days.

And yet given this list, how could I point my new brothers and sisters to any COG organization? And if I couldn't do that, what could I do? I was not interested in building an independent religious organization. Even if I had been, I was not ready to move to India and live in poverty. And how would that help people who had serious physical needs? This whole situation was foreign to my own experience.

In looking for examples that might help me understand what my responsibility was, Paul's statement about different men planting and watering but God granting the increase seemed to fit my situation.[11] I would consider myself to be "nothing" and would assign God the responsibility for the spiritual

---

11. I Corinthians 3:5–7: "Who then is Paul, and who is Apollos, but ministers by whom ye believed, even as the Lord gave to every man? I have planted, Apollos watered; but God gave the increase. So then neither is he that planteth any thing, neither he that watereth; but God that giveth the increase."

growth of those whom He had drawn to His Word. And yet there were two key problems that needed to be resolved in India.

First, Leon Sexton's Legacy Institute had the spiritual leadership role in managing these small but growing congregations in Southeast India. His approach to church organization and structure was not all that different from the WCG model. My answer to this first problem was ostrich-like at the moment. Since I did not feel I had an oversight responsibility, per my new belief system on these issues, I could afford to be silent and detached. It was ultimately God and the Holy Spirit's responsibility anyway.

The second problem was, without a tithing system and in an impoverished area, how could a foundation of love and service be used to support an operation that would need money to survive—and a steady, reliable flow of it to thrive? My answer to that was to connect those who had both love and funds. There were people in the West whose hearts could be touched by God and the Holy Spirit. These people could be motivated to meet the needs of their less materially fortunate brothers and sisters. Could some of these be found in the COG movement?

After leaving David Hulme's group, my options on where to fellowship with others who believed as I did had been limited. There was no point in going back to the UCG or seeking to join one of the more extreme splinters from the WCG. But there was a small, local group that had separated from WCG in the '70s, led by David Antion. He had been an evangelist in the WCG back then and was related by marriage to Garner Ted Armstrong, the silver-tongued preacher who had first interested my dad. GTA, as he was known, was the son of HWA and had been the heir apparent to the organization before his personal failings had led to his being disfellowshipped by his father.

My previous opinion of the groups who left the WCG at that time was that they had been unwilling to work things out with the established leadership of the WCG. Without really knowing them, I had judged them as the kind of people more likely to insist they were right than to discuss and reach agreement. My more recent experiences, as well as my 180-degree change of perspective on the issue of the Government of God doctrine, led me to become more open-minded. And my dad had associated with David Antion's Church of God, Southern California, for a while, so I had a connection.

What I found when I introduced myself to the group was underwhelming but appealing. My assessment was that David Antion had felt a moral obligation to continue to serve those who looked to him for guidance and had continued to provide a weekly church service to accommodate their spiritual needs. He had also established Guardian Ministries, in which his recorded messages were sent out to a small but widespread group of listeners scattered around the country and even in Europe.

This was somewhat similar to what had attracted me to David Hulme at the time of his split from the UCG. He had initially expressed a humble desire to serve those who had looked to him for leadership. David Antion appeared to have actually carried out this intention. The humble, run-down rented facility and the small, disheveled group of people that attended (with a high percentage of them older and in marginal or even poor health) seemed evidence that David Antion was a servant willing to help others with no benefit accruing to him. This, along with —by COG standards—a relatively high level of cultural diversity in evidence within the group, led me to see David Antion as different. It appeared that he was giving to these people, not taking from them.

After attending for only a few weeks and speaking with David and others on a number of occasions, I found they were open to receiving my help, including as a speaker. This was important to me, due to my belief that I had been called and anointed to preach during my time in the WCG. Despite my rejection of the hierarchy of the WCG, I still believed that my own ordination into the ministry represented a solemn covenant with God. And with so much going on in India, I welcomed the opportunity to share my perspectives on what I was learning along the way.

I was careful not to appear to be trying to steal David Antion's thunder with stories of India. Despite his attitude of service, David might be sensitive to the appearance of trying to divert resources away from his local church or Guardian Ministries. My focus was on spiritual principles that would be of benefit to anyone in the audience, but my messages were spiked with interesting examples and stories from my recent trips and current activities.

Dad, who had not responded well to David Hulme's reserved, intellectual approach to theology—which differed from his own more aggressive, and even combative, dogmatic approach—was happy to hear that I had hooked up with David Antion. In Dad's eyes, David Antion's connections to Garner Ted

Armstrong, and his having gotten out long before the apostasy of the Tkach era, amounted to old-school credibility. None of that mattered or even appealed to me. I was encouraged that David Antion was educated, with a counseling degree and an independent counseling practice on the side. While Dad and I had different reasons for liking David Antion, it was nonetheless a positive development for our relationship.

Regarding the efforts in India, Rali and his Chennai company, Rajasri Systems, had begun work on a prototype website, with content developed in conjunction with Michael and Ryan Foster. Tutoring locations and protocols, a pending curriculum, a training manual for tutors, a logo, promotional materials, and much more was in flight. Ryan and another Legacy faculty member, Amy Hufton, were both enthusiastic about the program and very energetic. Commitments were also beginning to come in from our first monthly sponsors of students and tutors who were excited about the prototype website. My focus was corporate sponsorships to fund the official launch of TeachAKid the following spring, to coincide with my return to Chennai for the Passover and Days of Unleavened Bread. Branded backpacks, T-shirts, and media attention would generate enthusiasm and establish our presence.

While Michael's efforts to help a few homeless kids had been the genesis of the idea behind TeachAKid, he was also the cause of increasing concern about its future. He continued to shift his focus from idea to idea without following through on his commitments to any of them. He made unilateral decisions on the ground and explained later, despite my insistence that this was unacceptable. It would be impossible to build a sustainable program in this manner, as donors, sponsors, and participants in the West had a right to expect that the results would be auditable.

TeachAKid would not survive an incident like the one we had experienced with the cushion-cover program. I asked Michael to provide a brief biweekly report so that all team members could align and pull together, adapting as a group to any changes in the plan. The report template I provided was very simple: it requested an outline of his accomplishments during the last two weeks, his plans for the next two weeks, and a list of whatever challenges he was facing along the way.

Quite simply, Michael needed to exhibit personal and professional growth to successfully administer and manage a growing program, as opposed to ad hoc projects. The growing team needed to be able to depend on each team member to follow through on individual commitments. Verbal agreements on the phone weren't working. Biweekly reports, documenting agreed-upon plans and progress against them, with dates and expectations, were necessary.

Michael initially agreed to this, but after six to eight weeks of frustrating e-mails and phone discussions, he had produced only one report and it was so broad and vague it was useless. He seemed to resent having to adhere to a set plan and was increasingly uncooperative. My time and emotional energy was spent in discussions with him, creating a negative dynamic, and keeping me from focusing on what I should be accomplishing. To resolve this, I reached out to a talented friend whom I had met during my time as David Hulme's assistant during my junior and senior years at Ambassador College.

She had wide experience in project management inside WCG TV operations and AICF, and later with nongovernment organizations in Thailand and elsewhere. She would act as project manager, coordinating Michael's efforts, freeing me up from those responsibilities, and removing some of the tension that was building between Michael and me. She had the credibility, skills, and talents needed to pull this off.

One of my personal tasks was establishing a board of directors. It would include the project manager, Michael, and me, but also experienced supporters on both sides of the ocean, including Leon Sexton, Rali Panchanatham, and others. The Board would help resolve any differences of opinion that might continue to arise between Michael and me.

Michael and I also discussed the importance of having me take the lead in establishing formal relationships between TeachAKid and universities and financial institutions in India. Together, we were to handle this on my upcoming trip, but Michael, instead, took matters into his own hands. He informed me by phone that, instead of waiting, he had met with an official of the primary university where several of our tutors attended. According to Michael, the Director demanded an endowment on deposit in India of at least $50,000. Until that money was in place, Michael said they were stopping him from continuing with the pilot program currently underway.

Without a functioning cost-effective pilot program to showcase TeachAKid in the West, we wouldn't be able to raise that amount of money. More importantly, the purpose of a pilot was to solve the many operational problems we would face and provide proof to investors and donors that our project was viable.

After eighteen months, multiple trips to India, significant amounts of money, and an enormous amount of work and energy, the pilot program had been completely shut down. There was enormous progress and potential, including the prototype website, which was impressive, and, at that time, available for review at TeachAKid.org. But now, even though several of the tutors Michael had been working with were not even students at this university, Michael refused to proceed until I produced the endowment they demanded.

Over the course of three months of attempts to get Michael to hold himself more accountable, my trust in him had eroded. Michael was aware that I wanted the board of directors, which I was putting in place, to manage fund allocation. The timing was suspicious.

There was no way I was going to agree to deliver $50,000 into an account in India outside the legal framework of a foundation, without a board of directors, prior to having a viable pilot program underway. That would be a program guaranteed to fail to meet minimum standards of accountability for a 501(c)(3) foundation, even if there was a way to effectively launch it, which there wasn't.

I had been eagerly marching toward a majestic mountain peak, fueled by an inspiring vision, and following a route I knew would take me there safely, with the wind at my back. Just as I was arriving at base camp, Mount Everest suddenly loomed in front in all its fearful glory. Looking around, there was no equipment to get to the top, and the Sherpa suddenly demanded $50,000 I didn't have.

Returning to India right now was pointless. Michael had handled all local contacts. I had no phone numbers or addresses and didn't even speak the language. Michael had effectively shut TeachAKid down.

As the deadline to purchase tickets to India approached, my wife and I were locked in painful discussions (via our attorneys) about finalizing the divorce and splitting our assets. She was familiar with the master spreadsheet that tracked exactly where every dollar of our money was. It detailed our assets, including a net-worth figure down to the penny. I had proposed a clean, 50/50 split. She had rejected my proposal.

By this time, I was earning significantly more than she was. In California, she was entitled to demand alimony from me, due to our income disparity.

And since she worked within the legal system and was connected to lawyers and judges, she was pushing hard for this. She justified her position with her accusation—bolstered by my step-uncle, our tax preparer—that I had somehow hidden income and/or assets from her.

I recalled my dad's appearance before the Supreme Court of Sweden during his divorce case in which he had thought God would back him up.[12] There was no need for me to repeat Dad's past mistakes, so I quickly agreed to a lump-sum settlement giving her 75 percent of all assets, in return for a clean break with no alimony.

When she moved out my soul was shattered. It had been central to my identity that I would never do what my parents had done; I would never get divorced. In the ensuing two years, I had been through the gamut of emotions. There had been anger, grief, and despair. On March 12, 2004, the day the divorce settlement was final, I felt lost.

---

12. See *TPotS*, chap. 2, "Run for Your Life."

7

Sgt. Pepper's Lonely Hearts Club Band

Denial ain't just a river in Egypt.

— ATTRIBUTED TO MARK TWAIN

God wanted me to learn something from this that I was still unable to grasp. Knowing that God's original intent did not include divorce, and that He had gone on record as hating it, I suffered under the inner conflict of knowing He would have wanted me to avoid it yet it had happened anyway. Whatever I had learned so far, distilled from my processing of this failure, was depressing.

Twist and Shout

In my reinvention as a player in the booming world of corporate technology, my career and financial ups and downs, my marriage, and now the failure to come to terms with Michael in India, my focus had been on myself. What mattered was what I wanted and didn't want. In my marriage, for example, the idea of the sanctity of marriage had been central to my worldview, but only in an egocentric context. In the end, I was not all that concerned about or even aware of what my partner wanted.

My moral compass, when it came to marriage, was further skewed by many years of believing that I was the head of the family, which meant I was in a superior position in the Government of God. In that sense, my wife reported to me. She was my responsibility. It was up to me to bless or overrule her decisions, and to comment on or express my perspective on even her wants and desires. If they didn't agree with mine, then there was a good chance God wanted me to resist them. The combination of my fixation on what I didn't want—divorce— coupled with a misinformed and misguided perspective on what the relationship was, had pretty much doomed it to failure from the start.

It was only a positive outlook that kept me from being instantly sucked down into a self-destructive vortex of depression. Previously, there were multiple sources of optimism: hope that it wasn't really over, success in my career, anticipation of financial independence, and, most of all, the belief that God was guiding me forward spiritually and was blessing my efforts in India. Now, the marriage was legally dismantled, and my plans for setting up a foundation for homeless children in Chennai, into which I could pour my heart and soul, were likewise destroyed.

The divorce settlement was the final nail in the coffin of my planned trip to India for the Days of Unleavened Bread and the launch of TeachAKid. If it weren't for the effect of that cash settlement on my personal financial situation, I might have been tempted to come up with the money that would break the logjam created by Michael's premature and unauthorized actions, which led to the entire program being held hostage for $50,000. But even if I hadn't felt that it would be foolish to invest any more money in Michael and his programs, I suddenly had none to invest.

My dad seemed actually happy that I was divorced from my wife. He had never embraced my choice in marriage nor had he gotten along with her. But perhaps he was just trying to be positive and was pleased that we were now spending more time together. With my divorce finalized, we were able to focus on our joint real estate investments in Spokane.

I was bringing objective financial analysis to my dad's experience in construction. Between the two of us, we had a winning combination for jointly buying and managing single-family homes. In this light, my prospects for a quick recovery from the divorce settlement looked good.

In 2003, we were already several years into a lengthy phase of easy mortgages, coupled with appreciating real estate valuations. At the time, very few were aware of the circular nature of this equation. The securitization of mortgages was just beginning to turn this extended bull market in real estate into a massive bubble that would create enormous wealth before threatening the foundation of the interrelated global financial markets. For my dad and me, it was a positive time of father–son participation in easy wealth creation, amidst dreams of financial independence. For my dad, this meant the fulfillment of a lifelong dream of "making it in the big country out West." For me, it represented a possible solution to the impasse that had settled around my dreams of establishing a viable foundation to help the homeless children of Chennai.

Despite cancelling my trip, I was hoping to salvage the TeachAKid situation somehow. I was in close contact with Amy Hufton before she left Thailand; she was scheduled to be in India during the Passover and Days of Unleavened Bread. I commissioned her to work closely with Michael to try to complete the manual we had initiated. I also asked that she interview and evaluate those tutor candidates who were not currently in the university program. With a manual and tutors, it might be possible to operate the pilot as an extension of Legacy Institute if I could get it moving in the right direction again.

What Amy reported after her trip to India was disturbing. Michael had tried to solicit her to become his ambassador to the US to help him to make contacts and raise funds for the TeachAKid program. Yet even though he was trying to convince Amy that he was committed to the tutoring program, he had also stepped up his campaign to reach out to anyone and everyone via e-mail to solicit funds for a variety of projects. One day it was the goats for the AIDS village; the next, aid for farmers facing drought, or women's initiatives, or a variety of orphans' and homeless children's assistance projects.

His appeals were designed to entice individual donors to send a one-time donation for a short-term, tactical need. This was depressing. After three trips, long discussions, countless e-mails and phone calls, all in an effort to build a long-term sustainable program, Michael was unwilling or unable to achieve this. There would not be a viable program delivering lasting improvements. There would be no foundation able to support a growing program.

Confronted with Michael's return to a focus on soliciting unaudited donations and the failure of my vision, I began to question my own motivations. Were my efforts really stemming from a pure desire to help these children, or was I trying to prove to the world and myself how good I was? Why was it so important to me to turn these efforts into a foundation that would gain the respect and support of the West? Why did I want corporate sponsors to believe in what I was doing and be willing to support it in a big way? These rhetorical questions really had no clear answer.

Whether there was any impurity in my motives or not, a huge cultural and philosophical divide existed between what Michael and I were trying to do. Then I learned from Amy that despite the money sent for goats by one of the founding members of TeachAKid, there was no such program, as far as she could tell. This was the last straw. I severed the relationship with Michael and put all TeachAKid efforts on hold.

I was now at a sadly familiar dead end.

The only way I could interpret events and circumstances in India, which had been on the outside edge of my control and understanding, was to believe that God had been guiding me. In the process, I felt closer to underlying spiritual realities and felt certain that God had been directly involved. It was evidence that Christ would back up anyone willing to follow Him with the "signs following" them.[1] It had been only the beginning of what I thought was possible, and I was certain that God wanted me to continue to walk in faith down the gangplank I was on.

But how?

I could not continue to work with Michael. The differences I experienced, whether based in cultural perspectives, ability, professionalism, or standards of integrity, were too big to be bridged. Yet, without him and the hope of a viable charity in India integrated with the ongoing efforts to assist believers, I had no vision for how to proceed.

Was my faith adequate? Was it a lack of faith to want physical funds in place before walking down the gangplank? Or was I practicing faith balanced with wisdom and experience? Was it wrong to seek to establish a reputable,

---

1. Mark 16:20: "And they went forth, and preached every where, the Lord working with them, and confirming the word with signs following. Amen."

sustainable program, using not only faith, but also a minimum of experienced participants and resources?

I decided that to approach this differently would be foolish and would not have God's blessing. Even when Christ admonished His disciples to forsake all and follow Him, He used a practical example about counting the cost, in order to insist on something other than blind faith.[2] This seemed to tell me to focus on my career while waiting for God to provide clarity on how to dedicate my economic success in service to Him.

With trips to India, my pending divorce, the house sale and move, progress on my MBA had been slow. Despite the managed chaos, one class at a time I had reached the halfway point, with a grade point average close to 4.0. What I was learning was translating into success at Deloitte. The engagement that had opened the door to the millionaire's club was continuing to pay dividends. It's time to share that story.

I Don't Want to Spoil the Party

A senior team of Deloitte associates had previously delivered a technology road map to the IT department of a large regulated utility company. It had cost about $1 million and was deemed "fluffy thought-ware" by the client. Deloitte was shown the door while the client figured out how to take a more realistic and grounded approach.

In the meantime, the real estate division of this utility company had separately issued its own request for a proposal for an IT strategy and road map for its real estate operations. I had won and delivered this engagement, out of which came the proposals for the $2 million worth of work I had sold. The utility's headquarters facility happened to be no more than twenty minutes from my home, making it easy for me to put in extra hours without the usual travel expenses. And I was hitting my stride in my field, pulling together diverse elements of my experience and skill set to create an efficient and innovative delivery system for the products and services Deloitte had to offer. But most

---

2.   Luke 14:28–30: "For which of you, intending to build a tower, sitteth not down first, and counteth the cost, whether he have sufficient to finish it? Lest haply, after he hath laid the foundation, and is not able to finish it, all that behold it begin to mock him, Saying, This man began to build, and was not able to finish."

importantly, in proposing my work to the clients, I had realized something important about Deloitte that I was consciously avoiding.

My proposals had to be put through an internal risk management review, to minimize risk to Deloitte and maximize our profit. Risk management had a word-processing tool called The Terminator. It flagged certain risk words and replaced them with terms that were more acceptable. When I got my proposal back, I studied it—and was dismayed at what I learned. Words like *deliver*, *direct*, and *ensure* were changed to words like *support*, *advise*, and *oversee*. The net result was to water down Deloitte's commitment to deliver value to its clients. In other words, while my efforts were focused on convincing my client that we would be delivering services guaranteed to be valuable, risk management sought to minimize Deloitte's contractual obligations to actually do so. Deloitte wanted to avoid any commitment other than to ensure delivery of invoices for payment.

This went against my grain, so I did what I could to make sure Deloitte was on the hook to deliver, and then worked tirelessly to make sure we did. My primary counterpart on the client side, the VP of Finance for the real estate division, liked my approach, and it opened up the door to some interesting and enlightening discussions about the nature of corporate America. He showed me an article that provided a scientific basis for some of the observations I was making. The article was a discussion of the book *Moral Mazes* by Robert Jackall, on how and why managers in large corporations lose their moral compass.[3] I shared cultural values with my customer that I found lacking at Deloitte. Reading the article on *Moral Mazes* led me to evaluate the pyramid structure of Deloitte in the light of what I had learned about the institution of systems of rulership in the Bible.

---

3. The book description on Amazon.com includes the following: "This classic study of ethics in business presents an eye-opening account of how corporate managers think the world works, and how big organizations shape moral consciousness. Robert Jackall takes the reader inside a topsy-turvy world where hard work does not necessarily lead to success, but sharp talk, self-promotion, powerful patrons, and sheer luck might. What sort of everyday rules-in-use do people play by when there are no fixed standards to explain why some succeed and others fail? In the words of one corporate manager, those rules boil down to this maxim: '*What is right in the corporation is what the guy above you wants from you. That's what morality is in the corporation*,'" accessed September 26, 2017, https://www.amazon.com/Moral-Mazes-World-Corporate-Managers/dp/0199729883/. See Robert Jackall, *Moral Mazes: The World of Corporate Managers*, 20th anniversary ed. (Oxford: Oxford University Press, 2010).

As mentioned, the use of the word "rule" and its introduction to human society was a curse. It was never God's intent that human rulership, which was granted over the earth and the animals, would be extended to other human beings. Rather, it was a result of sin and disobedience. We sin our way into a condition in which we become ruled, in a variety of ways, by our fellow humans. We lose our individual sovereignty.

Since it is impossible for sinful human beings to rule with justice and integrity, Adam and all after him bring down "greater condemnation" upon themselves for having the responsibility of rulership but failing to exercise it properly.[4]

Our movement from sovereignty to slavery happens when we, like Adam and Eve, abdicate our responsibility to rule ourselves. We abdicate our obligation to operate according to the Golden Rule and to act with integrity according to a moral compass. When we do, we allow others to determine the set of rewards and punishments that become our new orientation. When we abandon our personal internal compass, we, like Israel, begin to wander in the desert.

A cycle of oppressive rulership and slavery was initiated in Eden. This cycle leads to God freeing the enslaved by humbling and removing the rulers, as when the power of Pharaoh was destroyed so he had to let Israel go. Even then, Pharaoh made one more desperate attempt to bring them back under his dominion, which cost him the remainder of his army, his power, and his glory.

Once freed from Egypt, the former slaves were led toward the Promised Land, toward sovereignty under God. Sadly, in the desert, they soon erected a golden calf; idolatry takes us back under the rule of sin, symbolized by Egypt.

The Egyptian system of systems enabled oppressive god-rulers to enslave others in efforts to extend their dominion even into the next life. Their slaves, including the Israelites, were deployed to erect massive monuments into which the wealth of the nation was poured, in the belief it provided the rulers wealth and power even beyond the grave. They sought to extend their abuse of power into eternity.

Yet the Israelites, who had just been freed from this oppression, were soon longing for it. That is how powerful this illusion of freedom created by abdication can be. Like an addict longing for the fix that frees his mind and senses from

---

4. James 3:1: "My brethren, be not many masters, knowing that we shall receive the greater condemnation."

the reality of his responsibilities, so the illusion of being under the protective care of another human being causes us to abdicate personal responsibility over our own lives, leading inevitably to slavery. In kidnappings, this is referred to as Stockholm syndrome.

And as mentioned, those willing to assume the role of ruler bring themselves greater condemnation. Instead of ruling over others who abdicate their sovereignty, we should be serving them in a sacrificial way, increasing their independence so they will outgrow the need to be ruled. This is what Christ did. This is the essence of being a Christian.

Sadly, as highlighted by a quote attributed to Helen Keller, "People do not like to think. If one thinks, one must reach conclusions. Conclusions are not always pleasant." Eve's way of dealing with the difficulties of having sinned was to "desire" Adam. It is much easier to offload our personal responsibility onto someone else, even if it means making that person our ruler. Generally speaking, this is how the system of hierarchies that governs this planet is empowered today. The aggregation of abdication, in varying degrees, by those who cede responsibility, creates the pyramid of pyramids.

My goal is to help us all to do that which Helen Keller said we preferred not to do. These principles extend from families and personal relationships, through churches, governments, and increasingly in our day, large multinational corporations. One of the reasons I have spent time on this is because reflections on these connections empowered my understanding of prophecy, especially the relationship of church, state, and commerce in the biblical system known as Babylon the Great. The merchants and the rulers are distinct from the Beast's power, but they were all colluding. Knowing all this, I was having an increasingly hard time supporting the values of the firm I was representing. At the same time, almost schizophrenically, I was enjoying the perks that went hand in hand with success at Deloitte.

For example, the engagement at the utility company proved so profitable and promising that our practice leader authorized a trip to Las Vegas for me and my team. It had to be brief, so we were on the ground for no more than twenty-four hours. Still, the seven of us easily blew through our $10,000 budget, which of course included the flight, transportation, and hotel rooms but still left plenty of green for fun. From the time we hit the tarmac and stepped into our limo, we painted as much of the town red as we could during our whirlwind stay.

Between the meals, the clubs, the show we took in, and the time we spent at the casino, there was no time to sleep, so we barely saw the inside of our rooms. The reason for mentioning this trip is that Vegas was a microcosm informing my view of how the system of systems called the global economy works.

The Paris Hotel is a good example. The hotel is a massive complex, which includes all the restaurants, shops, and facilities needed to keep people from ever having to take any of their dollars outside the hotel. And the ceiling inside is painted like sky so guests think it is still daytime long after they should be in bed. In the casino itself, free alcohol and oxygen are pumped into the environment, further enhancing the illusion.

The result is exactly what the owner-operators desire. A mini-universe, carefully crafted to feed the fantasy that the players can win. It entices and disorients the guests to start gambling and keep gambling. That is, it ensures they act against their own best interests in a way that benefits the owner-operators of the system.

My insider experience with capitalism in action exposed more and more evidence that the ultrapowerful and influential of the planet had created a similar system spanning our global society. They were aligned in their efforts to bring every ounce of intelligence, creativity, and power to bear upon the goal of motivating the citizens to eagerly participate in activities that work against their own best interests, ceding their power, wealth, creativity, energy, and allegiance to those who treat them like sheep to be shorn and slaughtered.

As these ideas were being formulated and developed, I was enjoying and relishing my own limited success within the capitalist system. My success with the utility brought the magnitude of opportunities now open there to the attention of more senior partners in the firm who wanted in on the action.

Piggies

My management had always communicated that my job was to become a trusted advisor to my clients, and I had. As a result, the client was investing several million dollars in following my proposed strategy and road map. Having proven that Deloitte could deliver value, the door was open for the team that had tried (and failed) before to come back in and pursue the large-scale systems integration initiative within IT that had originally attracted Deloitte's attention. Such an engagement would be enormously lucrative to Deloitte. A powerful energy industry partner within Deloitte decided to leverage my success, so I was appointed process lead on the team.

Once the client signed off, however, a more senior individual closer to the partner was positioned to fulfill the role. Within the utility there was a similar dynamic, as folks familiar with my work on the five-year road map were forced to take a back seat to the more senior leaders who were now driving the broader initiative. Although Deloitte was only paying lip service to what the client wanted, this did not become an issue at first. Our initial proposal and presentation went well, and Deloitte won the engagement. But when the Deloitte team explained their process framework, it wasn't the same as what I had developed. Worse, a UC, Berkeley, professor who was the brother of a very senior executive within the utility was helping Deloitte with this pursuit. The money that flowed from the project budget for his services made me uncomfortable.

The client naturally raised questions during the discovery and strategy sessions, trying to hold Deloitte to the standards already deployed. Deloitte partners were reverting to Deloitte's standard methods, which had earlier been rejected by the client. When project stakeholders came directly to me and asked pointed questions, I answered carefully but truthfully. This generated rumblings that were not well received within Deloitte.

As I sought to address the problem, I was accused by certain parties in Deloitte of "going native," of putting the client's interests before Deloitte's. I was directed to make statements that I felt would mislead the client. Things soon came to a head.

An off-site session was scheduled at which the Berkeley professor was a dominant figure. The meeting was to align everyone and deliver marching orders on how we were going to proceed. At one point during this session, attended by four Deloitte partners, I was called on the carpet for having discussions with the client and was given the party line on what to say. In no uncertain terms, I was instructed to affirm that the methodology being proposed for the larger pursuit was exactly the same as the one I had been using. In my opinion, however, this was, at best, a significant stretch of the truth.

I explained that the client's questions were very specific and that I was not comfortable bending the truth. The rather large professor rose from his chair, and as he leaned his entire imposing frame toward me, yelled across the table, "If you can't get on board, then shut the f—k up!" No one, myself included, said a word. Having thus settled the matter, he sat down and continued outlining the approach he recommended on how to manage the regulated institution in which his brother was a very senior executive.

The next day one of the four partners who had been present called to apologize for the way I had been treated. He had felt uncomfortable that no Deloitte partner had stood up to defend me. This seemed odd, since he was one of them. It wasn't clear if he was trying to offer me a lifeline or protect himself. Still, I was confident in my abilities and my position with the client. I was also confident God would back me up, since this was, in my mind, a moral issue. And I felt that my success within the firm spoke for itself. In terms of the financial numbers I had racked up over the last two years, I was outperforming most of the senior managers in my practice area.

Given my relationship with my manager, I fully expected to be promoted to senior manager in the spring. But in a meeting with our practice partner, I was told, "Promotion to senior manager is reserved for those who are on track to make partner. I need to know in my heart that, if you are promoted, you have what it takes to make partner. I'm not sure I can say that about you."

Somewhat foolishly and arrogantly, I maintained the attitude that I deserved to be promoted. Gone was the humble person who had huddled under his desk, praying for God's help. I felt I was being cheated and wanted justice. This attitude quickly led to a pissing contest with my manager, who had formerly been one of my biggest supporters. It was a battle I was destined to lose.

When I came in to work one morning in March, about a month after my divorce was final, I was offered a severance package by human resources. I really had no option but to sign it. Then I walked away from a company and a job that had transformed me from a promising novice into a professional management consultant with one of the most respected brands in the world.

I'm not supposed to discuss the terms, but the severance was a fraction of the bonus that should have resulted from the sale and delivery of projects over the last year. I was shown the door right before it was due. So as I approached my forty-fifth birthday, I was unexpectedly in a dead end in almost every area of my life, including my career.

My rapid rise to success at Deloitte had been short-circuited by internal conflict. This on top of my marriage of twelve years ending in a bitter divorce and a battle over the assets we had accumulated. My thirty years of association with God's True Church and its splinter groups was also coming to an end, as I had shifted focus to support and launch programs in India, investing enormous energy into pursuit of God's path for me in a far-flung area of the world. These plans had collapsed under my feet. I had placed my spiritual bets and now saw absolutely no path forward with the projects and programs.

In all of these areas, I could do a decent job pointing at the other side as the cause of the friction.

But I was the common denominator.

This was weighing very heavily on me as I began, for the first time since age sixteen, three months of idle time with no gainful employment or goals.

And then, of course, there was the small matter of money. After shelling out a large percentage of everything I owned in a divorce settlement, I was now unemployed. As discouraged as I was, and as depressing as the setbacks were, I had no doubt God was in some mysterious way—completely hidden to my logic at the moment—walking me down another gangplank of faith. And where there is faith, there is hope.

My housing situation as a majority owner of a three-bedroom house in Pasadena meant that my mortgage was 50 percent paid by the other two tenants. As a single guy, I could keep my living expenses low. The free time resulting from my severance with Deloitte made several trips to Spokane possible, during which I could work out the details of the real estate investing business with my Dad. So I figured I might as well take it easy for a while and enjoy the time off, as a blessing from God.

Even before my hypnotism experience, I had always had a fascination with golf. Golf is a sport where you work on yourself. Golf courses seemed as good a place as any for God to help me sort the mess out. Spending some time using golf to get to a place where I wasn't fighting myself, dragging myself down, being my own worst enemy, might yield benefits off the course as well. I had a number of great leads through my work at Deloitte and thought that my next career step might come to me while I focused on golf. Within a few weeks, this paid off.

I had made a few friends along the way, including the CEO of a celebrated and fast-growing real estate technology start-up, now called Accruent. Accruent had many Fortune 500 clients. The CEO invited me to attend their annual customer summit held at Shutters Hotel on the beach in Santa Monica. During the golf outing, I was paired up with Rollin, who introduced himself as the chief financial officer (CFO) of one of Countrywide's divisions—Countrywide being a celebrated and rapidly growing company.

During our round of golf, Rollin explained that he was the CFO of the corporate real estate division of Countrywide. He asked me if I knew of anyone who might be interested in assisting Countrywide with its real estate system needs. It felt like Rollin was fishing to see if I was interested in the role since I had been introduced as an expert in real estate systems. The role Rollin was discussing would have been a great chance to take on a responsibility for an important area of business operations with a major impact on a set of large budgets. But one of the lessons I had learned at Deloitte and the utility was that I needed to transcend the label of systems expert.

The intersection of business operations and business strategy was at the heart of company growth and was a superior career path than being tied to specific systems. I wanted to make sure that my next career move was to a role that could influence corporate strategy. I recommended to Rollin a fellow manager from Deloitte who had been on my team as I delivered the work I had scoped and sold at the utility.

The Accruent event, however, proved to be my first and last opportunity to rub shoulders with business leaders on the back nine. My hope had been that my future career move would materialize on the horizon of the eighteenth hole, but the reality was solo golf and pickup games with whatever twosome or threesome happened along. These were usually older, retired duffers who, like me, seemed not to be heading anywhere in particular, and certainly nowhere exciting. To make matters worse, after an initial promising spurt of improvement, my golf game started to go downhill along with my attitude.

What bothered me most was the impasse in India, and the dissolving dream of TeachAKid.org. My career trajectory had funded my optimism, and now the foundation seemed doomed. My discouragement, and the lack of a daily schedule provided by gainful employment, sent me into a tailspin. First, I began staying up late and playing cards with others on the Internet. The next area of my life to trend downhill was my diet. My dinner was often a large bowl of chili and a beer, consumed in front of the computer. Dessert was a large bowl of Häagen-Dazs cappuccino ice cream with a hefty dose of Kahlua.

The sugar and caffeine kept me up late.

This led to me sleeping in and gave me the excuse needed to blow off the golf course, which led to more time spent sitting online playing spades. One beer with my chili turned into two or three, and the dose of Kahlua got larger. My days started late and ended later, with me crashing into bed in the wee hours on a full stomach with a buzz. I was actually kind of shocked to see myself failing to make any progress on the myriad ideas and things we tell ourselves we'll do if we ever have time, but it didn't stop the downhill slide.

I had imagined myself to be a self-made, self-motivated man, and it was very discouraging to find myself in this place. At the time, I was not able to cut myself any psychological slack, despite the relatively dramatic changes I had recently gone through. Putting on weight for the first time in my skinny life was the least of my worries. Even as my waistline was expanding, a gnawing guilt began to eat me up inside, which along with my lifestyle began to affect my health. For the first time in a decade, my health was trending in the wrong direction. I was worried about a relapse of the Ankylosing Spondylitis that had been in complete remission for seven years.

This concern was an increasingly valid one. The Holmes and Rahe stress scale lists forty-three stressful life events that can contribute to illness. Each of these events carries a numerical score, and a total of 300 correlates to a high risk of illness. I recently took this test, based on the events of that time, and my score was over 550. This didn't include the stress I felt at having baptized, and then abandoned, groups of people in India who had looked to me for guidance. Apparently, the Holmes and Rahe stress scale had not previously encountered this particular type of stress.

I'm not sure what a midlife crisis really is, but this seemed a good approximation. My ego and inflated sense of my own capabilities had kept me from taking the opportunity with Countrywide that God had put in front of me. This perspective further increased my doubt and despair. It began to feel like my future would consist of living in the past, with regrets. And in terms of my biggest failure, my relationship with my wife, my new understanding of God's intended relationship for men and women seemed hollow. I now knew what it meant that we were both created in God's image—that one of us was not a subhuman species. Despite this insight, I was now alone, and it is not good for a man to be alone.

In this time of failure and self-doubt, there was no female at my side to help or encourage me. I had pushed them all away in my arrogance and superiority. I had traversed so many bridges, burning them all in my zeal and the confidence that I was on the right path, heading in the right direction. And now I found myself on an island, alone with myself, and I was neither as right nor as good as I had previously thought.

What pulled me out of the black hole was a call from Rollin, the Countrywide executive I had met golfing. He called to thank me for recommending the Deloitte manager, whom he had hired as vice president of space planning. My happiness for this respected colleague and friend was bittersweet, as he had moved out and up, while I had moved out and down and was continuing to sink. But Rollin had not called just to thank me; he wanted to talk to me about another role. He needed to fill the strategic planning position for the growing division. This time he had my attention, and not only because I was feeling desperate. This position might be the answer to the prayers I should have been saying instead of spending all my time playing spades.

Then Rollin went dark on me. For more than two weeks, I heard nothing. Despair again began to creep in. All my confidence and zeal, and the faith that I had so consistently relied upon, might have been no more than ego-driven fantasies. The situation was eerily similar to the time I had resigned from the WCG and planned a vacation on the island of Maui, confident that God was going to provide me with the director position at UCLA.

Just as my checks from Deloitte were drying up, Rollin set up an interview with the chief administrative officer at Countrywide, a man who reported to the CEO, Angelo Mozilo. The interview went well, and the chief administrative officer let me know that meeting him was a formality. Rollin was authorized to hire whomever he wanted.

Suddenly I emerged from the black hole. I was now vice president, strategic planning, with Countrywide Financial Corporation (CFC), helping shape the strategy of one of the fastest growing and most exciting companies to work for in 2004, at the heart of a rapidly expanding economy driven largely by a growing real estate bubble.

I soon realized I was on the inside of something big. CFC's mission statement was one I could feel good about. It focused on making home ownership possible for the average American. This was my chance to make a positive difference. I would be helping the bottom rung within society—the disenfranchised and underprivileged. And I would secure my own financial future in the process.

I was flush with confidence at having stood up against the moral ambivalence of the corporate world, most notably with the partners at Deloitte Consulting. My new position was divine confirmation. I had followed what I believed to be right and had walked off the end of the gangplank, only to be rescued right before the sharks had gotten hold of me. I would make my mark at an up-and-coming firm and reap the rewards of my material success. This was an elevated platform for greater service to God.

This time things were going to be different. [5]

Good Day Sunshine

I could not have been more excited in the summer of 2004 as I completed Countrywide Financial Corporation's new hire orientation. Moving into my office and ordering business cards featuring the title "Vice President—Strategic Planning" brought to mind the long and winding road that had brought me here. It had taken almost ten years, but my transformation from minister and midlevel executive in the defunct and discredited Worldwide Church of God (WCG) to corporate executive was complete.

Within a few weeks, I had grasped the lay of the corporate land and the essential issues I needed to address in my CFC division. The fast-paced, high-performance environment of Deloitte had prepared me well. In no time, I was facilitating an off-site strategic planning session with division leaders, the main outcome of which was a strategic plan covering operational and capital budgets of around $400 Million.

---

5. Most readers are hopefully aware of the role Countrywide Financial Corporation played in the global economic crisis of 2008. CEO/Chairman Angelo Mozilo was featured on the cover of *Time* magazine in January 2009 as the first on a list of "25 People to Blame for the Financial Crisis," *Time*, accessed September 26, 2017, http://content.time.com/time/specials/packages/article/0,28804,1877351_1877350,00.html. Let's just say I had landed at another interesting juncture.

There we reviewed the mission, vision, and objectives for our division. I seized upon this discussion to push for a new name for the division that would tie the various groups and departments together and communicate who we were and what we did to the rest of CFC and our many external partners. The name selected was Countrywide Administration and Real Estate (CARE). Our new logo reflected the diversity and unity of our group and was viewed very favorably, solidifying our division's identity as serving and supporting the growth of all the customer facing divisions.

Countrywide was founded on the principle of "making home ownership affordable"— which appealed to my social consciousness. And as CFC grew beyond its mortgage company roots, it was extending its offering across the financial services spectrum. CFC was now, for example, also a bank—expanding into areas of personal finance for its customers. In the strategic planning community, we were working to upgrade the vision and mission beyond "making home ownership affordable" into "enabling the American Dream"— for the average American.

And CFC had big growth plans. We had thirty thousand employees, but strategic plan numbers were being thrown around internally that went as high as one hundred thousand. This was truly exciting stuff for me and my team, two of whom had previously reported to Rollin, and two whom I personally hired. My first hire was a young man with a degree in English who had worked as a report writer within a technology firm.[6] Report writing, in this case, meant working with technology systems to query data to deliver information to management to enable better decision making. He had since spent almost a year pursuing his dream in the film industry— working as a producer of a movie that was filmed in Hungary.[7] I quickly recognized a true talent, with the capability to assist with my vision on how to help CFC achieve its mission.

I loved the opportunity to operate at this level in business, and others noticed that I not only enjoyed what I did but was darn good at it. After my first eight months, I was awarded the CFC Rookie of the Year award for 2004, for Strategic Planning. This became a springboard to take on additional challenges.

---

6.   Michael Schindler.

7.   *Metamorphosis*, starring Christopher Lambert, featuring an interesting twist on hell and time.

One of the problems CFC was trying to solve was where, geographically, to add the next ten- to twenty-thousand employees. The VP of space planning (my former Deloitte colleague I had introduced to Rollin) and I proposed Deloitte for a potential location strategy engagement. Considering my recent negative experiences at Deloitte, I wasn't exactly pushing them to succeed, and they ultimately failed to win the business. Instead, I convinced management that I could deliver a tailored solution to the problem by hiring and building the expertise internally. So my team began delivering reports to the various divisions based on gathering and evaluating data from every Metropolitan Statistical Area in the United States. These reports were in answer to the question on where each group would ideally locate its centers of operation, as we expanded beyond our home base of Southern California.

This was a chance to support the strategic planning efforts in the other divisions of the company. In return, I gained access to information, plans, and strategies related to all aspects of CFC's business model. Against these plans, my team ran data models to produce optimized recommendations on how and where they would best be able to achieve success in hiring for and operating profitable business centers across the country. This was quite a spectacular vantage point to gain an overview of how the company was both helping to expand and profit from the rapidly growing real estate bubble within the US economy in 2005.

As I was growing into my strategic planning role, I also connected with leaders outside the company, including an experienced forward thinker I had met at an industry event. He had been responsible for strategic planning at Ericsson, the Swedish telecommunications giant, and advised me to expand my reading across disciplines. He explained that by reading widely strategic planners could identify important trends that give critical insight into future events. One of the magazines he recommended was *Scientific American*, as it features research that can provide key insights into important trends for those with an eye to envisioning likely future scenarios.

Up to now, I had only skimmed the surface of the prophetic interpretations that have always lurked just below the surface of this story. Those most interested in the religious and prophetic aspects of this story might wonder why I instead spent so much time on my career path. It's time to connect some dots. CFC was a gigantic pump for the expansion of the bubble at the core of an economic meltdown within the US, which would spread to the entire planet. I'll highlight again that CFC's mission had grown beyond "making home ownership affordable" to "helping the average American achieve the American Dream." The CFC version of the American Dream, it turns out, was a nightmare. As bad as it was, we'll see as we move forward that it is but a precursor of that which was foretold when the forces of a corrupt form of Islam brought down the twin trade towers.[8]

In that regard, the timing of my immersion into strategic planning also coincided with the statute of limitations being reached, as far as I was concerned, on all past WCG predictions. HWA had advanced scenarios developed prior to WWII which foretold the rise of Europe, its union, and the reunification of Eastern and Western Europe. This had provided adequate evidence for his followers to believe him to be right in interpreting prophecies through the lens of Europe as the Beast that would instigate Armageddon. I had spent a decade in Europe under the influence of this scenario, aggressively expanding the media outreach and supporting the growth of the denomination. At the end of that decade, in 1995, I had resigned during the dramatic schism that emasculated that institution.[9] In 2005, after a decade of walking across the splintered fragments of the wreckage, I finally began to abandon the idea of Europe as the Beast without, as of then, having found any viable alternative scenarios.

The discipline of strategic planning assisted with my transition to a more open-minded viewpoint. This occurred naturally, as my work required me to objectively incorporate current geopolitical, economic, religious, and technology trends into corporate planning. My subscription to *Scientific American*, for example, brought leading scientific discoveries, along with the speculations and conclusions of thinkers at the forefront of research, right to my doorstep. These

---

8.   I won't go so far as to say that "I saw it all coming" in 2005, but the realization that this was a bubble that would end badly did help me protect my investments as well the investments of a few associates who followed my advice. It would be a year or two before I became fully aware of CFC's role in the global meltdown. The impact of this convulsion in the global financial system of systems would illustrate the stranglehold capitalism has on America and the danger of our multidecade bubble-driven era of prosperity. The middle class in America would be seriously threatened when it burst, as would the world economy as a whole.

9.   See *TPotS* for details.

became catalysts in condensing the swirling fog of my own spiritual impressions and experiences.

I had spent nearly forty years wandering in the desert. My efforts to follow the lead of the cloud and pillar, God's manifestation to the children of Israel during their own journey in the wilderness, had stalled due to my being trapped in a mixed bag of incomplete or erroneous beliefs. This had resulted in a circuitous route to the Promised Land, leaving me in many ways no closer to entering it than I had been at the beginning of my journey. But the clearer it became that I needed to lift up my eyes and scan a wider horizon, the more I sensed new routes opening up. At the same time, I was examining things in a fresh light with a willingness to abandon even my most sacred cows, if they proved to be already dead.

Think for Yourself

Adding several magazines to my reading material was a powerful catalyst to reassess my own varied and diverse experiences. Having lived in seven countries, learning multiple languages and assimilating elements of a variety of cultures along the way, I had personal insight into a considerable sampling of the components God had symbolically separated in the story of the Tower of Babel. I was like a mini-me of the diversity represented by that melting pot of the global population, the United States of America. If the reader is gleaning that this might matter, based on prior references to the Tower of Babel, this is intentional.

There was an overriding answer out there somewhere, and I was going to find it. The fact that each failure nonetheless ended up with me starting over in a much better place was a major source of encouragement. At the time, I was associating with David Antion's Church of God, Southern California (COGSC). After failing to influence David Hulme's group from within and failing to establish a humanitarian-based organization practicing true religion in India, my tail was tucked a bit more humbly between my legs. Without having achieved meaningful results in my efforts to serve God in ways I had imagined He wanted, I was content to sit near the back and listen.

David Antion provided for his local flock and ran a parachurch organization called Guardian Ministries, which had the "preach the gospel" commandment covered, at least minimally. Though tiny, his international evangelistic organization enabled, on a shoestring budget, local members and a few hundred scattered people to feel like they were part of something big. From my vantage point in the back pews, it seemed David Antion, unlike other WCG-trained ministers, was content to let the Sabbath and Holy Days play a supporting role to an emphasis on spiritual principles related to our interactions with others. He also seemed intent on helping his flock live life focused on charity and righteousness, rather than worrying about emphasizing doctrinal differences. This was the exact path I had begun advocating since before the 1995 collapse of the WCG.

Considering the small size of the congregation and the fact that Antion's ministry went beyond the local congregation, a relatively large percentage of local people were involved in service to the local church and assisting Guardian Ministries. This hands-on approach meant a higher degree of personal ownership. By sitting back as a spectator, I was the exception to the rule. I was impressed that David seemed to want each of the church members to be participants rather than just cheerleaders.

There was also a Guardian Ministries–sponsored Feast Site. Since I had nowhere else to go, I made plans to attend there in the fall. This made it even easier to simply relax and evaluate, over time, whether my favorable impression of David's approach was accurate, even as I was getting more actively involved. My positive attitude toward this small group quickly led to friendships, and I invested a lot of time and thought in preparing a message that reflected my current thinking, rather than delivering canned messages from the past.

In one particular sermon I explored the contrast between the WCG focus on God's calling being limited to a select few, supported by a hand-selected set of verses, and Jesus's clear statement that many are called. My adventures in India had broadened my perspective and opened my mind and heart more fully to the idea that God was not limiting His efforts to the COG movement. I'll circle back to this sermon in a minute, after discussing what triggered the thinking that went into it.

My subscription to *Scientific American* was ironically providing insight into matters of faith. One article I read at the time covered artificial intelligence and the insights from molecular biology that leading researchers leveraged to create ever more sophisticated computers.[10] It focused on a basic, binary element, the difference between negative and positive feedback loops, inherent in all living matter.[11]

Having an understanding of the basic operations of life at the cellular level in microbiology was a powerful lens with which to examine any number of issues in a new light. It was possible to extrapolate the principles back even further, in evolutionary terms, to the physical materials that provide a foundation for life and even the structure of the laws of the universe. There are even theories that view the universe as consisting of, at its most basic level, information, as though the universe itself is a kind of monumental gigantic computer, running a program which has resulted in the arrival, at this point, of human consciousness and an emerging universal consciousness. If this is true, humans are now approaching the ability to harness a similar computing power to that of the universe, as we build simulations of artificial intelligence with computers.

Most fascinating was the insight gained on the cognitive processes within human beings. The article caused me to reflect on why people tend to be unshakable in the dogmatic belief that they are right and all others are wrong, a point driven home during my trip to Leningrad during the time of Gorbachev's abduction.[12] What I took away from the article was that we tend to process negative feedback loops, while leaving positive feedback loops unprocessed.

By way of example, let's imagine you believe the moon is made of green cheese. A picture of the moon that looks greenish becomes a positive feedback loop. You will tend to accept this as confirmation of your belief, without questioning or processing it. If, however, you see moon rock at a museum, which is clearly not made of green cheese, this represents a negative feedback loop, and your reaction is quite different. When our beliefs are challenged, our primitive fight/flight responses are activated. All our considerable energies and resources launch a counterattack against this assault on our belief system. If there is a way to refute it, or a plausible, or implausible, way to deny the evidence, we find it.

---

10. Unfortunately, I have tried to find this and other articles I read at the time, without success.

11. These insights were validated and enhanced a number of years later when I encountered Bruce H. Lipton's book *The Biology of Belief: Unleashing the Power of Consciousness, Matter, and Miracles* (Carlsbad, CA: Hay House, 2016).

12. See *TPotS*, chap. 8, "Back in The USSR."

In this example, some would even go so far as to embrace the elaborate theory that the moon landing was faked in some Hollywood studio. Or we just flee the intellectual challenge, surviving to fight another day. In recent years, this idea has found mainstream acceptance under the label of *confirmation bias*.

Several lightbulbs lit up in my head after reading this. Here was scientific research that supported the idea that the ego is the enemy of truth. One of my favorite scriptural passages immediately came to mind, which outlines how the "mind of Christ" is the opposite of a mind controlled by ego.[13] At this point, I began to view the Ego as the Antichrist.

There was another concept I came across in that article, or another article I read around the same time. Scientific research on our dream state highlighted that we typically process positive feedback while sleeping. The article explained how during sleep our bias toward positive feedback and/or our resistance to negative feedback are brought back into equilibrium. In considering the effects of sleep deprivation, the hypothesis presents itself that being spun up on self-referential positive feedback loops leads to psychosis, if not held in check. In other words, selectively accepting data points which seem to reinforce existing beliefs leads to an increasing detachment from reality.

The ego feeds on self-validation to feel strong and in control, rather than submitting itself to a higher power. My reading indicated that our ego shuts down, to a degree, during our sleep cycle, allowing us to recognize our beliefs about green cheese as ludicrous. The bizarre and amazing dream language and typology, as discussed and elaborated in the research of Carl Jung, are symbolical ways in which we resolve and process psychological issues.

This fed into an ongoing awareness that I and others from the WCG background had been locked in a self-referential confirmation of our understanding of numerous Scriptures. For example, I suddenly saw a passage in Romans in a different light, "Because that which may be known of God is manifest in them; for God hath shewed it unto them. For the invisible things of him from the creation of the world are clearly seen, being understood by the

---

13. Philippians 2:3–7: "Let nothing be done through strife or vainglory; but in lowliness of mind let each esteem other better than themselves. Look not every man on his own things, but every man also on the things of others. Let this mind be in you, which was also in Christ Jesus: Who, being in the form of God, thought it not robbery to be equal with God: But made himself of no reputation, and took upon him the form of a servant, and was made in the likeness of men."

things that are made, even his eternal power and Godhead; so that they are without excuse."[14]

Paul's statement that God has shown even the worst sinner "that which may be known of God" was diametrically opposed to one of the foundational teachings of the WCG. The WCG had taught that humankind was cut off from God and that God was not revealing Himself to those who were not called. But this passage in Romans taught something quite different. This meant that the way in which God was working with humankind, the reason for a church, even the interpretation of what the sign of the Sabbath meant, were all very different from what the WCG had taught.

None of this was surprising to me at the time. Readers who have not experienced immersion in an all-consuming ideology, and the difficulty in digging one's way out of it, might wonder why it took a full ten years since the foundations of the WCG, as an organization, had been shaken and then shattered for me to come to this point. There had been a gradual awakening, accelerated by trips to Thailand and India. What I had experienced there, along with what I was learning had accumulated adequate proof that God was not providing exclusive insider information via this His One True Church.

It's Only Love

At each step on this journey, and with each new clarification of what the Bible actually reveals about God's guidance for humanity, I was extremely careful not to throw the baby out with the bathwater. There was no rejection of God's authority, His Word, faith, or even religion. My desire to walk with God and to learn from Him was more intense than ever. For example, while I was finally ready to fully abandon the viewpoint that true Christians kept the Sabbath and Holy Days, which enabled them to have an exclusive relationship with God, my understanding of them still required me to keep them. The insights I had gained from my walk with God still gave me a sense of a unique identity, which might be ridiculed by others but which to me was enormously valuable. And along with that identity there was still a desire to share what I saw, for the betterment of all.

---

14. Romans 1:19–20.

Moving away from this claim to exclusivity didn't nullify the fact that many, if not most, rejected the message about God that the creation revealed. The passage cited above shows that while God reaches out to all parts of creation, one reason He does so is to hold us accountable.[15] Paul is highlighting that, in spite of God shedding His light on all of us constantly, it is our failure to acknowledge and glorify God that leads to our preference for darkness. Clearly, our own actions, and not the intent of God, keep us from seeing what God is constantly trying to show us. This distinction might seem just a minor semantic nuance between many being called but few chosen. But WCG theology placed great emphasis on this distinction. Man does cut himself off from God, which means that HWA and the WCG were not exactly wrong. They just overstated the case, declaring that man had no access to God whatsoever, except the few God was handpicking out of the mix.

The WCG belief was based on the Genesis story of the angel barring entrance to Eden, but Christ removed that barrier by His death when the veil in front of the holy of holies was rent in two.[16] I highlighted this in preparing to deliver my first sermon to David Antion's group, connecting the fact that the heavens declare the Glory of God to the logical conclusion that God seeks to work within every individual and all humankind collectively.

In other words, when God created the sun, moon, and stars, and set them "as signs to mark seasons and days and years," it was for broad consumption, not for some tiny subset who could figure out some set of esoteric secrets.[17]

On the other hand, the WCG and its splinters believed access to God was limited to those who followed the Jewish lunar calendar. The Holy Days, which were derived from it, were prophetic in nature, and only those who diligently organized their lives around them were in tune with God. Through them, one could understand the plan of God, the events related to salvation, and the establishment of the Kingdom of God on earth.

---

15. Romans 1:21–23: "Because that, when they knew God, they glorified him not as God, neither were thankful; but became vain in their imaginations, and their foolish heart was darkened. Professing themselves to be wise, they became fools, And changed the glory of the uncorruptible God into an image made like to corruptible man, and to birds, and fourfooted beasts, and creeping things."
16. Genesis 3:24: "So he drove out the man; and he placed at the east of the Garden of Eden Cherubims, and a flaming sword which turned every way, to keep the way of the tree of life."
17. Genesis 1:14.

It began to dawn on me, pun intended, that the brightest illumination we allowed in through the aperture of our understanding was the light of the moon, so to speak. But wasn't the moon, after all, the "lesser light"? What about the vast universe of stars? Excluding these from our view is a monumental disservice to the declaration of God's true Glory, as it leaves only our tiny solar system. What about the light of the sun? Its light reveals everything and is so blinding in its intensity that we can't even look at it.

The implications of all this were not pleasant for those of us who drank at the COG trough. The image that comes to mind is that of a Jewish priest squinting to make out the emergence of the new moon in order to fix the beginning of the lunar calendar accurately. To be successful in this activity, it was necessary to situate oneself within the darkest night. This also brought to mind the pyramids, which were astrological instruments that allowed the occupant of its dark inner chambers to use the shafts as telescopes.

So while it is accurate to say that God's Glory is most visible while viewing the heavens at night, it is also accurate to say that to understand what God is doing here on earth it is better to get as far away from the darkness of night as possible. This means we should focus on that which can be seen in daylight, by the light of the sun. I'm getting ahead of myself, though, because the extent of this wasn't clear to me at the time.

What was very clear, even then, was this: No matter which way the earth would be spinning through the universe, some light was shining on earth, at all times and in all ways. Even in the darkest nooks and crannies. In other words, the creation was figuratively screaming God's name and His attributes, any- and everything of importance about Him, to all people, at all times throughout history. We might be deaf, but that was not God's doing.

This was something I felt comfortable sharing with my new friends in David Antion's Church of God, Southern California. These were people who had already rejected a number of tangential so-called truths, a rejection made easier due to the mistreatment many of them had personally experienced at the hands of the WCG and its founder, HWA. This made them more open to other insights that those more fully wrapped in the WCG cloak were quick to reject out of hand.

COG theology, for example, believed most of humanity was not called, and thus were not being judged. If "many" (using HWA's definition of the word "many," as when he explained that Christ's statement "many are deceived" meant 99.99+% of humanity were deceived) were called, then the vast majority of mankind, throughout history, was destined for the lake of fire—the so-called third resurrection, where the incorrigibly wicked were burned up completely—body, soul, and spirit.[18] My shift in focus might lead my hearers to believe I was calling our teaching on the resurrections into question, and while I was looking into this, I was careful to avoid challenging this doctrine because that was not my point. It was important to let people understand what the Bible was saying before pushing a cognitive negative-feedback-loop button that would cause them to reject the clear message out of hand without even understanding the issues involved.

The point of my sermon was much subtler, in a two-fold way. The first step was to open up our understanding to the truth that God was working with everyone, right now, today, in different ways. This alone was challenging enough for COG folks.

By overstating the case around our calling, we built an inappropriate attitude around it, one that supported the view that we and we alone were handpicked to perform the task of preparing the world for the return of Jesus. But the second part of this was the most important. Rather than a handpicked squad, my message openly clarified, in direct contrast to what the WCG had taught, God was calling out to everyone. All the time.

The key to helping the audience accept changes to these beliefs was to focus on God's love. By focusing on love, I was able to help those in the audience who were otherwise not ready to let go of the special feelings of exclusivity. And I made sure not to put my dirty feet on the heavenly signs established by the greater and lesser lights and the stars, which were given authority to "establish

---

18. Scripture references are Matthew 24:5, 11; Mark 13:6; Revelation 19:20; and 20:10–15. In terms of doctrine, the WCG taught that there were three resurrections, using numerous Scriptures. I Corinthians, 15, for example, was "the resurrection chapter." In it, we claimed, we could see all three of them. Those alive and dead "in Christ" would be in the first resurrection. This was an elite group, in which we included ourselves. The vast majority of mankind throughout history were "not called." They would have their first chance in the second resurrection, which would give them a chance to show fruits of repentance. Those unfortunate souls who had been called and had rejected their calling would be resurrected in the third resurrection. They would be brought back to life for the sole reason that God would then pass judgment upon them and cast them into the lake of fire. They would be consumed and would cease to exist.

signs, seasons, and days." This is a strong endorsement for the Sabbath. But through the lens of love, I clarified that these signs point us to something. They are not, in and of themselves, the thing of importance.

As a minister in the WCG, I had studied the covenants and their relationship to each other. At the time, the lens had been the understanding of how they all pointed to Christ. The sign of the Noachian covenant, the rainbow, promised that God would never again wipe out humankind wholesale.[19] This was a promise of Grace, fulfilled in Christ. The sign of the Abrahamic covenant was circumcision—which among other things pictured the blood that was required for the removal of sin. And of course, the Sabbath, which we always said pictured the Millennium, one thousand years of peaceful rule by Christ, at his return.

I've emphasized that the sign that identified a follower of Christ, contrary to our generally accepted belief, was not the Sabbath. It was the sign found in John 13:35: "By this shall all men know that ye are my disciples, if ye have love one to another." Now the full force of that understanding was about to finally change my perspective more dramatically.

The Sabbath, the sign of the Mosaic covenant was, like the face of Moses, a reflection of the divine light, of our love for God. It was visible in the darkness, but the sign Christ brought was more direct, more clearly visible in the light of day, from the outside, by "all men." And "all men" obviously had to include both those who claimed to be Christians and those who didn't. The WCG was likely correct in stating that the Sabbath foreshadowed the one thousand years. But it was perhaps more significant that it foreshadowed Christ Himself.

What wasn't well known, at least in the WCG world, is that two of Christ's well-known proclamations—that He was "Lord of the Sabbath" and "Come unto me, all ye that labour and are heavy laden, and I will give you rest"— were connected, despite being separated by an unfortunate chapter break. In Matthew 11:27–30 Christ explains that He reveals the Father, evoking the sign of the Sabbath, the identifier of the true God and then invites them to find

---

19. Genesis 9:13: "I do set my bow in the cloud, and it shall be for a token of a covenant between me and the earth." Genesis 9:14: "And it shall come to pass, when I bring a cloud over the earth, that the bow shall be seen in the cloud." Genesis 9:16: "And the bow shall be in the cloud; and I will look upon it, that I may remember the everlasting covenant between God and every living creature of all flesh that is upon the earth."

rest in Him. [20] Chapter 12 then opens up with the story of Jesus defending His disciples, who picked corn to eat on the Sabbath, and Jesus openly proclaims Himself to be "Lord even of the Sabbath day." He goes on to discuss healing on the Sabbath and turns the tables again on the judgmental Pharisees, pointing out that their approach risks the unforgivable sin of "blasphemy against the Spirit."

Jesus was directing His disciples to begin to observe it in a completely different way. In other words, Christ seems to be redefining the Sabbath, the sign of the Mosaic covenant, in a manner similar to how circumcision, the sign of the Abrahamic covenant, was redefined as being of the heart instead of a physical rite.

This realization might have been the end of my allegiance to the COG movement, had I had it then. But at the time, I wasn't quite there yet. Even so, a number of insights I had been straining to see had become clear to me. So long as we believed that we were special, handpicked, different, and uniquely connected to God, it was impossible to wear the sign of love visibly. We had to get to the point where we realized that we were essentially no different from anybody else.

God is calling all. But we all have both an innate attraction and resistance to the call. We are all generally unwilling to take the next step off the gangplank of faith. The ball is in all ways and at all times in our court. By the time we imagine we've hit a ball back into God's court, it's already back in ours. None of us are fully enlightened. We all have some degree of foolishness and darkness in our hearts. While God would like to see us move forward, we're at any given moment unwilling or not ready—or both.

God is, at all times and in all places and in all societies, in and through all religions, throughout history, working with each individual. God is not limited by our beliefs, creeds, morals, or lack thereof. In one way or another, He is constantly drawing people to Himself, drawing people to the light. To our minds, the road might be circuitous or even lead in the wrong direction for a

---

20. . Matthew 11:27–30: "All things are delivered unto me of my Father: and no man knoweth the Son, but the Father; neither knoweth any man the Father, save the Son, and he to whomsoever the Son will reveal him. Come unto me, all ye that labour and are heavy laden, and I will give you rest. Take my yoke upon you, and learn of me; for I am meek and lowly in heart: and ye shall find rest unto your souls. For my yoke is easy, and my burden is light."

while, as momentum and trajectory can carry us away from it. But all objects are ultimately drawn toward the center of mass.

This was true before Jesus, and it is true after Jesus. It was true regardless of anything Herbert W. Armstrong had to say about it. There are many implications to moving away from exclusive exceptionalism (a belief in being part of an elite group from which others are excluded). Perhaps the most critically important one for me was the rejection of doctrinal criteria, which made insiders feel closer to God while judging others as being further away from Him. Whatever knowledge I had that others lacked didn't make me one whit a better Christian than they were. Knowledge wasn't what Christianity was all about.

But the biggest problem was one the COG had in common with the dogma of mainstream Christianity. This fatal flaw at the heart of all dogmatic Christian interpretations of Scripture was judging others. And this is what we do when we declare them as either in or out, going to heaven or hell, saved or lost. It was becoming painfully clear that this is not a perspective God wants us to engage in.

I know some of you are thinking, "Wait—Christ separates the sheep from the goats." Don't worry—we'll get to that. For now, suffice it to say, we are to love, and leave the judgment up to Him.

One general outcome of this, influenced by reading *Scientific American* and the many theories related to the nature of the universe, was a growing understanding and awareness of love as its primal force. To me, love seemed to lie at the heart of the nature of the universe, and to manifest itself in the creation in profound yet very subtle ways. This augmented my view of Paul's statement in Romans about the invisible things of God being understood by humans through those things which are seen.

Even as I was focused on the orderly progression of evolutionary forces generated by divine love, my personal life still seemed to reflect the opposite. I was recently divorced and living in a house I shared with two single guys. At this stage in my life, I was a loner in so many ways—confused about what was attractive to me, and not attractive to others.

A lyric from Pink Floyd's *Animals* album, which I had shoplifted while working as a cashier at Safeway many years ago, in my wild, dark days, had always stuck with me. The song was called "Pigs" and the line was "Just another sad old man, all alone and dying of cancer." I'd always tried to live a life that would lead away from such a fate.

Now it seemed my life was taking exactly that path.

Despite a focus on love and spirituality, my divorce left me feeling isolated and lonely.

From this dark and lonely elliptical orbit, I would soon accelerate back to the center of gravity.

8

I Saw Her Standing There

There be three things which are too wonderful for me, yea,
four which I know not:
The way of an eagle in the air; the way of a serpent upon a rock;
the way of a ship in the midst of the sea; and the way of a man with a maid.

—PROVERBS 30:18–19

A recently divorced friend of mine from David Hulme's group, Syrisa (pronounced "Swisha") hosted a dinner party and invited me to attend. I sat next to one of her close friends, Angela. We chatted during dinner, and I was intrigued by the fact she had traveled to Europe several times and had worked in London for a summer. The conversation was enjoyable, but that was about it.

I did invite her, however, to go with me and some other girls on a group date to an all-you-can-eat sushi place owned by the family of my former colleague and friend from Deloitte, who had preceded me in joining CFC. I enjoyed the dinner quite a bit and have a photo of me, as a proud single guy, surrounded by the beautiful faces of six young ladies.

Lovely Rita

When Syrisa invited me to go kayaking with a group of her friends off the Malibu coast, I jumped at the chance. Angela was there, too. Something about that afternoon, perhaps seeing her wearing a bathing suit in a kayak on the ocean from a short distance away, suddenly ignited my interest. A couple of weeks later, I managed to meet Syrisa and Angela again at the same beach, where I learned that Angela, who was a physical therapist, was also pursuing certification as a yoga instructor.

I asked her if she would look at my shoulder and suggest a few exercises to help me with the problem that was hampering my crawl stroke. She did, and after practicing various yoga poses together on the beach, I was hooked. The timing of this coincided with my newfound freedom from the restraints of COG theology concerning who God was and wasn't working with. This meant that it really didn't matter that she was not a believer in COG doctrine. And that surely contributed to the fact that I fell head over heels for this woman.

Angela, however, viewed me very differently than I viewed her. Her perspective of me was anything but that of a young Adonis in a bathing suit. While we were both unmarried, she had never taken that plunge. I saw her as young and free, while to her, I was old and divorced.

This upped the irony of my theorizing about love in spiritual and philosophical terms, while failing to grasp the physical implications. It highlighted both my challenges in practicing love in my human interactions and my recent epiphanies about not being a specially chosen person.

Decades of arrogant thinking had brought me to this painful impasse. It was a different world outside the COG bubble. It was a good thing I was full of faith because it would take a miracle for me to win this girl over.

Faith kept me going, while hope and love were my constant meditation at that time. A focus on love in my first sermon in David Antion's group had helped downplay the controversial components of my message. It was well received, and I was invited to speak again. Faith was the follow-up topic.

The sermon took my previous thinking a step further and into territory that extended quite a ways from classic WCG theology. This brings us to the second article that dramatically influenced my thinking at this time, on a topic even more abstract than the first. At the time, it seemed ironic that science would enhance my view of faith, but it most definitely did.

A December 2002 article in *Scientific American,* about the ideas of a young, Greek rising star in theoretical physics, Fotini Markopoulou Kalamara, grabbed my attention.[1] To me, the article addressed that long-standing philosophical question of whether a tree falling unobserved in a forest makes a sound. It discussed her mathematical framework that, to me, illustrated that the universe does not exist until it is observed.

This appeared to be a wonderful confirmation of the simple, yet so elegant, creation story in Genesis where God, by proclamation and observation, brought the universe into existence: "And God said, Let there be light: and there was light. And God saw the light, that *it was* good."[2]

This was a catalyst to examine concepts from other articles I was reading about string theory, parallel universes, and quantum particles migrating between them, in a free-associative and speculative way. I suppose it's not unusual for a novice in a given area to extrapolate, in an undisciplined manner, based on a rudimentary understanding of complex ideas. And the name of the author of the article, so reminiscent of Marco Polo—the childhood game where kids locate each other by sound—lent levity to reconsidering that tree in the forest conundrum, which I had from time to time contemplated.

Science seemed to be confirming the idea that the universe exists because God conceived it, without, of course, recognizing this. It was fascinating to me how humanity seemed to draw closer and closer to understanding the nature of creation, and thus God, yet without acknowledging Him. Aside from being intriguing, it seemed important—and so it occupied my thinking.

What if, I reasoned, the theory that there can be an infinite number of parallel universes is not only true, but also related to our own creative powers? Clearly being created in God's image, by One who refers to Himself as our Father, means that He has imparted abilities that, in some infinitesimally small and vastly inferior way, are nonetheless similar in nature to those He possesses. What if we, like the Father who conceived of us, actually conjure up our own version of the universe since we each observe the creation differently? What if

---

1.   Amanda Gefter, "Throwing Einstein for a Loop," *Scientific American*, December 2002, https://www.scientificamerican.com/article/throwing-einstein-for-a-l/.
2.   Genesis 1:3–4.

we are actually and literally the creators of our own, unique universe? Turning the hearts to the Father to bring our universe in alignment with God takes on a greater importance in this light.

And while it felt like this was an important insight, I recognized the risk of hubris associated with such trains of thought, along with the fantastical and unprovable nature of the model they suggest. The mental construct was certainly more of a fun analogy than a real theory. Still, other areas of scientific research and theory seemed to reinforce this hypothesis.

Could this idea represent a bridge between the theoretical and actual implications of Schrödinger's infamous cat?[3] Theories being generated from quantum mechanics, for example, included ideas around quantum particles moving between dimensions and universes. Could this be the physical manifestation of how our own imagination, beliefs, and/or faith, as created within our own individually perceived universe interact with the universes created by others? Was that an indication that consciousness physically affects creation in this manner?

What if we, by flexing our faith muscles in the right way, can literally take command of our own universe, and bring our entire reality into greater conformance with the bedrock of our beliefs? Clearly, certain dominant personalities, from Alexander the Great to Hitler and Stalin, managed to force reality to bend to their will, overcoming the viewpoints and ideologies of millions of others, bringing their reality into conformity with their own vision. This occurred as the perception of widening circles of conscious beings adapted to the one that they used to distort and shape the universe directly under their own observational control.

I don't mean to diminish more positive, liberating examples by putting forward examples of military leaders and tyrants. But sadly, it is often the ones living in relative darkness who learn to leverage their amazing, God-given creative powers for ungodly purposes. And in a perverse way, liberated from the shackles of morality and introspection, these wayward souls can enslave those more attuned to their own humanity.

The point is that overcoming our own self-doubt is paramount to faith, and a prerequisite to embarking upon a path to subvert and overthrow such tyrants. After all, Christ said the faith of a mustard seed could move mountains,

---

3.   We'll discuss this quantum physics thought experiment in some detail shortly.

and the WCG's interpretation of prophetic references to mountains in the Bible being symbolic of governments seemed reasonable enough.[4]

In business, Steve Jobs comes to mind. The creator of the famous "Microsoft is Big Brother" commercial in 1985 was also the creator of what was the most valuable company on earth at the time of drafting this section. Jobs famously generated a "reality distortion field," forcing others to conform to his vision even as they believed it to be impossibly wrong. In the humanitarian arena, examples such as Mother Theresa and Albert Schweitzer come to mind.

But the most obvious and powerful positive examples are spiritual leaders such as Gandhi, considered the founding father of a liberated India. His influence literally overthrew the dominion of the British Empire, simply by force of will and the exercise of a powerful idea. Other religious figures, whose visions displaced many mountains (the regimes that once dominated the people who came to adopt their ideas), include the Buddha, Moses, and Christ. Their creative power energized cultures, overthrew leaders, and raised entire civilizations through the force of the spiritual energy they unleashed.

Moses liberated the enslaved tribes of Israel, and they became a regional superpower in short order. While ancient Israel as a nation ultimately failed to become the city on the hill that God intended it to be, all of Western civilization is built upon what are considered "Judeo-Christian values."

The Israel of Christ's day failed to recognize Him and called for His crucifixion, which was carried out by the Romans. Christians picked up the torch, in the wake of the failure of the people of the Mosaic covenant to recognize Christ, and this religion permeated what became known as the Holy Roman Empire.

The ideas generated by the Mosaic covenant, which were carried forward into and enhanced by the Christian covenant, have permeated the world, like leaven, preparing the way for the Kingdom of God. As we fast-forward two thousand years from Christ, many non-Christians somewhat justifiably hold Christians in contempt for failing to represent an objective standard of love. Yet Christianity spread and was embraced by hundreds of millions of people throughout the ages, spawning many, many Christian nations across the planet that have dominated social progress for many centuries. And these Christian

4. Matthew 17:20.

nations are playing a significant role in the prophetic mosaic that God is unleashing.

And even though the world is not Jewish in any sense of the word, the power of the sign of the Mosaic covenant, the seventh-day Sabbath, helped the Jewish people retain their identity for four thousand years, along with the hope and faith that their prophetic restoration to the Holy Land was secure. Their faith has been vindicated by their return to their ancient homeland, to again become a regional superpower in our day—with enormous prophetic significance.

Savoy Truffle

The point of these examples is the power we have to create and shape the nature of our world. Christ confirms it by saying we could do greater works than He did after He ascended to heaven.[5] There is much more that could be said to explain and flesh out the ideas and perspectives I was developing at this time, but I'll limit my philosophical and scientific noodling to just those elements of the ideas generated by these two articles which had a direct impact on my evolving theoretical framework.

First, my views were now much more open, enabling a broader and deeper understanding of how God is working out His plan for mankind. The walls of the box in which I placed God and His people had been broken down. Second, my view of faith was being dramatically expanded by the insights gained from research on positive and negative feedback loops (which form the basis of our beliefs), and the more speculative thoughts on the nature of the universe (or universes). The former was solid science while the latter was unsubstantiated extrapolation from new scientific insights. But they both enabled me to look at the Bible in a fresh light, revealing that in many cases it did not say what I had previously thought it said.

But rather than dive into specific doctrinal error, let's return to the subject of the sweeping progression of Judaism and Christianity and what it revealed about WCG/COG theology. We had been anachronistically mining the depth of the revelation of God prior to and with special emphasis on the Mosaic

---

5.   John 14:12.

covenant. We were like a Monday-morning quarterback, if Monday had been four thousand years ago. We sought to examine each play in slow motion, under magnification, to gain a full understanding of all it was supposed to picture. This was, on the one hand, a very positive approach, especially as we did so with an acceptance of Christ. Our deep appreciation of Christ benefited from an amazing grasp of the richness and depth of the Old Testament.

On the other hand, we were maximizing the value of an old, outdated covenant. And we limited our reinterpretation of it by minimizing the fact that Christ's covenant was newer by two thousand years and had, in many ways, an opposite focus. Christ warned about old wineskins being burst with the expansive fermentation of the new wine, demanding that the gatekeepers allow the waters of the river of life to flow freely.[6] In this sense, we were the opposite of Job, whom I spent considerable time discussing in *The People of the Sign* and whom I described there as being ahead of his time.

His struggle was to grasp that which Christ would bring in the then-future covenant while anchored in a world still governed by a prior covenant. We, on the other hand, seemed to be asking for a "do-over." We wanted to reimplement the system of systems which God had delivered four thousand years ago but which He had radically transformed two thousand years later.

What would happen, I began to wonder, if we in the COG movement had been a bit more like Job, mining the wealth of the prehistory and posthistory of the Mosaic covenant, but focusing on truly understanding the Christian covenant? This was something I had loosely and generally sought to do over the last ten to fifteen years. But with what I was learning now, this was becoming a brightly burning passion. And with it came the prospect of exciting faith-filled adventures yet ahead. I began, once again, to become energized, spiritually.

As 2005 approached, I was involved in David Antion's small, and relatively ineffective, COGSC, trying to serve and support the spiritual growth of our community by speaking and spending time getting to know the other members. It was a comfortable spiritual place to be, nice to be involved, but not too involved, after my experiences in the WCG, UCG, and David Hulme's group. Gone were the pretensions and the delusional sense of self-importance on the part of the leadership. And it was relaxing after almost two years of intensive activity in Thailand and India.

---

6.   Matthew 9:17.

My personal situation also became more comfortable. My roommate and friend who had participated in the purchase of the house in Pasadena had gotten engaged, so we sold the house. Given the perfect timing of our purchase in an inflating housing market, we did quite well on the sale. I moved to Woodland Hills, halfway between Pasadena and my office at CFC, leasing a brand new two-bedroom apartment in a beautiful gated complex.

Aside from more than cutting my commute time in half, I now had access to a large, sparkling pool; a fitness room, which I desperately needed; and a luxurious common area for parties. It was a perfect opportunity for me to retreat to lick the wounds of my recent divorce, the failure of TeachAKid, and my separation from most of my church friends. And in this setting, I could welcome and entertain those few friends who hadn't given up on me, or the new ones I was making. This was perfect for a conscious shift toward treating those around me with greater love and respect, the sign of Christ.

At the same time, I had never been one to be content with comfortable. With the money from the sale of the Pasadena house, I bought the two fourplexes in Washington state that my dad had built. Dad had been trying to sell these since his remarriage, and I was happy to help him out. The rents provided cash flow into the real estate investment business owned jointly with my dad and his new wife, and he would continue to manage them.

With our joint investment portfolio growing, we began helping other investors do what we were doing. I connected them to our broker in Washington, who understood the profile of houses we felt would work best within our model. My dad and stepmother earned additional income as property managers. And all of this was taking place in an area of the country that my location strategy work at CFC highlighted as one of the best in the country in which to make long-term residential property investments. Meanwhile, the clock was ticking on completing my MBA coursework within the required time frame, so I threw myself into completing the program.

Despite increasing clarity on both my physical and spiritual paths, living by myself felt like treading water. Speaking of treading water, a shorter commute and swimming laps in that awesome pool wasn't improving nagging issues I was having with my neck. Within a week of taking up a swimming regimen, I experienced escalating pain and tightness in my right shoulder that forced me to stop swimming altogether. Along with these physical problems, living alone amplified the emptiness I felt without a female companion. That my ex-wife played but a cameo role throughout this two-volume story was by intent, and partially driven by her legal demand not to be mentioned by name, not because she wasn't important to me at the time. Without a significant other, I felt incomplete and adrift.

The pain in my neck and shoulder was a call to action, physically, and it gave me an excuse to bring a woman into my life, whether she wanted it or not.

If I Needed Someone

Angela had completed her yoga certification, and was looking to build a private yoga practice. She agreed to take me on as her first client with a weekly private lesson on the basic principles and poses. She was a physical therapist by day, and in her yoga classes, she emphasized avoiding injury through alignment, while increasing both strength and flexibility. My neck and shoulder pain began to recede and after the first month, we increased the sessions to twice a week.

Tuesday and Thursday nights were the highlights of my week. The more I improved, the more I enjoyed the yoga. But Angela was the real reason for my anticipation of these sessions. I fell hard for her, so hard it was a little bit terrifying. All the more so as she continued to view and treat me strictly as a client, and only over time, maybe a little bit like a friend. There was no doubt, no room for misunderstanding. I was nothing to Angela, other than a sort of client/friend.

Another haunting aspect of this was the inner conflict in feeling as if I were moving away from God just because I was interested in a woman. It wasn't just that Angela did not believe in the traditional COG dogma, as I was really moving away from my concerns in that regard. It was deeper than that. It went all the way back to my childhood baggage and my feelings of guilt as a rebellious teenager. After God saved my life in the high-speed car chase, I had dedicated myself to God and, later, what I believed to be His Work.[7] My extreme focus on this precluded the kind of personal relationship with a woman that God actually wishes for every man. I was more aware, now, of how my view of my special calling had put my marriage relationship in the back seat.

---

7. See *The People of the Sign.*

God had brought Eve to Adam exactly because it wasn't good for a man to be alone. Yet I was as conflicted about this as certain religious organizations that teach celibacy as a higher calling. That which is both normal and natural, and actually pleases God, was something I was denying myself. One way to describe this is through Scriptures that describe God as a "jealous God." An improper understanding of these verses would lead to feelings like this. It was as if one had to choose between God and a desire for a "soul-mate" relationship with a woman. This insight was the thin wedge of even deeper insights yet ahead. For now, I began to get a handle on long-standing feelings, going back to the start of my failed marriage, of having withdrawn from the edge of where God was working. And this helped me gain deeper insight into why that marriage had failed.

Still, this was uncharted water for me. It wasn't clear where Angela stood spiritually. She seemed very open, which was one reason she was studying yoga. But did this translate into a kind of submission to a very real Creator of the universe, or was her spiritual intent of the fuzzy, diffused New Age variety? I was only just now coming to view such interest as genuine, if unfocused, versus a form of satanic deception, which was a tough transition to make. But was God, and obedience to Him, important to her?

Allowing myself to fall head over heels for Angela was a starting point in resolving many internal conflicts—including the feeling that I had wrongly abandoned the efforts in India, even though there was no path forward in that direction. But for now, this was still really bothering me. After all these years, and so much effort to purify my heart and my ways so I could be of use to God, I still couldn't get my bearings. The fog was beginning to lift, but I couldn't make out what was being revealed.

In hindsight, what was happening was that my fledgling yoga practice, coupled with falling in love with Angela, was opening my heart, my emotional self, to the truth in ways my efforts to please God through obedience to a set of commands, even if they were His, had not.

One input to this opening, during this time, was the Conversations with God series of books, in which author Neil Walsh claims to have asked questions of God and received direct answers by revelation. The first book had appeared in 1995, but it came across my radar screen in 2005 by way of a recommendation from my little sister. These books were intriguing in light of what I had experienced in India and helped open my mind further to the fact that God would work with whomever, whenever and however He chose. Sincerity and purity of heart, not specific beliefs or Biblical knowledge, made the difference between those who could connect with God and those who were unable to do so. And it was obvious that thinking we already have the answers shuts that access down.

My recent efforts in India, even though they had not resulted in an ongoing program, gave me opportunity to discuss these insights within Antion's group. I developed a presentation in PowerPoint to augment a sermon on the Feast of Pentecost entitled, "Letting God out of the Box." The main point was that we limit God through our own conceptions of Him and His Work. When it comes to the power of God's love, we limit it by not recognizing Christ and God in every human being we meet.

What was left unsaid in this message was just how cancerous is the attitude of exclusivity. It poisons our relationships with others. But more importantly, it paradoxically limits our actual relationship with God, even though this delusional attitude of exclusivity leads us to believe that our relationship with God is more special than the relationship others have with Him. What was explicit in my message was that our failure to acknowledge God and Christ in our fellow human beings, even in an abstract way, limits God from working with us.

And if we don't honor people spiritually for who and what they really are in God's sight, we actively disrupt their perceptions of God. If we're around them, we create a distortion field about God. When we claim to be close to God, while others perceive, consciously or not, that the love of God is not flowing through us, then our relationship with them is polluted and dysfunctional, as is our representation of God.

These insights, a result of my reflections on why things hadn't worked out in India, gave me hope that I might find a new and different way to return to pick up the pieces and rebuild. If I could figure out what God had really wanted, apart from my ego-driven goals to save the world, I would know what God wanted me to do next. He would lead me back to reengage with those who had asked for and welcomed my help, along with others who could benefit from the channeling of God's love for humanity. If, that is, I could get out of my own way as I had done when playing golf hypnotized.

The response to the "Letting God out of the Box" sermon on Pentecost in Antion's group was very favorable. But I knew that the path forward was not in conjunction with David's group, the way I had been working with Leon Sexton's Thailand-based Legacy Institute. David used the local church as a base of operations for his own evangelistic efforts through Guardian Ministries. The Feast that prior fall of 2004, up toward central California, had been a nice experience, but even this larger gathering didn't seem poised to generate any forward momentum for David's own efforts, much less my hopeful aspirations to somehow still launch a program in India. And he wasn't about to share his stage.

In the early summer of 2005, I heard the UCG was planning a Feast site in Estonia, where I had served as the first WCG pastor at the time of Estonia's independence from the Soviet Union. This gave me the opportunity to reconnect with an old friend, Victor Kubik, and he welcomed my offer to travel back to Estonia to support his efforts to expand a small but growing UCG group there.

That Victor, the UCG, and I were able to put aside differences was encouraging. And I was able to convince my dad and stepmother to join me in traveling, which would reunite us at a Feast site for the first time since his departure from the WCG ten years earlier. All of these were very positive developments as I approached the 2005 Fall Holy Day season.

Meanwhile, Angela and I continued to work with each other on becoming more flexible. While she focused on my physical condition, I focused on changing her rigid opinion of me as nothing but an older, divorced client. Along the way, I came up with the idea of offering to help her structure and manage the launch of a private yoga and wellness practice, and she agreed. We would usually discuss her business after yoga over dinner at one of the restaurants near my apartment complex. Tuesday and Thursday nights became even more magical for me.

But while I had ulterior motives, Angela was all business. She continued to let me know in no uncertain terms that she was not interested in me as anything but a client and friend, and not even very much as a friend. Since there were certainly no physical indications that my aspirations for more of a relationship with Angela would ever materialize, all I had was hope. The biblical definition of faith is the substance of things hoped for, so I decided to back my hope up with faith. I banished all doubt and determined to treat Angela, despite my normal insecurity, with complete respect, loyalty, and trust.

My goal was to be a true friend to Angela, expecting nothing in return. I grew to treasure every moment she was willing to spend with me and tried to make every one of them special, while honoring her need for space and independence. This was not easy, but yoga provides an apt metaphor.

Yoga is a balancing act between what are often considered opposites: strength and flexibility. It achieves this through an exquisite synthesis of the physical and spiritual, the inhale and the exhale, the masculine and the feminine, the practical and the mystical. The practitioner's limits are tested on a 30" x 70" battlefield called a mat, on which grueling individual mental and physical challenges translate into spiritual growth. It requires intense concentration and complete relaxation at the same time. Openness to change becomes the key that unlocks progress.

For me, yoga was essential to resolving the underlying cognitive dissonance on my internal battle for sovereignty and achievement, a desire to both progress and be above the fray. As I was conquering the basics of yoga and, with Angela's assistance, developing my own individualized yoga practice, I was being stretched in a variety of ways I had never before experienced. Physically, mentally, and it turns out, spiritually, I was becoming both stronger and more flexible in ways I had thought impossible all my life.

My lifelong internal conflict and turmoil had manifested itself in an autoimmune condition, Ankylosing Spondylitis, which had threatened to put me in a wheelchair.[8] A decade ago, I had overcome its mastery of me by transforming my daily swimming routine from an obligatory challenge into a dance. Now it continued to recede into full remission as I took control of myself in a new and completely different way, a way that let me be who I really was while enjoying the transformation into what I might yet become.

During this transformation, Angela maintained a friendly, polite, and persistent distance, even as continued to fall in love with her and sought to overcome her resistance. Along the way I understood, instinctively, that the many demonstrations of testosterone, which had seemingly worked (or not) for me in the past, would not help me here. Instead, I had intense hope, mixed with

8.   See *TPotS*, chap. 7, "Flying," and chap. 8, "Revolution."

faith, and a focus on expressing true love to her in ways she might be able to appreciate and understand.

Along with these subtle shifts in my physical and emotional state, my attitudes towards God, my fellow human beings, and religion were experiencing a profound shift as well. My fledgling yoga practice and Angela may have triggered this shift, but they were enabled by my experiences in India, and a deeper and clearer understanding of certain Scriptures. Some of this change was a result of extending beyond my comfort zone, as I had done in India. But this time, instead of pursuing true religion in remote places, with names I could barely pronounce, I was following an amazing person that God had brought into my life, in her pursuit of spiritual enlightenment, to explore areas I never would have chosen on my own.

Let me give you an example.

Once I had a grasp on the basics of yoga, I joined Angela Sunday mornings at City Yoga in West Hollywood. There, I was confronted with having to decide to participate in an opening mantra, in Sanskrit, the meaning of which I didn't understand but which surely invoked, or at least appealed to, deities I would consider pagan. For someone schooled in WCG theology and practice, this was like running headlong into the lake of fire. Many a sermon had been given on the dangers of flirting with false gods. Satan was a devouring lion, eager to catch unawares anyone who strays away from the herd.

This is why, as strange as it seems, exploring yoga in my neighborhood made me more nervous than the danger I had encountered while baptizing a combined nineteen people under the hood of the cobra God and at an AIDS village in the backwaters of India. This time I wasn't worried about my physical health and safety. I was worried about my spiritual standing with God.

I took one of the mantra cards home and studied the words and their meaning. My fears were partially confirmed, and yet I chose to look at the intent, not the detail. I decided to go ahead and participate in the request for opening and awakening, invoking a prayer-like state for myself, and dedicating my practice to drawing closer to the true God.

Here, like in India, I was following my heart, not my head. It was an expression of faith that went beyond my prior understanding of a "safe zone" in which I had 100 percent certainty of being in conformance to my narrow conception of God. Participating in yoga in this way expanded my desire to draw closer to God, beyond explicit adherence to defined actions. I trusted that God was guiding my steps, even though they took me into strange, uncharted waters.

Golden Slumbers

The next step in my awkward exploration of a more open approach to God came quickly by way of a girl named Paith. Angela met her in a yoga teacher training program, and Paith invited Angela to attend a women's group with a spiritual focus. This was a Baha'i-sponsored discussion group that was currently going through a strange-sounding Baha'i book called the *Kitáb-i-Íqán*, the English translation of which was *The Book of Certitude*.

Angela did not have any luck interesting any of her other friends, and so she invited me to attend this and other similar events. Any chance to spend time with Angela was a godsend to me, so I gladly accompanied her to these. I knew even less about the Baha'i Faith than I did about yoga, though I recalled having seen from a distance the golden-domed building at their World Center in Israel when I traveled by boat to Haifa from Athens.[9]

While Angela drove us to the event, a talk show happened to be on the radio in which an expert was interpreting the dreams of callers. This brought a somewhat disturbing recent dream to mind. I had been an old homeless man— grizzled, with weathered, wrinkled, overexposed skin—wearing drab, grimy clothes in desperate need of a wash. We quite naturally give such people a wide berth, and that is how others treated me in my dream. My response in my dream was to become somewhat obsessed with trying to connect with people in an effort to find my home. This naturally led them to distance themselves and shun me even more.

In my dream, I felt the pain of being completely alone, a homeless outsider. And at the same time, I had very vivid impression of learning, in this process, how to interpret the way others looked at me. In real life, I'm not actually a good judge of other people's emotional states. But in my dream, I could discern their thoughts and motivations through their facial expressions and their eyes. They were judging me, in a number of ways, and it gave me insight into the judgment they brought upon themselves in the process.

---

9. See *TPotS*, chap. 5, "Getting Better."

And as this insight grew, I grew younger, my skin became paler, and I sported a full head of long, thick black hair. This was quite strange as in real life my hair was fine, brown, and had been thinning since I had turned sixteen. As I grew even younger in my dream, my hair grew thicker and longer, and I grew stronger, like a young Samson. The dream ended with me being far more different, in fact, from my actual self, than the older, homeless, grizzled version of me had been.

This dream had made quite an impact on me, and from my earlier studies into Jung and his archetypes, I knew it had significance. As I excitedly shared with Angela about my dream, the coincidence of hearing this show, since I so rarely listened to the radio, seemed providential. I had to call in, and against all odds, I got right through to the host. Angela was probably irritated, but as I just mentioned, I wasn't a good discerner of such matters. I asked her to pull over so I could focus on discussing this dream, live on the air, before arriving at her event. The host rather enthusiastically predicted that I was entering a very positive phase in life, in which new opportunities and vistas would open up to me.

Had I been more attuned to Angela's emotions I might have toned down my enthusiasm over this positive omen about my life taking off in exciting new directions. The passion I felt during this public confession on the radio was not lost on Angela, sitting stone-faced next to me in the car. It was probably obvious to her that my enthusiasm was pointed in her direction, eager for it to infectiously open her up to the romantic relationship I so strongly desired.

This didn't produce the effect I had hoped for. If anything, Angela was reacting to the old, homeless version of me, not the young, handsome hunk me. She was taking mental notes to stay a safe distance away from this strange guy she had tagging along with her who just could not take a hint.

On the way home, she asked, "What did you think of the meeting?" Knowing she admired these people, I considered my words carefully. The meeting had been different than I expected and was actually quite stimulating in a number of ways. Even though women were predominant at the open discussion, there was no feminist axe being ground, nor did I sense any tension or undercurrent around distinctions between testosterone- and estrogen-fueled perspectives. A Baha'i emphasis on the principle of the equality of men and women certainly contributed to this, and this generally accepted vague platitude was beautifully illustrated by the metaphor of men and women being the "two wings of one bird." Baha'is seemed to have a certain je ne sais quoi that helped them bring this principle to life in a way that warmed the heart.

On the other hand, I had challenged them on several topics, perhaps a bit more than Angela would have preferred. "The people were refreshingly sincere and humble," I offered. Then I realized she might have gotten over the awkwardness of me sharing my dream with her right before the event and might even be fishing for a friendly tagalong to more of them. I added, only slightly disingenuously, "The topics were really interesting. I'd love the chance to meet up with some of them again, because I have some other questions I'd like to ask."

"They told me about another event I'd like to go to," Angela said. "It's a talent show at the Baha'i Center called 'The Best of Crimson Spot.' Crimson Spot is a weekly open mike at the Center, and their annual showcase is coming up."

I couldn't believe my luck. This was as close as Angela had ever gotten to asking me out. "Sounds awesome," I replied, adding perhaps just a little too enthusiastically, "I'd love to go to that."

The entire time I had been chasing Angela, I was held at bay by a lack of romantic interest on her part. One "date" we had highlights how excruciatingly awkward this sometimes was. My former roommate from Pasadena was a graphic artist who worked for a Hollywood magazine called *Backstage West*. He had access to tickets to movie screenings for Oscar contenders, attended by potential influencers—which were also attended by the actors, who answered questions. As a result, I got to meet Mark Ruffalo, Anthony Hopkins, Paul Giamatti, and others. One time there was a choice between several movies, which I presented to Angela. She picked *Kinsey*, starring Liam Neeson and Laura Linney, largely because it was on a night she had available.

I found this an interesting choice, knowing that Kinsey was the famous pioneer in sexual research. You can imagine my hopeful thoughts related to taking Angela to a movie of this nature. As it turned out, Angela had no idea who Kinsey was and neither of us expected the incredibly graphic sex scenes, some of them presented in stark black and white, including homosexual acts and sex between senior citizens. Both of us were squirming in our seats, and I made a lame effort to overcome the awkwardness with humor. I whispered a joke to Angela about the movie "she chose" for us to watch together. Words cannot describe the look of distaste on her face. She either didn't get the joke, or didn't like that it was on her.

But it was not the kind of event at which one could get up and walk out. The rest of the audience were the in-crowd trendsetters, eager to lavish praise on a film which presented the controversial "father of the sexual revolution" as a kind of saint, rescuing us all from the oppression of Victorian morality. To put it mildly, the result of such hopeful efforts to draw closer to Angela seemed to result in her pushing me away. The one interest we had in common, it seemed, was religion, which meant I could move in closer by attending such Baha'i-sponsored events.

While I'm sure some would call it denial, I was inspired to keep ignoring Angela's resistance. Still, my confidence that I could overcome her doubt about me was nothing compared to the faith needed to propel me beyond fears of the negative spiritual implications with chasing her in this way. It wasn't only the residual fear of wanting to be close to a woman who was outside the hermetically sealed confines of the WCG and its splinter groups. In order to get closer to her, I was now cozying up to religious ideas that were foreign to me.

But there was no turning back now.

In addition to not wanting to be alone, I was concerned that being alone represented a failure on my part to conform to Christ's commandments. His true followers would not be lonely, because they would be recognized by others as being full of divine love. The dream about overcoming homelessness had encouraged me that I was making progress in coming to understand how to stop judging and start loving. Falling in love with Angela was my chance to change. It was now or never if I ever wanted to fulfill the sign of the Christian covenant.

Over the course of our friendship, my intentions were not only thinly veiled; I had let Angela know, directly, multiple times, that my interest went beyond friendship. And I cornered her with such discussions, despite the counsel of our mutual friend Syrisa and any others who saw what was going on. They could see that Angela was simply not interested. For her part, Angela repeatedly said, "thanks, but no thanks," letting me know in polite but very clear terms that we would, at best, never be anything but friends. Syrisa drove the point home, explaining in a decidedly unfunny way, that Angela had given me the "talk to the hand" speech on three separate occasions.

Got to Get You into My Life

While each of these speeches resulted in a temporary emotional tailspin on my part, rather than being discouraged or depressed I shook them off like a dog shaking off his master's rebuke, rebounding with enthusiasm and loyalty repeatedly. This was not my usual style when it came to relationships, but it was anchored in faith, hope, and love. I was going to break the chains of past bad habits, the ones that had led to so many short-term and dysfunctional relationships, including a failed marriage. Along the way, a most amazing thing happened. It was the simple realization that I would rather have Angela in my life as a friend than not have her in my life at all.

This was no calculated psychology experiment. I was allowing my feelings to lead me, which was completely foreign. Always quick to analyze what I was experiencing, I realized that bitter childhood experiences had led me to find adult relationships in which I could dictate the terms. If I did not have the illusion of being in control, I didn't want the relationship. This had been most explicit when, in Europe I had outlined to my then-fiancée what our relationship was going to be like. She had gone along with my dysfunctional approach, until she just couldn't anymore.

So I reassured Angela that if a friendship was all she wanted, I would welcome spending as much time as possible together. This approach is found in romantic comedies I had previously found pithy or silly at best. My wounded male psyche preferred macho bravado, but I was different now. I began to internalize the classic "if you love her, let her go" cliché. In true romantic comedy fashion (the movie *Groundhog Day* comes to mind), Angela got just enough value from our friendship to not toss me out of her life altogether when, as happened several times, I promptly ignored my agreement to give her space, forcing her to deliver another "talk to the hand" speech.

We were spending quite a bit of time together during this period. Yoga was the focus, including private tutoring, Sunday mornings at City Yoga, a class she was now teaching, and me providing business guidance. Then there was the occasional Baha'i-sponsored event. At the "Best of Crimson Spot" performance Angela had invited me to, a singer/songwriter named Devyn performed original compositions based on Baha'i prayers. I was impressed with the power of these prayers set to his music. One of them was titled "A Prayer for Waking" and opened with "I give praise to thee, O my God, for Thou hast awakened me out of my sleep." It struck me, quite powerfully that God was providing a spiritual awakening.

Along with moments of spiritual encouragement, there were signs of encouragement from Angela as well. She reciprocated my participation in Baha'i events by accepting an invitation to come to church with me to hear me deliver a sermon one Saturday morning.[10] She appreciated my message, which she felt was warm and open, in contrast to the other messages and interactions she experienced during her visit. As the summer progressed, I continued to spend time with Angela whenever I could.

I had now spent an entire year falling ever more deeply in love with her, even as all attempts to win her over caused her to pull away. Painfully, this was brought home during a visit by my younger sister. I took the two of them out to dinner together. It was a bold move, introducing Angela to a member of my family. You never know what's going to happen when you get together with my younger sister, but I thought the dinner went quite well. This was big.

So I asked her what she thought of my chances with Angela.

With genuine and loving concern, and typical Fransson tact, she said, "Give it up."

Things were slowly coming to a head.

As August approached, Angela volunteered to plan a big birthday party for Syrisa. She wanted someone to accompany her to Little India, in greater LA, to buy spices, decorations, gifts, and other items for an Indian-themed party. Guess who volunteered to help? Here was yet another chance for me to show Angela that I could be her best friend.

As the day approached, my excitement about spending an entire day with the woman I loved got the best of me. In spite of (or perhaps because of) the fact that my love was unrequited, I determined to once again overtly try to win her over. I wrote a poem for her that I wanted to share in yet another attempt to help her see the potential we had together. The poem, titled "Thursday Night—Senses at Attention," expressed my anticipation of her arrival at my door for our weekly private yoga session.

The personal and confessional nature of the poem made me understandably nervous about giving it to her. Perhaps I should have paid more attention to that

---

10. At David Antion's Church of God, Southern California (COGSC).

little voice, but there was no stopping me. From the moment she picked me up, I somewhat obsessively looked for the right time, or the chance to create the right opportunity, to share the poem. This made it difficult for me to be "in the moment," and Angela sensed my nervousness and awkwardness.

Unbeknownst to me, Angela was second-guessing letting me join her. My behavior made her uncomfortable enough that she planned to tell me that our friendship was just not working for her. My plan was to give her an intimately confessional poem, while she wanted to tell me to get lost—forever. By lunchtime, even I sensed the tension. Both of us were imagining that our lunch at an Indian food cafeteria in Little India was the right time to deliver a clear message to the other party. I didn't know how bad the situation actually was, but thankfully, I could tell the moment wasn't right for me to give her my explicit poem about longing to be closer to her.

While neither Angela nor I were afraid to speak our minds, generally speaking, neither of us managed to get out what we actually wanted to say to each other. So we sat at the cold chrome-covered table in the little cafeteria-style bistro, frequented only by locals, who sat all around us jabbering away in various Indian languages or dialects. The selections in the buffet line hadn't been visually appealing, nor were they necessarily what we expected. Our food sat on cheap, Formica, compartmentalized dishes on even cheaper plastic trays in front of us, looking as out of place as we did. We sat pushing the spicy, pungent, and marginally identifiable food items around with our institutional cutlery. Each of us was wondering why the other person was so tense and nervous, while looking for an opening to tell them what they were not ready to hear.

As the meal dragged on, each of us palpably wished we were anywhere else, completely frustrated and unable to express what we were feeling. Instead, we shared stilted small talk, interspersed with various ways of asking the other person if everything was OK, without really wanting an honest answer.

Somehow, we got through that lunch, exiting the depressing venue to enjoy the sun striking the brightly colored objects above and behind the windows of the many and varied shops of LA's commercialized version of a romanticized India. As the day wore on, I focused on making sure to show consistent positive support of Angela's efforts to make Syrisa's party one she would appreciate and remember. This would be a devotional sacrifice for any red-blooded American male, not to mention one who had spent most of his life believing birthday celebrations were selfish affairs, at best, if not outright pagan.

It was a struggle, not a joy, to keep up the façade. At the end of the long and emotionally draining day, Angela was as frustrated with me as she was agitated at not having found anything appropriate to wear for the occasion. She was tired and seemed upset about having signed up to organize the party. Ready to give up, she said, "Let's just go home, I'll deal with this later."

I was still invested in ending the day on a more positive note, sensing, quite accurately, that it was now or never. If I failed to turn the negativity around, this might be the last chance I would ever have to do so. So I urged her to keep looking just a little bit longer for that dress, though personally, I was enjoying the search even less than she was.

We proceeded down toward the end of a long street full of shops, at the far end of Little India. The search now seemed futile and hopeless, when suddenly, and against all odds, she found the perfect dress in the last shop. She loved the color, style, and fit, and her mood changed dramatically, realizing she had gotten everything done. Walking back to her car, a warm and friendly Angela thanked me for supporting her in her quest. The mood had become almost upbeat as I inserted one of the traditional Indian music CDs she had just bought, based on the storeowner's recommendation for the event, to give it a listen.

The sounds that issued forth from the car speakers were, to say the least, very different from what we expected. The songs had been transferred from old vinyl, complete with the hollow raspiness of a bad master, and they featured an older guru intoning in a flat voice with sparse instrumentation.

Angela's mood was swinging back into the negative, and I insisted we turn around and exchange it for something better. After some initial protests, Angela agreed. By the time we were again on the way home, with a much more upbeat CD of Bollywood movie music playing, her mood had turned around completely. Without knowing how narrowly I had already dodged a bullet, I decided to swing for the bleachers and shared the poem.

I'm sure it would be overstating the case to say my poem touched Angela's heart, but I felt she appreciated the gesture of presenting her with a poem about how much she meant to me. It finally felt comfortable referring to her as my friend.

I've Got a Feeling

At Countrywide (CFC) I had now completed a full annual strategic planning cycle and had built a successful team. My work was both interesting and challenging, and in addition to my MBA work, I focused my spiritual efforts on the COGSC, working to counteract the lack of warmth and openness Angela had noticed. My relationship with my dad was also improving, as we worked to develop the real estate business in Spokane. My goal was to gain enough financial freedom to pursue my vision of an international organization based on the biblical definition of true religion.

But my focus was still on Angela.

The next thing I knew, it was Syrisa's thirtieth birthday, and I was helping Angela host it at the home of one of their friends. The atmosphere was festive, and the guest list was large and diverse, including people from Syrisa's and Angela's world of physical therapy and friends that Syrisa and I had in common from our WCG and COG days. I've always found mash-ups where cultural worlds collide enjoyable, and there was a tingle of excitement in the air, which, initially I couldn't quite place.

My job was outside on the grill, cooking the tandoori chicken Angela had prepared, which lent itself well to casual chats with various guests. The heavenly scent of the chicken and the free-flowing beer and wine enhanced the flow of conversation as well, and a festive party vibe unfolded. Angela looked radiant in her new dress, and I had never seen her smile so broadly. In her wonderfully understated way, she was the perfect hostess of a carefully planned and well-executed party. And since I was her designated assistant, I had lots of opportunity to show my support of her while also getting to interact with that beautiful and inspiring smile.

After amassing a healthy batch of ready-to-serve tandoori chicken, I popped into the kitchen to get my next set of instructions from the commander in chief. She was talking to an older coworker of hers from Glendale Adventist Hospital, a woman I instantly categorized as a sweetheart—the kind of gentle, loving soul everyone loves to be around. Both were smiling broadly, but Angela had a slightly guilty look that I was not accustomed to seeing. Angela's friend asked, "Were your ears burning?"

My initial reaction was a self-conscious fear that they were making fun of my attraction to Angela. The words "Angela was talking about you" had always meant that another slap down of my romantic aspirations was in the works. Syrisa, in particular, had seemed to take perverse pleasure in exactly these kinds of embarrassing moments. My momentarily confused discomfort seemed to last an eternity.

But it actually quickly gave way to a more positive form of confusion as Angela's friend said, "Congratulations," and reached out to give me a reassuring hug. I gave Angela a quizzical look and noticed her guilty smile was now centered in a face that sported a decidedly rosy tinge. My confusion turned to elation, as the coworker continued, "Angela was just sharing with me that you two are an item. You are one lucky man."

And I was.

A pleasant tingling started at the base of my spine and ran up my back, setting off a pleasurable mini-fireworks session at the base of my skull. After an entire year of chasing this beautiful woman, the moment I learned that there was real hope of drawing her closer to me, and into my life, was indescribable. It is imprinted permanently on my memory. I managed somehow to express the words, "I am, I truly am," in a somewhat relaxed voice, while internally doing double backflips, and externally extending my non-drink-holding hand around the shoulders of a woman whose face was decidedly expressing a happy embarrassment.

Elvis Costello, on his *Costello & Nieve* five-CD live collection, explains that when people ask him about the meaning of his songs his answer is, "If I could have said it in words other than are in the song, I would have written a different song." Similarly, if I could explain what it was that changed Angela's heart, I could speculate, but the best I can do is point you to the quote that opens this chapter and say that if I did know what it was, I would have done it sooner. But I do know that I will be eternally grateful to God for giving me the hope, faith, and love I needed to win this beautiful angel over.

Just Like Starting Over

Love: a single word, a wispy thing,
a word no bigger or longer than an edge.
That's what it is: an edge; a razor.
It draws up through the center of your life, cutting everything in two.
Before and after. The rest of the world falls away on either side.

– LAUREN OLIVER, FROM *DELIRIUM*

I have a picture of us from Syrisa's party on my desk in front of me as I write this. We're standing very close, my arm around her shoulders, both of us beaming. From then on, Angela and I spent more and more time together, getting to know each other on an entirely different level. However, in just a few short weeks, it was time for me to leave for the UCG Feast of Tabernacles in Tartu, Estonia.

I had bought a new digital camera for the trip, and I have many wonderful photos of a visit with my relatives in Stockholm during a stopover my dad, stepmother, and I made en route. The short visit was reminiscent of the naïve and wonderful time as a student at Ambassador when my stepsister Julie, her mom, my dad, and I traveled through Sweden during the summer—the perfect picture of a happy family. So much water had crossed under the bridge since then, including the death of Julie's mother, and my dad's remarriage, but Dad seemed to be reliving those glory years.

His proud happiness was exceeded by my own, which came from a much different place. Despite being a bit worse for the wear, I was embarking on a glorious new journey, and my expectations about the Feast, and my focus during the time in Sweden were very different now. My priorities had changed.

Long gone were the days of believing I was part of an elite group—the One True Church. My focus was exclusively on living my life in such a way that the love of God might be manifest. And there was no better way to do that than to focus on the most important physical relationships I had.

So I wasn't just sharing pictures of Angela with my parents and relatives in Sweden, I also made sure to arrange to be in touch with Angela by phone, which, with international cell phone charges and the time difference, was not that easy at the time. Even before leaving, I had written several cards to her and continued to do so en route, timing my mailing of them so she would receive one each day I was gone. It was disappointing to be leaving on a trip alone just then, and though my perspective on service to the church was much more balanced, this Feast represented an exciting and highly anticipated step forward for me, in several important ways.

Revolver

I've left it to the reader's imagination to interpret my use of Beatles' song titles as chapter and section headings, but there's an exception to every rule. The Beatles seventh studio album, *Revolver*, provides an appropriate reason to break it.[1] Among many other distinctions, *Revolver* was ranked number one in the "All-Time Top 1000 Albums" by Colin Larkin, editor of the *Encyclopedia of Popular Music*, and is often regarded as one of the greatest achievements in music history. With it, the Beatles reinvented themselves and completely transcended any stigma of being a "boy band."

The title represents turning things around, standing things on their head, looking at life in an entirely new and different way. When I heard this album

---

1.   Released on August 5, 1966 and remastered on September 9, 2009.

during the winter of '73–'74, in Alaska, at age 13, it struck me in the same way "Hey Jude" did four years earlier in Sweden. As a deeply troubled adolescent, the words and music amplified my feelings of being utterly alone and lost, while also allowing me to accept these feelings. Music from that point on became my solace, and in diving more deeply into it, illegal drug usage had followed it in quick succession. *Revolver* as a title was also a premonition of a craze that was yet to develop around hidden messages and backwards masking, fueled by paranoid fears of satanic influence. The Beatles had embedded the word "love" in the title, spelled backwards. Fans felt it, but critics couldn't see it. They couldn't relate to the fact that the Beatles' intentions, despite their humanity, were pure and noble. This phenomenon they were expressing—of being outside the mainstream and misunderstood, even from within it, was the inverse, the mirror image, of my own experience.

For ministers within the COG movement to reconcile, after parting ways in a cloud of disagreement and accusation, was revolutionary in COG circles. It would be wonderful to see Victor and Beverly Kubik again, as well as a number of other people I had known during my brief time as the first pastor of the WCG church in Estonia. It was gratifying to be involved once again in an area I had served while in Europe, and it was a chance to improve my relationship with my dad and stepmother. But I was most excited about the chance to share the insights I had recently gained, which seemed so spiritually important to me personally. These perspectives, gained, communicated, and reworked during my explorations and discoveries inside and outside of the COG groups I'd been a part of over the past ten years, were hard fought and won. I was excited to share them within the COG movement, starting with the UCG, at the Feast in Estonia, Friday, October 21, at 10:00 a.m.

My sermon, titled "Faith, Hope, and Love," was delivered with a heart full of my recent experience with Angela. Faith is the substance of things hoped for, and true faith manifests itself in actions that express our belief that our hopes have already been realized. My view of faith had been expanded, as referenced earlier, by Markopoulou Kalamara's article in *Scientific American* presenting the case that the universe did not exist until it was observed. This is connected to the account in Genesis where all things were brought into existence when God conceived them.[2] Other articles I read, on string theory, parallel universes, and quantum mechanics, provided quotes and examples. Our own creative power, in an infinitesimally inferior and fractal way, was literally of the same nature as God's. Faith enabled us to exercise our tiny portion with tremendous potency, to create a new reality for ourselves, even if that reality was not (yet) perceived by others.

During my seventy-five minutes (yes, Feast sermons in the UCG were that long), I also covered my perspective on how the sign of the Sabbath had been replaced by the sign of Love, under Christ. I had often covered this topic over the previous decade, and I assured my audience that this did not diminish the validity of the Sabbath. Even delivered carefully, without diminishing the importance of what the Sabbath meant to those who kept this particular sign, the topic made most of the audience cringe, or at least squirm. I quickly moved on to the topic that I was most excited about. It was a subtle perspective that I had recently teased out of a very important and powerful parable told by Jesus, with far-reaching implications.

The realization of what this parable meant for us, in the COG movement, had come to me as many of my past spiritual insights had tended to do, as I had prayed and worked and then prayed some more during the preparation of my sermon. The *Scientific American* article on how we process feedback was also a key to looking at this parable in the way I did. So was the shift in my thinking on Paul's reference to Psalm 19 in Romans 1:19–20, discussing the way the creation reveals the invisible things of God, to all men, not just the tiny subset of humanity that the WCG had previously counted as "called."[3]

To do this discussion justice, it will be helpful to look at the entire passage/parable of the sheep and goats, found in Matthew 25:31-46:

When the Son of man shall come in his glory, and all the holy angels with him, then shall he sit upon the throne of his glory: And before him shall be gathered all nations: and he shall separate them one from another, as a shepherd

---

2. Genesis 1:3–4: "And God said, Let there be light: and there was light. And God saw the light, that *it was* good."
3. "Because that which may be known of God is manifest in them; for God hath shewed it unto them. For the invisible things of him from the creation of the world are clearly seen, being understood by the things that are made, even his eternal power and Godhead; so that they are without excuse:"

divideth his sheep from the goats: And he shall set the sheep on his right hand, but the goats on the left.

Then shall the King say unto them on his right hand, Come, ye blessed of my Father, inherit the kingdom prepared for you from the foundation of the world: For I was an hungred, and ye gave me meat: I was thirsty, and ye gave me drink: I was a stranger, and ye took me in: Naked, and ye clothed me: I was sick, and ye visited me: I was in prison, and ye came unto me. Then shall the righteous answer him, saying, Lord, when saw we thee an hungred, and fed thee? or thirsty, and gave thee drink? When saw we thee a stranger, and took thee in? or naked, and clothed thee? Or when saw we thee sick, or in prison, and came unto thee? And the King shall answer and say unto them, Verily I say unto you, Inasmuch as ye have done it unto one of the least of these my brethren, ye have done it unto me.

Then shall he say also unto them on the left hand, Depart from me, ye cursed, into everlasting fire, prepared for the devil and his angels: For I was an hungred, and ye gave me no meat: I was thirsty, and ye gave me no drink: I was a stranger, and ye took me not in: naked, and ye clothed me not: sick, and in prison, and ye visited me not. Then shall they also answer him, saying, Lord, when saw we thee an hungred, or athirst, or a stranger, or naked, or sick, or in prison, and did not minister unto thee? Then shall he answer them, saying, Verily I say unto you, Inasmuch as ye did it not to one of the least of these, ye did it not to me. And these shall go away into everlasting punishment: but the righteous into life eternal.

In reading this, I noticed that the sheep and the goats were identical in almost every way.

Both groups knew who Christ was and wanted to please Him. In that sense, the sheep and the goats claimed to be Christians, yet both groups failed to recognize Christ. The sheep and the goats all asked Him, "When did we see you?" Both sheep and goats had seen people in need, but neither had seen Christ in these people.

The only difference between the sheep and the goats was in how they responded to the people in need, despite the fact that they did not see Christ in those people.

I also want to stress the universality of this. Look at Paul's words in a passage familiar to WCG veterans, a passage used to support the role of the ministry in preaching the gospel: "So then faith cometh by hearing, and hearing by the word of God. But I say, Have they not heard? Yes verily, their sound went into all the earth, and their words unto the ends of the world."[4]

The quote Paul is using here, about their sound and words going to the ends of the world, is taken straight out of Psalm 19:1–3, "The heavens declare the glory of God; and the firmament sheweth his handywork. Day unto day uttereth speech, and night unto night sheweth knowledge. There is no speech nor language, where their voice is not heard."

The Psalmist states that the universe itself is declaring, showing, and speaking with a voice that carries around the planet in a universal language the Glory of God. This declaration, this communication, predates Moses and Christ, going back to the foundation of the world. A universal message has been delivered, able to be understood by all mankind.

And here Christ is summarizing what that message really is, in a parable that determines whether we you will be "in" or "out" when He establishes the Kingdom of God on earth:

You either treat your fellow human beings with love, or you don't.

Period.

That's all that matters.

Paul channels David's appeal to the message of the cosmos, showing that the signs in the heavens are in alignment with the sign we are to convey, the sign of love. This is the sign which the sheep fulfill in their actions, while the goats only profess to believe it. And what you do is infinitely more important than what you profess. This is not to say that our intentions, our motives, our hearts, don't matter. It's actually the opposite. The heart matters most of all. So what was the difference in the heart of a sheep versus a goat?

As I pondered and read and pondered some more to discern exactly what it was that caused the goats to miss the boat, I got my answer.

I concluded that the safest way to avoid being a goat was to stop trying to make a distinction about who is or isn't a Christian in the first place.

We simply had to understand that all men and women are equal and treat them that way.

---

4. Romans 10:17–18.

The only way this could be consistently accomplished would be to approach all people as though they already have Christ in them. To see Christ in everyone with whom we interact.

The whole idea of trying to figure out who is or is not a true Christian, it seems, is a poisonous pill to swallow. Depending on why we look for the sign, we may be guaranteed to miss it. This is why Jesus, when asked to identify Himself by a sign, identified the askers as evil and adulterous.[5] It was also why Christianity inadvertently built an explicit denial of the sign he gave, the three days and three nights, into its very definition of orthodoxy.[6]

The amazing irony, as indicated by including a denial of the sign Christ gave, in the definition of who is and who is not a heretic, is that by drawing a circle to exclude others we end up outside of the circle that Christ drew.

My understanding about how judgment of others worked was in alignment with my understanding of quantum mechanics, which describes how the universe functions at the particle level. Whereas Einstein had studied the large-scale cosmos to develop and test his specific and general theories of relativity (which outline the opposite of what is often understood popularly by those who say, "everything is relative"), Max Planck and, later, Niels Bohr looked at the tiniest components. It was Bohr who won the Nobel Prize in Physics in 1922 for describing the molecular model, which he compared to our solar system. Today we take our understanding of these systems for granted, and often don't reflect on the hand of God, who created these astounding structures at vastly different scales as the framework that supports our existence.[7]

---

5. Matthew 12:38–40: "Then certain of the scribes and of the Pharisees answered, saying, Master, we would see a sign from thee. But he answered and said unto them, An evil and adulterous generation seeketh after a sign; and there shall no sign be given to it, but the sign of the prophet Jonas: For as Jonas was three days and three nights in the whale's belly; so shall the Son of man be three days and three nights in the heart of the earth."
6. See *TPotS*, chap. 4, "A Day in the Life," and elsewhere
7. The history of quantum mechanics is a rich and fascinating study. The groundwork was laid in the fields of physics and chemistry, beginning in 1838, which led to Einstein's experiments in studying the nature of light. He postulated in 1905, consistently with Planck's quantum hypothesis from 1900, that light was composed of quantum particles. These were labeled photons in 1926.

The Inner Light

Bear with me as we dive just a bit deeper into scientific theory and explore a fascinating paradox of quantum mechanics—a mysterious feature built into the fabric of the universe. Let's not lose the context, which is that the cosmos loudly and proudly declares God's Glory, even as we examine an important component needed to understand the nature of our free will, and therefore, our relationship to God. We'll use the thought experiment designed by Austrian physicist Erwin Schrödinger in 1935 to illustrate both the principle and its application in this context.

Some readers will have recognized the name of the physicist and are already opening the lid on the box which contains Schrödinger's Cat. Schrödinger used this cat in a box to illustrate what he saw as the problem of the Copenhagen interpretation of quantum mechanics applied to everyday objects, which resulted in a striking contradiction with common sense. In the thought experiment, a cat, a flask of poison, and a radioactive source are placed in a sealed box. An internal monitor detects radioactivity and if a single atom decays, the flask is shattered, releasing the poison that kills the cat. The Copenhagen interpretation of quantum mechanics implies that, after a while, the cat is simultaneously alive and dead.

If you're new to Schrödinger's Cat, you might think this is incredibly loopy. The idea does contrast drastically with common sense and logic, which is why Einstein, in a debate with Niels Bohr in 1927, invoked God, by writing, "I, at any rate, am convinced that He does not throw dice."[8] Yet many profound and fascinating discoveries have shown that, whatever we think of this thought experiment, it is accurate. The conundrum lies indeed at the heart of what we, as human beings, experience and call reality. As soon as we look in the box, the cat is alive or dead, but not both.

From a theoretical perspective, this poses the question of when exactly quantum superposition ends and reality collapses into one possibility or the other. Although the original experiment was imaginary, similar principles have

---

8.   Matthue Roth, "Albert Einstein," My Jewish Learning, accessed September 27, 2017, http://www.myjewishlearning.com/article/albert-einstein/.

been researched and used in practical applications.[9] Let's explore a practical application with spiritual implications.

First, at the most fundamental level, this paradox supports the position I took earlier that each of us has the creative capacity to restructure our personal universe literally, the one in which we, as individuals, live and which is different from the known universe, as understood collectively. Our faith in our God-given power to create a new reality can significantly increase our power to perform a creative restructuring, one in which we increasingly "see it differently." So let's examine this in the light of the parable of the sheep and goats. Let's consider how eliminating our judgment of others, removing the distinctions between "us" and "them" is a prerequisite to recognizing Christ.

By analogy, seeking to discern by whatever distinction we might choose, who is and isn't of Christ, is the decay of the atom that triggers the release of the poison. If we are unable or unwilling to see Christ in each human being, the cat will likely be dead every time we open the box to peek inside. We will form a negative opinion of that person's spiritual status.

As children, we are like sheep. We grow up without prejudice. Then we learn to distinguish and judge.

Education is necessary for survival. God has worked with humanity since creation to bring us to higher levels of maturity. Cain slew Abel. Abraham sent one son into the wilderness to die and took another to be sacrificed on an altar. Jacob's sons threw their brother Joseph into a pit. And on and on it goes. Even those specifically chosen by God suffered violence at the hands of those closest to them. The religion delivered by Moses to Israel was designed to create every distinction possible between God's chosen people and the rest of the world. This included the sign of the Sabbath that gave the first book in this trilogy its title. There was a reason, a time, and a place for such lessons and approaches.

Even as God has taught these lessons throughout what has been a very painful and bloody history, along the way we learned and adopted all kinds of negative, unhealthy, ego-driven ways in which we compare and contrast ourselves to others. Then God assessed that we were ready to achieve the next step in our path to full sovereignty. Christ introduced a new level of acceptance of others.

---

9.   This illustration was adapted from *Wikipedia*, s.v. "Schrödinger's Cat," last modified September 22, 2017, https://en.wikipedia.org/wiki/Schr%C3%B6dinger%27s_cat.

Christ put our battle with sin to rest, in that those who rested in Him were already declared overcomers. And then He admonished us, over and over again, to stop judging others, and to stop using the law as a crutch, as a schoolmaster, as a measuring rod to support the vile, bigoted, ego-driven attitudes we, in all too many cases, picked up along the way.

Then He commanded us to get out there and practice His approach. The field of application is a set of baby steps in the new direction—a glass of water, a kind word, and a bit of our time— in support of others, especially those whom we would normally consider "the other." To do so, we simply need to see Christ in them, no matter who they are. Speaking of a glass of water, if I've lost anyone with all the discussion of quantum mechanics, just use the famous glass half-full vs. glass half-empty analogy. When it comes to our assessment of others, we need to view the glass as half full.

WCG theology had conditioned me to see the glass as completely empty, in fact, sealed up with no possibility of having any water whatsoever. Ironically, this was now flipped on its head.

I had been the blind one, unable to see Christ or God in my fellow human beings. My blindness was my belief that Christ couldn't possibly be in them unless they knew the secret Sabbath handshake. This handshake was a willingness to obey numerous obscure commands from four thousand years ago. Obedience to these commands might not seem to make sense today. And only a few believed they were still required. Nonetheless, we believed those unwilling to swallow everything we taught, hook, line, and sinker, were not called by God. They were completely cut off. God was not working with them in any way.

Again, there is an ironic twist to all this. The parable of the sheep and the goats, along with Jesus's command not to judge, meant that those who are members of the COG movement also have the potential to see such spiritual truths. That's why I was so motivated to share what I was learning.

But, in Estonia, both my sermon and a PowerPoint presentation on India the following day, entitled "Letting God out of the Box," were met with mixed reactions. Some felt these were exceptional, eye-opening messages that granted them new spiritual insight. A few eagerly told me so, seeking time to discuss these matters with me over the remainder of the Feast. They shared ideas and positive energy about God, the Bible, and how they should impact our relationship to our fellow humans.

But most kept their distance, as though I were an enemy operative attempting to lead people astray. Unfortunately, but not unexpectedly, my father and stepmother belonged to the latter group, which affected their enjoyment of the Feast, and mine as well.

I made numerous attempts to help my dad understand more about how important love is, but it seemed impossible for him to move in that direction. He genuinely feared moving toward a new understanding of love, which the WCG had defined as keeping the Ten Commandments (the first four defining love toward God and the last six defining love toward neighbor). Any departure from a rigid focus on these ten simple commandments into what he viewed as a murky, questionable area made him instantly nervous. This was a sad but undeniable object lesson on the sheep and the goats and of the spiritual principle that perfect love casts out fear.[10]

Given that this experience happened in Estonia, I was reminded of my time in Leningrad. The young students I met there were convinced that the Soviet satellites, such as Estonia, would "return to Mother Russia" in a crisis.[11] Those who still believed in "Mother Russia" were like the goats, viewing themselves as positive in thought and intent as an empire, regardless of certain details related to how they had actually behaved. Christians who typically try to identify others as in or out, true or deceived, saved or not saved, have similar delusions of how others view them.

Christ's parable points out that the only way to be sheep is to systematically and diligently avoid such comparisons altogether—or end up on the goat side of the equation in our interactions with our fellow humans. The ideologies and theological constructs that had so captivated me most of my adult life, and still did, were secondary, by a margin of unlimited width, to the importance of connecting at the level of the heart with our fellow human beings, no matter what their political, racial, social, or religious creed might be.

As interesting as these insights were, and as exciting as it was to be back in the region formerly known as the Eastern Bloc, which I hadn't visited since the

---

10. I John 4:18: "There is no fear in love; but perfect love casteth out fear: because fear hath torment. He that feareth is not made perfect in love."
11. See *TPotS*, chap. 8, "Back in the USSR."

Iron Curtain came down, the Feast lost its luster after I delivered my messages and experienced the reaction to them. Most of the listeners were locked into a doctrinal system of denial. They were unable to see that the Scriptures actually said something different from the meaning assigned during their conditioning within the WCG system. Most of the people had decided that my glass was half-empty, that I wasn't really "one of them." It was depressing, and as I felt the weight of their judgment, my thoughts turned more and more to Angela.

Upon arriving in Estonia, I had bought a SIM card and minutes for my phone, and continued to arrange my schedule around the time difference, so I could spend as much time as possible on the phone with my beloved. The daily cards I had begun sending her even before I left for the Feast had also heightened her anticipation of my return. For Angela, my trip to Estonia highlighted how much she enjoyed having me in her life.

One of my most treasured memories from that Feast is a picture of the moon I took over the city; it made me feel connected to Angela, on the other side of the world, and it symbolized the elements of the story that will bring this chapter of the story, and a very lengthy chapter of my life, to a close.

Nowhere Man

At this stage in this narrative, my dogged adherence to the COG system surely seems strange to any reader who has not experienced being inside a construct claiming the kind of definitive authority the "One True Church" had over my life. In fact, despite my experience in Estonia, I was still not ready to give up on a fundamental premise. I still clung to the idea that God had selectively called me and seemed to be continuing to reveal truth which was hidden to the rest of humanity. I was hopeful that in reaching out to veterans of the WCG I would find others who were open to similar insights. So when I returned to California, I delivered a similar sermon as the one in Estonia on faith and again used the PowerPoint presentation on "Letting God out of the Box" within David Antion's group, even though these had gotten mixed reviews in Estonia.

The messages were received with more openness—perhaps because these folks knew me and perhaps didn't see me as an outsider/interloper, or perhaps because they already viewed themselves as the outcasts of the old WCG. Whatever the reason, as we moved from 2005 into 2006, I was elected to the Council of the Church of God, Southern California. From within the Council, I proposed assisting the church with a strategic planning initiative, using the framework I had learned and modified at CFC. The proposal was accepted with eagerness, and a number of engaging sessions resulted. These assisted in establishing and outlining an identity, vision, strategy, and objectives, which helped everyone feel a bit better about who and what the COGSC was and could become. Because of these exercises, the tiny group became infused with a renewed sense of energy and purpose, and I was excited with where it might be leading.

One reason for my excitement was that I was still eager to form a base of operations from which to return to India. At the same time, I was concerned with what I was learning through my new access to the inner working of the church, including its finances. These two situations would work together to help me with the last remaining piece of the puzzle I had been trying to put together for the previous ten years.

The main issue I had with what I was seeing in David Antion's operations was the relationship among him, Guardian Ministries, and the Church of God, Southern California. The governance structure of the organization ensured that despite the church Council, David and Guardian Ministries controlled what was done and how. This was problematic and disappointing, but what was more immediately disturbing to me was the proportional cost of David Antion's salary as church pastor, relative to all other expenses combined.

This quite naturally became an issue when we moved from strategy and objectives into the next step in the strategic planning process, which is to set specific goals for the coming year. There was a massive financial roadblock in our way. The budgetary history revealed a small but chronic and increasing deficit even as certain expenses were coming due related to needed repairs to the facility they had been leasing. Despite this immediate and obvious problem, the other council members all viewed David's salary as the one sacred cow in the budget.

I didn't take issue with the salary itself, which was not exorbitant for a full-time church pastor. It was that we had a serious problem that needed to be dealt with. In analyzing the situation in an effort to formulate a meaningful and well-thought-out recommendation, something else became very clear.

David was using the resources of the local church to stage his recorded sermons, which were owned by Guardian Ministries and used for its purposes. Yet none of the local members had any real benefit from the recordings, owned and used independently as part of a national and global outreach program. David did occasionally provide updates and encouraging news that resulted from his efforts with Guardian Ministry, but the local church had no insight into the accounting of income that resulted from those efforts or anything else which might make the relationship more mutually beneficial. Further, David often traveled to visit and speak to other groups connected by, and presumably supporting, Guardian Ministries.

In addition, David was a practicing licensed counselor with paying clients. David's activities as pastor of the COGSC probably represented a relatively small percentage of his time, and in that light, the money being paid to David seemed excessive. As I began to understand this structure and the dynamic it created, I felt confident I knew not only how to approach the small deficit but how to shift to a healthier foundation.

It was easy for the Council to see the increasing challenge to balance the current budget against current expenses. How would we be able to fund any of the goals we had just established? The first step was to use our strategic planning sessions to call out the gap between what the congregation had said it wanted to accomplish and what it was actually focused on. From there, a budget committee could be established with responsibility to make a recommendation to the church Council on how to address this situation.

As this was happening, one of the Council members decided to warn David that a budget committee had been established to make a recommendation to the Council on how to address these issues, that I was on it, and that I had called attention to the fact that a high percentage of church income was committed to his salary.

David reacted quickly and forcefully, with an attempt to stop the work of the committee. He used the same old tired biblical analogies used by the WCG and all its offshoots to support the supposed authority of the one in charge and then applied various Scriptures about fighting off wolves that were out to attack the shepherd and scatter the sheep.

In simple terms, in the end, it was just the same old story playing out one more time.

At the time, I was shocked by his unexpected reaction. How had I had so misjudged him? Why had his reactions caught me off guard? What was I missing?

I Me Mine

Originally, I saw David Antion's enthusiastic ongoing efforts to support and serve the somewhat shabby little community of believers as altruistic. Now I saw him as a user, not a giver. The COGSC was in a financial crisis that was sapping its energy and power to act, meaning Guardian Ministries was a kind of spiritual vampire, sucking the spiritual life force from the local congregation. It was being bled to death financially by David's salary while his main interest was not the congregation at all but rather Guardian Ministries. The question that puzzled me was how someone who obviously felt, believed, and wanted to be a benefactor to these people, a "helper of their joy," could be so blind and calloused to the reality of their spiritual situation? David had suffered greatly because of such treatment at the hands of those in command back in the old WCG.[12] It was disturbing to realize that he seemed blind to the fact that he was treating others in the manner that he had been treated.

And I struggled to understand how David Antion could react so angrily against a professionally and ethically sound approach to helping a local congregation that was dependent on him for its spiritual nourishment. In thinking this through, it didn't seem to me that the money was most important. What appeared to be most important to David was the need to present and represent himself as an evangelist in the WCG tradition, both to the outside world and to those inside the COG fold. The need to live up to this image seemed to trump activities which might actually serve the sheep in his care. He needed to convince himself and others that he was right with God and was fulfilling the commission God had given him. But the things which he needed

---

12. *TPotS*, chaps. 3, "The Continuing Story of Bungalow Bill," and 4, "I'll Be Back" and "Love Me Do," provide examples and background. Note that David Antion was a brother-In-law by marriage to HWA's son GTA, through his wife, who was a sister to GTA's wife.

to do to convince himself of this were different from those that actually served other people.

He naturally assumed that others saw things the way he did and so imagined that my strategic planning work would have energized and increased the motivation levels of the congregation to support him and his efforts as an evangelist. If the local church were thriving and growing, it would also raise and contribute more money to his efforts, providing an improved foundation for those things that I believed were actually most important to him: his own status and accomplishments as an evangelist. Instead, the strategic planning process defined him as merely a local pastor, and he felt very threatened at the core of his spiritual identity.

I say none of this to disparage David. I've placed him under a microscope not because I believe he is a bad man, but because I identified with him. And it further cemented what I had come to learn about those who felt they had a special calling from God, me included.

I was doing similar things, taking similar approaches, making similar decisions, which explains why I'm being so hard on him.

At the end of *The People of the Sign*, I wrote, "Why does the God Daniel called 'The Revealer' have such trouble showing us the truth about ourselves?"[13] It had taken God an entire decade, and the entire course of events described in this volume, to help me uncover a critical, but deeply hidden truth about myself. My realization of what was motivating David was a mirror showing me how blind I had been.

My attachment to the COG movement, the people in it, and even my behavior toward those outside it, was because of my belief that God had called me specifically to fulfill a mission with regard to all these things. All the discussion about Jonah, throughout these volumes, was an internal struggle with my own feelings of having been called by God during my time at Ambassador College, along my own ordination into the WCG ministry.[14] I had been ordained to the rank of preaching elder within the WCG Government of God hierarchy. As such, my calling was to preach the truth, primarily among those called and converted. I was held captive, enslaved by these beliefs.

---

13. Daniel 12:47.
14. See *TPotS*, chaps. 5, "Do You Want to Know a Secret," and 7, "You've Got to Hide Your Love Away."

The degree to which this was ingrained in my psyche had finally become clear.

Though I had cast off various components of the COG ideology, I had held tightly to my own special calling. I refused to let go of it, despite the constant negative feedback the universe delivered to me. Reflecting on my failure to build a viable foundation in India, I realized that my desire to be actively involved in God's Work, which had appeared to be a positive catalyst, was actually preventing success.

The need to play a role in God's Plan was an ego fantasy.

This insight was stunning—it stopped me in my tracks.

No one can claim the kind of special relationship with God needed to presume to be doing His Work. It pollutes the pure working of the Holy Spirit. On the surface, this had been clear to me for more than a decade, but I was still far from the detachment I needed from the outcomes of whatever God might be accomplishing in or through me.

In India, for example, perhaps Michael had bristled less at the idea of needing to adhere to Western standards than at my hands-on, ego-driven efforts to force an accomplishment that was never going to happen in the way I imagined. God may not have wanted things in India to happen the way I was driving them, or I may have been my own worst enemy—preventing God from assisting with a vision that had come from or been endorsed by Him.

Who knows which of these was true, but in the process of trying to figure it out, Moses came to mind. The Mosaic covenant, and his experience in the wilderness, had fallen short of getting the people of Israel to relate directly to God, in favor of a reliance on a priesthood. I had resigned from the ministry because I had seen the WCG/COG Government of God construct as an instance of this type of idolatry. But my role as a developer/promoter of programs in India seemed to continue a pattern of me viewing myself as an important component in the relationship between people and their God

If David was anything like me, then he naturally felt a compulsion to preach successfully the gospel of the Kingdom of God on an even broader scale, commensurate with the role of evangelist. And he would naturally feel justified in his use of the local congregation in the same way that the WCG and its other offshoots had justified various forms of a "pay and pray" base of operations for their activities related to the preaching of the gospel.

This conclusion was my personal opinion, but it was actually a positive not a negative assessment of David Antion. Despite his volatile reaction to the establishment of a budget committee, he was sincere in his approach. It wasn't really about the salary at all. He had a calling and an ordination from God, stemming from the One True Church, and the hands of the duly appointed and anointed ministers in the Government of God. He was bound to this calling, and had to fulfill it in order to be right with His Creator.

For my part, I had partially escaped from this logical trap. David had been ousted in a power struggle not of his making, while I had been fortunate enough to resign for reasons of conscience. My rejection of the WCG's belief in its authority to collect tithes liberated me from the idea that I deserved to be paid by others to fulfill the commission God had granted. David didn't have the luxury of seeing how the presumptive right to benefit from the tithing model to fulfill a commission to perform a modern "Work of God" was a poisonous idea. I had escaped from these logical traps, and from the organizations practicing them, but not from myself. The last chain that held me enslaved was this powerful residual belief about my personal calling from God.

I had spent decades believing that the outpouring of the Holy Spirit hinged on obedience as tested by the Sabbath and Holy Days.[15] That God gave richly of His Spirit to those in the COG movement because we obeyed Him more fully, more completely than anyone else on the planet. But the fruit of the Spirit was summarized by traits such as love, joy, peace, gentleness, meekness, etc.—not exactly the first descriptors which objective observers of us would be likely to use.[16] The splintered, squabbling, egotistical followers of the sign of the Sabbath showed no evidence to back up the idea that we were filled with the Spirit of God.

Quite the contrary, actually.

---

15. Acts 5:32: "And we are his witnesses of these things; and so is also the Holy Ghost, whom God hath given to them that obey him."

16. Galatians 5:22–23: "But the fruit of the Spirit is love, joy, peace, longsuffering, gentleness, goodness, faith, meekness, temperance: against such there is no law."

Chains

It had taken me a decade to understand that my ego, not God, had driven me to travel the world, building castles in the sand which the ocean of truth was destined to wash away. To my credit, I had been willing to put everything on the line, which had led me to build these sand castles at great personal sacrifice, in places where I believe God had ultimately led me. Those exotic locations and experiences had slowly, but ultimately, radically and dramatically opened me up to accept all my fellow human beings as children of God, with access to Him. I had come to see that all human beings had, in the ways that really mattered, attitudes and approaches in no way inferior to mine.

I was becoming more like a sheep, after having inhabited the pasture of the goats during most of my adult life. All human beings were obeying God in their own way and had access to His Holy Spirit in varying amounts known only to God and for the purposes which He intended, regardless of anyone else's opinion.

My experience with David Antion helped me see the profound extent to which we in the COG movement had the pyramid upside down. The rulers sat at the apex, just below Jesus Christ, the chief cornerstone, and enjoyed a lofty position supported by all those at the base, the foundation of the pyramid. Christ, however, had come to illustrate that a spiritual pyramid is inverted. Christ planted the cornerstone at the bottom.

In fact, Christ had stood at the apex of the planet at one point, while surveying all the kingdoms of the world. He had declined to become their ruler, choosing instead the path of humility, which led to humiliation and death at the hands of those He had determined to love instead of rule.[17]

Sadly, in the COG movement we had this backwards and upside down as well. Our focus had always been on the gospel of the Kingdom of God, in which Christ would return as conquering King to assume exactly the role He had, in fact, rejected. We loved the verses that supported this view, such as Psalm 2:8–10, "Ask of me, and I shall give thee the heathen for thine inheritance, and

---

17. Matthew 4:8–10: "Again, the devil taketh him up into an exceeding high mountain, and sheweth him all the kingdoms of the world, and the glory of them; And saith unto him, All these things will I give thee, if thou wilt fall down and worship me. Then saith Jesus unto him, Get thee hence, Satan: for it is written, Thou shalt worship the Lord thy God, and him only shalt thou serve.".

the uttermost parts of the earth for thy possession. Thou shalt break them with a rod of iron; thou shalt dash them in pieces like a potter's vessel."

And while this is about Christ at His return, as King of Kings, we would be right there with Him, as stated in Revelation 2:26–27, "And he that overcometh, and keepeth my works unto the end, to him will I give power over the nations: And he shall rule them with a rod of iron; as the vessels of a potter shall they be broken to shivers: even as I received of my Father."

These inspiring verses of victory give us encouragement—the hope and confidence that the forces of evil will be overcome, and that peace and justice will win out. But they do not win out by using the means and methods of the enemy. In the COG movement, we were preparing for leadership roles in the Kingdom of God. Our training paid a degree of lip service to the characteristics of the sheep. But the main focus of our preparations to rule with Christ was working within, and in some cases, climbing a false hierarchy structure which we had labeled the "Government of God." In training for these roles, we were preoccupied with the administration of the law in our lives and our own families and our own tribe, whichever COG color our particular tribe happened to wear. This was all preparation for the time when we would be elevated to positions of authority that would be rightfully ours.

We were the opposite of Christ, who had abandoned His position on the highest mountain, the station He had with God prior to His birth. He had opted to become the lowliest of servants, washing the feet of His disciples. He reached out to the outcasts and fed the poor. Christ's choice to reject the mantle of authority was perhaps one reason John the Baptist, who came to announce Him and said he wasn't worthy to lace His sandals, became doubtful when he found himself in jail. It seems that John was among the many who believed, in a similar fashion to the COG-movement beliefs in our day, that the Messiah was to forcefully overthrow the governments of that time, and establish the Kingdom of God. John sent two of his disciples to ask if Jesus was "the one":

Then Jesus answering said unto them, Go your way, and tell John what things ye have seen and heard; how that the blind see, the lame walk, the lepers are cleansed, the deaf hear, the dead are raised, to the poor the gospel is preached. And blessed is he, whosoever shall not be offended in me.[18]

---

18. Luke 7:22–23.

Jesus served the needs of those who looked to Him. Not the other way around. He descended from the highest mountain to our level. And lower. He entered the lowest valley, the valley of death, on our behalf. And on His way to becoming the dust under our feet, He washed the dust off ours.

While John was doubting and asking for a sign, Christ told John's disciples to tell them what they saw. In the end, the only sign that mattered was John 13:35, "By this shall all men know that ye are my disciples, if ye have love one to another."

How truly pathetic we of the COG movement were, compared to that example.

At that point, it didn't matter to me that I had run out of viable options among the churches of the COG movement. In preparing my final sermon as a COG minister, at what turned out to be my final Feast, my focus had been the parable of the sheep and goats. It had become obvious that a focus like the one we had within the COG movement, a concern with being "right with God" was a surefire way to become a goat. God had helped me see that He did not want me to concern myself with who was or wasn't a true Christian, a "Person of the Sign." Spiritually, I was homeless, just like in my dream. This realization was like the hypnotism that had overwritten my ideas about my inability to play golf, which had previously prevented me from playing well. Now I was free to see Christ living in others and in myself.

This also meant that I was now fully liberated and empowered to treat my fellow humans in ways that might enable them to recognize the love of God within me, without worrying about whether they had the love of God within them. *Namaste*—a word shared at the end of each yoga class—expresses this beautifully: "The light within me respects and honors the light within you."

I Want to Hold Your Hand

This also enabled me to more freely give myself over to my relationship with Angela, without worrying about whether my life with her would allow me to continue with this or that COG group and its eccentric and difficult people. The chill of fall turning to rainy California winter brought the warm realization that Angela and I were made for each other. One morning, on my way to work, the sun broke through and inspiration hit. While driving I composed a poem for Angela on a scrap of paper held to the steering wheel with my left hand, recording the words that flowed through me with my right.[19] As soon as I had it written down, I called to read it to her on the phone.

When I read the thoughts that had moved me to Angela, they moved her as well—and our relationship moved with us to another level. The progression was so fast, and seemed so good, that within a month, I rather abruptly decided to propose. Valentine's Day, 2006, was only a little over a week away, and I quickly hatched a plan.

The Caioti Pizza Café was just around the corner from Angela's apartment in Studio City. This unassuming local restaurant was a favorite of ours. We had once run into the ultrareclusive Beach Boys legend Brian Wilson while walking into this restaurant; it was an almost magical place for us. There was a wonderful table for two on a little wooden platform about a foot high, just inside the door and to the right. It was nestled in a sort of open but hidden way right in front of the window overlooking Tujunga Blvd. The silverware and napkins were kept in a wooden box on the tables, the perfect place to hide something in advance. This is where I would propose.

The idea of Angela discovering the ring in a fortune cookie occurred to me, and I spent two days tracking down a place that could make a big, chocolate-dipped one in which I could hide the proposal and the ring. Another two days were spent tracking down a suitable promise ring, and selecting and printing quotes to put in both fortune cookies—one for me and one for her, with the intent that I would open mine first. Then there was another trip to the specialty baker to drop off the goods and schedule the pickup of the cookies for the day of the big question.

Another day was spent meeting the waitress who would be on duty that night. It took almost no persuasion for her to agree to join the romantic conspiracy. She even signed up to try to pull off the admittedly implausible scenario that a casual Italian restaurant was offering giant chocolate-dipped fortune cookies as a Valentine's Day treat.

When the day arrived, I scrambled to pick up the cookies; thankfully, they were not only ready; they were exquisite. From there I broke several laws in my rush through the traffic to reach Studio City in time to arrange everything

---

19. Included as appendix VI.

with the waitress. We carefully walked through the protocols and the exact timing, the exact wording, choreographing everything carefully, with specific cues. Then I deposited flowers on the table, inserted a card in the silverware box, and placed a special bottle of wine next to the flowers to complete the ambiance. Then I asked my coconspirator to guard the table until we arrived

Jumping back in the car for the three-minute drive to Angela's apartment, I glanced over at the book we were using in my MBA class on negotiations, *Getting to Yes*, placed strategically on the passenger seat. To sit down, she would have to pick up and move this hint, and it would be followed up by another subtle hint on the card in the silverware box.

After ten days of frantic but focused activity, I was wound up like a top. But when I opened the car door for her, there was something in how she grabbed the book without looking at it when she sat down that made me start to question why I had felt we were ready for this step. The difference in our demeanor was suddenly striking. Not only didn't Angela get the hint, but we weren't on the same wavelength.

Not at all.

A wave of nervousness descended upon me, which had turned to near panic by the time, only three minutes later, I parked the car at the restaurant. The feet that swung around from the driver's seat and touched the pavement had turned decidedly cold and a feeling of intense terror came over me. Walking the half block to the restaurant, I had flashbacks of the restaurant in Little India. It suddenly struck me, to my horror, that she had given me no real indication whatsoever that she was interested in marrying me.

What a fool I was to get ahead of myself in this way again, living in my own self-referential fantasy, completely oblivious to the inner world of the person I supposedly cared about.

Everything felt wrong, as I opened the door to Caioti Pizza Café. My excited yet careful planning would surely end up with a humiliating "No!" in response to my proposal. Rushing into this step was going to set the relationship back. It might backfire completely. I starting looking for a way to back out, to call off the proposal. But it was too late. Everything was prearranged, as the sly sideways glance from my accomplice, the waitress, made painfully clear.

There was our table, complete with the rose, the special bottle of wine, and the box with the hidden card with its unmistakable hint. Back in the kitchen were the chocolate-coated fortune cookies, dark for me and white for Angela, like a bride and groom, which the waitress was planning to deliver. It would be awkward, difficult, and embarrassing to try to undo all that without Angela noticing.

If Angela caught on that something was planned and then cancelled, it would most certainly cause what my mind was now working overtime to avoid—a setback in the relationship. I faced a binary decision between two very bad alternatives. The only path forward was to white-knuckle my way through this foolish decision to propose, come what may.

Angela barely mentioned the decorations and the effort I had gone to. It seemed to make her uncomfortable that I had gone to such a fuss over dinner. Was it the public display of affection that bothered her or something deeper? When she opened the silverware box and found the card, she only glanced at the message, offering a polite thank-you that sounded more like a pained "Why are you doing this to me" than a pleased "Wow, you've made me feel appreciated."

Then she put the card down and studied the menu.

The dinner was enjoyable enough, now that the need for Angela to express appreciation had passed. As we came to the end of our meal, I became anxious again, still looking for a way to catch the waitress's attention and pull the plug on the carefully planned finale. But it was a fairly busy night, and there was no escaping the inevitable. Soon she was heading to our table holding a little tray with the very big and very visible bridal-couple fortune cookies perched on top.

Angela's expression turned to puzzlement, and not in a good way. As the waitress set down the tray and turned away, she asked, "Why are they serving us fortune cookies?" "It's a Valentine's Day special," I answered, but I could tell Angela didn't buy it.

I also sensed her apprehension mounting, as though she were perturbed that I was up to something she didn't understand. My apprehension was considerably more pronounced than hers was, and in my extreme nervousness, all I could do was open my cookie. Inside was a slip of paper on which was written the definition of true love, designed to heighten the anticipation for what was inside hers.

Angela is a meticulous planner who does not like surprises. I had built a series of them, each one designed to heighten the sense of mystery and anticipation.

What I believed would create the enjoyment of an increasingly spectacular series of fireworks had instead generated an escalation of awkwardness.

Angela was no longer trying to hide the fact that she was uncomfortable— even irritated. In response, the blood was draining from my head and face, which she sensed, putting her even more ill at ease. As the situation deteriorated, my only hope was to speed up the progression and short-circuit the mounting suspense that seemed to be making her so uncomfortable.

I urged Angela to open her cookie, and she grabbed the two large points on her white-chocolate-covered fortune cookie and pulled in opposite directions. As the cookie gave way, I watched two chocolate-covered fragments float down onto her plate and pictured an emotional train wreck, the cowcatcher and grill from the locomotive collapsing in slow motion before my eyes.

The phrase "ice running through his veins" denotes dispassionate, professional precision, and in a sense, that is what took over. There was a roaring in my ears as I watched Angela tug the slip of paper loose from the half of the cookie into which it was firmly pinched, between the side of the cookie and the ring which only I knew was still hiding inside, like a spider waiting to emerge and crawl up her arm. The note was going to ask her to marry me, and there was nothing I could do to stop this farce from proceeding to its bitter end.

As I mechanically got up from my chair, I felt the icy water in my veins, and it was anything but reassuring. My plan was proceeding exactly as planned, despite the intense feeling that it was all emotionally wrong. I might never recover from the wounds that were about to be inflicted on me, when Angela inevitably recoiled from my ill-timed proposal.

As I awkwardly sank to one knee in the cramped space next to her chair, I wondered if Angela's eyes were reflecting the terror in my eyes, or if what I saw in them was her own. By the time I was in position, the contents of the broken fortune cookie—the platinum promise ring and a quote from Anthony to Cleopatra, lay on top of Angela's open palms, her fingers as far away from touching the unwanted objects as possible. She stared at them with a look of consternation on her face that was several shades away from anything that could be called joyful.

My left knee was not quite resting on the eight-inch-high wooden platform on which our raised table stood. The muscles of my right leg struggled to maintain a half-bent and painful weight-bearing position. And in this terribly uncomfortable and embarrassing pose, time stood still as my mind raced.

I looked up at Angela, studying her face from the strange forty-five-degree angle created by my desperate position. Her eyes darted around the room at the other guests and the waitress. They were all staring at her as well, and at my back, wondering how this poor fool had gotten it so wrong.

Then her eyes met mine and seemed to beg me not to do what I was about to do.

There were two times in my life when I was in out-of-control situations in which I quite literally thought I was going to die. One was on a wild horseback ride on a plantation in South Africa in 1985. The second was in a massive surfing swell off the north shore of Kauai, Hawaii, ten years later. Both had lasted long enough for me to process fully the fact that I was in imminent danger. In each of those situations, like this one, I had time to become fully aware of my emotions at the time.

It really did feel like I was about to die. And yet I somehow managed, in a faltering voice, to utter the words, "Angela, will you marry me?"

In retrospect, this had more in common with an even earlier time when I really should have died—the time I ran off the road, miraculously passing through a light pole unharmed, in the high-speed chase where I was given a second chance.

Emerging softly from those beautiful lips, in a voice that can only be described as the whisper of an angel, I discerned a barely audible, "Yes."

I had found a soul mate—someone beautiful, kind, and perfect with whom to share my life fully and completely.

I was not going to make a mess of it this time.

Appendixes

I: New York Times Article on Deadly Runaway Bus Incident[1]

5th Ave. Bus Runs Wild; Messenger Killed and Cyclist Hurt

By N. R. KLEINFIELD
Published: October 03, 1997

A city bus driver with a history of medical problems and two suspensions for substance abuse a decade ago lost control of his bus at the height of the morning rush yesterday and it bounded wildly down Fifth Avenue in midtown Manhattan in a seven-block journey of destruction. The bus caromed off another bus and plowed into cars, a bicyclist and a messenger before slamming into a chinaware store at 27th Street.

The messenger, who had been pushing boxes of documents on a metal handcart, was killed and the bicyclist was left in critical condition. The driver of the runaway bus was not seriously injured.

The police said they believed that the driver, Charles Alston, 55, had suffered a seizure or heart attack, and an investigator who spoke on condition of anonymity said that he had "a long history of medical problems."

Angel Williams, the driver's stepdaughter, said that he was epileptic and had throat cancer and severe asthma. She said she believed he has had seizures about three times a year, though never while working. The Metropolitan Transportation Authority said there was nothing in Mr. Alston's medical file to suggest that he suffered from epilepsy.

The police identified the messenger as Alex Castro, believed to be in his 30's. The bicyclist was Neil MacFarquhar, 38, a reporter for The New York Times.

The bus's crazed trip was witnessed by scores of pedestrians and workers in midtown buildings who heard the screeching mayhem outside their windows.

---

1. *New York Times*, accessed December 15, 2013, http://www.nytimes.com/1997/10/03/nyregion/5th-ave-bus-runs-wild-messenger-killed-and-cyclist-hurt.html.

''It was like the movie 'Speed,' '' said Jason Rogers, an advertising design student walking to school. ''When I saw the movie, I thought it looked fake, but I guess they did a good job, because it looked like this.''

On another day or another week in what is customarily one of the city's more heavily trafficked areas, the frightening spectacle of a bus running loose down Fifth Avenue would undoubtedly have produced a far higher toll. But the flow of traffic and the number of passengers on the bus were lighter because yesterday was the first day of Rosh ha-Shanah, the Jewish New Year. Because of the holiday and the fact that the bus was nearing the end of its route, officials said, only four people were aboard when the episode occurred around 8:45 A.M., and none were seriously injured.

''With the loss of a life, you're never fortunate, but we are fortunate in that it was a holiday,'' Mayor Rudolph W. Giuliani said at the scene of the accident. ''I've been here at 8 or 9 A.M., and it's very busy.

II: David Hulme's Church of God Inaugural Letter

David Hulme, Evangelist April 15, 1998

Dear fellow elders of the Church of God,

I am delighted to be able to send this first official letter to you as a start is made on a viable Work once more. I don't need to tell you of the turmoil of the past few weeks. I hope that the pathway to better times will be as smooth as possible for everyone. Certainly the congregations that I have attended in the past few days have been at peace. Following are the attendance figures as we know them to date (additional groups are forming in a number of places as I write).

	Passover	First Holy Day
Arcadia/Glendale, CA	117	190
Oakland, CA	98	155
Modesto, CA	–	137
Salem, OR	22	33
Roseburg (& Coos Bay), OR	28	43
Coos Bay, OR	11	–
Boise, ID	13	15
Rapid City, SD	15	21
Franklin Lakes, NJ	23	42
Allentown, PA	13	26
TOTALS	**340**	**662**

The ministers who have committed to serving the Church of God include: John Anderson, Steve Andrews, Waldo Armstrong, Don Billingsley, Ted Budge, Wayne Carlson, John Christopherson, Steve Elliott, Dick Emery, Wade Fransson, C.L. Handy, Steve Le Blanc, Dave O'Malley, Brian Orchard, Mike Regan, Edwin Stepp, and Pete Wolf.

In relation to all that has happened, a number of questions continue to be asked by ministers and members. I thought it would be helpful if I would share some of my responses with you.

Q. It has been mentioned to me by a few people that you said you weren't going to leave United and now you have. To them, this demonstrates that you broke your word and can't be trusted. To me, it means you had a good reason! Could you please let me know why you left?

A. I resigned from the Council of Elders for reasons of conscience. I could no longer support a governance structure that I believe has failed. I have had to admit that

Herbert W. Armstrong was right in Mystery of the Ages, especially chapter six, where he describes a proven form of government for the Church, (see p. 247). It was also increasingly difficult to participate with men with whom I had less and less in common about how the job of president should be done. A council cannot run the day to day affairs of a church very successfully, and two cannot walk together unless they are agreed.

I don't think I said that I wouldn't leave United. I signed a unity statement in good faith in November, believing that we should give the relationship another chance. But in my opinion others did not exhibit good faith in their behavior through the next few weeks. Obviously I must agree with the apostle Paul that there should not be divisions among us. I have not created a division. On the other hand Paul and Barnabas separated over the matter of taking John Mark with them. There are times when brothers separate for their mutual good. There is also the example of Abraham and Lot when their herdsmen could no longer dwell in the same area together. The solution was to separate. There is no reason, however, that there cannot be cordiality and an amicable relationship.

Q. I thought you said you weren't going to start a church. I've heard that you incorporated on April 3rd.

A. There is no incorporation at this point, and no papers have been filed. It is very likely, however, that incorporation will occur in the near future. While it is possible to function as an unincorporated church, there are distinct advantages to incorporation.

My comments about not starting a church need to be given context. After my removal from office and my resignation from the Council of Elders and employment with the United Church of God, an International Association, it was not my intention to do anything in terms of taking up the leadership of a group of people unless it became clear that it was the right thing to do. I do not believe that anyone should take it upon himself to lead in that way. Through prayer and God's inspiration of His people, I believed it would become clear what the future would be for those who were becoming increasingly disaffected. The emergence of a group of people who are part of the spiritual organism was a spontaneous response to recent events. After several had asked for leadership, one group formalized the requests that had been made to me. I concluded that these were God's people who needed help, and that I would help them whether we became an official church or not. As things have progressed it has become evident that a new incorporation will be necessary. The ministry who have also stepped forward to help God's people, feel as I do, and agree that this is not a charge that can be ignored.

Q. What does the Church of God stand for? What are your plans?

A. For the past three years I have written about the Work of the Church in terms of 1) seeking out the maximum opportunities to preach the Gospel, and 2) becoming a Godly community in preparation for the coming of God's Kingdom on the earth. These are the priorities we intend to pursue much more vigorously. This will mean working diligently at producing publications designed for the world we live in, expressing the truth in terms people can understand. It will mean using television, the Internet, and new technologies, as they become available. It will also mean that the ministry will focus much more on building up and encouraging the spiritual resources of God's people in preparation for the return of Christ.

Q. What are the criteria for hiring ministers into the Church of God?

A. At this point there is so little in the bank and virtually no way of knowing what the cash flow will be, that it is premature to speak of hiring anyone. We also want to put high priority on getting out the message. The point of your question though is, I'm sure, whether or not ministers will be recognized and hired without some kind of credentialing process. I and an executive team of advisors will certainly discuss each person who might be considered for a paid position. We will also discuss each person who wishes to have his ministerial credentials accepted by the Church of God. Among other requirements, each applicant will have to give assurances on the basic doctrines that Herbert W. Armstrong learned and taught from the scriptures during his years as leader.

Q. Will all tithes from members of each congregation be required to be sent in to headquarters?

A. Yes. In the first few weeks it may be necessary to have local congregations handle some of their own costs until the accounting system is up and running, but the intention is to have centralized collection of tithes and offerings.

Q. What will be the Church of God policy on disfellowshipping? Will we have to have bylaws before troublemakers can be attended to?

A. The Bible is clear about the grounds for disfellowshipping. The Bible is the guide to policy. The Bible comes first, bylaws a distant second.

Q. Are there any Feast of Tabernacles plans in the making?

A. Plans are definitely in the making. This week tentative sites have been discussed. We may have one large site for the U.S. or two or more geographically spread. The choice of sites will be under God's direction – where He places His name. At this point it is too early to speculate regarding international Feast sites, except to say that it does appear likely that we will need some.

Q. It has been rumored that you made the TV pilot program without the Council's approval. I personally have a hard time believing this because we were given constant updates in Eagle Rock until suddenly it was never mentioned again. I told others this. But in my attempts to defend you, I would like to be accurate. Could you please tell me what happened?

A. In January 1996 the Strategic Planning Committee of the Council put the TV pilot on the fast track for action that year. The committee's chairman was Roy Holladay. The members were Jim Franks, Doug Horchak, Dennis Luker, Peter Nathan, and me. Sometimes Bob Dick would be involved in the meetings. This represented half of the Council. Also present at times were Steve Andrews, Edwin Stepp and Steve Sidars. I first mentioned the pilot concept in June 1995 to the whole interim council. It was written up in New Beginnings that month. The funds that came in at the Feast of Tabernacles in 1995 were designated mostly for preaching the Gospel with a lesser amount for the General Conference. So there were restricted funds set aside for preaching the Gospel. In April we leased video-editing equipment to do work on the TV pilot. This was fully one month before I left for Israel. Three members of the Executive Committee approved the lease. They were Bob Dick, Dennis Luker and myself. The fourth member of the committee, Doug Horchak, was not available that day. In May at the Birmingham Council meetings I informed the Council that in three days time I was leaving to go to Israel to begin taping the pilot program. Once there I sent back reports each week to the Council about the trip. Several Council members responded with encouraging comments. In June 1996 the Council reviewed the lease agreement for the video-editing equipment. A month or two later the Strategic Planning Committee saw the first edited version of the program. At the Feast in 1996 excerpts of the pilot, with commentary on the purpose and approach, were shown in the Feast video. It was not until December of that year that complaints about the pilot began to be heard.

Q. We were wondering if we could get on a mailing list to receive tapes of sermons or videos and could we also get the address?

A. Yes, you can get tapes. We will put you on the list for weekly audiotapes. If you need videos, please let us know. The address is:
Church of God, P.O. Box 150 Monrovia, Ca 91017

As you can see from the questions, there is a great deal of interest in where we are going and in what has happened over the past few months. This past week we processed the first few days of mail income and the Holy Day offerings from two congregations. We are very grateful for the generosity of God's People.

Thanks for your commitment to serving God's people in another difficult time. This coming Holy Day and weekly Sabbath my wife and I will be in El Paso. We look forward to meeting all of you where you are in the near future.

With love and respect in Christ's service.

III: Legacy Newsletter, October 1, 2002 Report on Madras (Chennai) 2002 Feast

Feast of Tabernacles 2002
Madras, India

As I said at the beginning of this letter, the Feast of Tabernacles was the most interesting and educational Feast I have had in years. It was different for a number of reasons.

It started out like any other Feast. Then unusual things began to happen. Visiting the HIV/AIDS center and preaching the Gospel of the Kingdom to them was only the beginning! The first Holy Day brought 27 adults and 4 children to gather in the rooftop hall built by Michael Hubert over his home. Included were Kevin and Sonali Fiske, Church of God members from southern California. Gloria and I were visiting from Thailand. Michael, his wife Terencia, and maybe 4 others regularly gather for Church of God services in Madras. All the rest were new—and they were all Hindus!

I have to be candid. I was surprised by this revelation when Mr. Hubert told me. I wondered why so many in attendance were Hindus and how they had come to be at the Feast of Tabernacles! It is a long story.

Last Passover, Gloria and I visited India and observed the Passover and Days of UB in India. The day before Passover evening Michael Hubert asked us to travel with him 5 hours by hired taxi to a small village southwest of Madras. Here we met a group of 4 or 5 Hindu farmers and briefly talked to them and their wives in their simple homes. Mr. Hubert explained to us that this group of men were interested in hearing about the Christian God. We could only spend a little over an hour with them before we had to head back to be in Madras before the Passover. I didn't think much about the meeting then. I was more worried about making it back in time for the Passover ceremony.

But they invited Mr. Hubert back to talk to them several times over the course of the 6 months between the Spring and Fall Holy Days. The result was that 11 men from this small village had come to Madras to keep the Feast of Tabernacles to learn more about the Kingdom of God.

The others in attendance (1 man and 8 women) were local people who were either relatives of those already attending services or people that had participated in one of Michael Hubert's Early Rain Foundation projects.

Only a few in attendance had ever had Bibles, so one of the first things we did was go look for Tamil language Bibles. We bought all we could find. We passed out 18 Bibles on the first Holy Day. Several feast-goers more familiar with Bibles helped them learn to look up scriptures. By the second day they all were enthusiastically finding scriptures and taking notes. The third day they were singing hymns in Tamil and reading scriptures aloud when called upon in services. The fourth day they were giving opening and closing prayers and writing poems to God. During the Q and A sessions after services, they were asking very thoughtful questions such as, "Where is Jesus now and what is He doing?"

I had to throw out all my notes and rework every sermon for an audience of people who were hearing the Gospel of God for the very first time! It was an incredible and humbling experience. Wade Fransson, a Church of God elder from California, came over from the Feast site in Thailand to give me a hand. Kevin Fiske pitched in with several messages. All of us experienced the same phenomenon, seeing God's Holy Spirit at work changing hearts and minds in people who were discovering the True God for the first time.

Don't ask me to explain where all this is going. I am still trying to digest it all myself! But if I am reading my Bible correctly (and I believe I am), this is not the first time pagan Gentiles have been called by God to receive salvation. In Acts 13, the Apostle Paul and Barnabas were asked to preach about Jesus in the synagogue in Antioch of Pisidia. When the Jews left the synagogue to return to their homes, "the Gentiles besought that the Barnabas were asked to preach about Jesus in the synagogue in Antioch of Pisidia. When the Jews left the synagogue to return to their homes, "the Gentiles besought that the Gospel might be preached to them the next Sabbath". The next Sabbath "came almost the whole city together to hear the word of God" (verse 44.) Then the Jewish leaders, out of envy, spoke against what Paul was preaching. Now let's look at what happened next. Verses 46-49:

> *"Then Paul and Barnabas waxed bold, and said, It was necessary that the word of God should first have been spoken to you: but seeing ye put it from you, and judge yourselves unworthy of everlasting life, lo, we turn to the Gentiles. For so hath the Lord commanded us, saying, 'I have set thee to be a light of the Gentiles, that thou shouldest be for salvation unto the ends of the earth.' And when the Gentiles heard this, they were glad, and glorified the word of the Lord: and as many as were ordained to eternal life believed."*

I never understood the power of these words in the book of Acts . . . *until now.* After the Feast in Madras this year, I understand better what was taking place then, and what looks like is taking place again today.

Is the arm of God shortened that He cannot call people directly out of the pagan religions in this sick world? Can God only call people who come from what we understand to be Israelitish nations today? Will God only call Gentiles with Christian backgrounds? Must they speak the English language before God can call them?

I keep reminding myself that God is far, far greater than the box we keep trying to put Him in.

What will happen next in India? We will keep you posted.

IV: Poem & Lyrics

The Quest

The man had one desire – find a maiden fair to save
From a fire-breathing dragon he saw crouching in a cave

He would slay each one he found. He was strong and he was brave
So he spent his whole life fighting just to glimpse the maiden wave

But his conquering banner couldn't wipe away the tears
That he never saw her cry as he marched on through the years

Ever straight and ever narrow, never stopping, never kneeling
For a man inside of metal lets his armor mask his feeling

He just piled the dragons higher hiding all the love behind them
Until she lost all her senses and then wandered off to find them

In their candle's dying light she threw off his religion
And in the darkness of the night she impaled their homing pigeon

And when he was old and weary he did curse the life he gave
To a broken hearted maiden who considered him a knave

He would never learn her secret. She would take it to the grave
He will never know his armor always hid the man she craved

— WADE FRANSSON

The Fight

Frightened by the lie
Running from what's true
Standing in the void
Lost without a clue

Like a cockroach on the floor
Like a cat's eye in the night
Not reacting to the light
We can't stand the sight
The sad truth is self-deception feeds the fight

All the words we use
Don't tell us what we mean
They hide us like a dirty cloak – no way we can come clean

Pushing rocks uphill
Filling words with air
Shading all we see
In colors of despair

Like a giant sucking sound
Like an asteroid in flight
Holding nothing with all our might
We're so empty when we're right
The sad truth is self-deception feeds the fight

All the words we use
Don't tell us what we mean
They hide us like a dirty cloak – no way we can come clean

We're out of luck
We're out of time
We are the victims of our crime

– WADE FRANSSON

V: Legacy Newsletter, October 1, 2002
Report on Gudiyatham

Community Care Center for HIV/AIDS Infected People
Gudiyeattham, India
Thursday, September 19, 2002

> "Money cannot help us.
> Medicine cannot help us.
> Only God can help us."
>
> M.S. RAJENDRAN, SEPT 19, 2002

Today, Gloria, Michael and I traveled away from the coast by hired taxi over 4 hours to a town of a population of 200,000 called Gudiyeattham. Here we met Mr. M.S. Rajendran, a civil engineer infected with the AIDS virus along with his wife and young son. Four years ago, Mr. Rajendran founded a HIV/AIDS shelter for people suffering with this disease and needing medical help and support from caregivers. In India, people who have AIDS are outcasts from their society. Many times even close family members disown them; the community shuns them; and their children are deprived of education because of fear the disease will spread among their children through close social contact.

Five years ago, Mr. Rajendran contracted the disease and passed it to his wife and unborn son. The negative treatment he received from family members and the society around him prompted him to found the center for treatment and moral support of victims and their families. The reason we are visiting the center today is to assess a very unique opportunity to preach the Good News of the Kingdom of God. Mr. Rajendran is a Hindu. Most of his patients and their families are also Hindu. Yet, through a mutual contact, Michael Hubert was invited to visit and encourage the patients and family members. He did this by telling them about the future return of Jesus Christ and the soon coming Kingdom of God. Interestingly enough, they are NOT looking for a handout to fund their center. They already have plenty of medicines on their shelves and sufficient beds and equipment. They are NOT looking for physical support.

Instead, they ARE seeking emotional support and spiritual answers.

Contracting AIDS in India is devastating. Once family and friends know you have it, it is an automatic sentence of banishment from society. Children with AIDS are not permitted to attend school, not by law, but rather by social pressure to stay away. They are afraid the infected child will somehow infect their children. Many feel the disease is a curse from the gods.

Gloria and I, along with Michael Hubert, were invited by Mr. Rajendran to visit and give a talk. After a wonderful lunch of traditional south Indian food prepared by center volunteers, we were escorted to the center where we met with the patients and their caregivers (usually a spouse or other relative.) We toured the facility and then addressed a small group of about 25 patients and caregivers.

I opened my Bible and read to them Genesis 1:26-27. I explained to them (*remember, the audience was HINDU!*) that their Creator made man to be in God's image; not the image of a cow or snake or dog. I also told them we all descend from the same two created ancestors, Adam and Eve. Therefore, we share a common ancestry and a common destiny. Since God is spirit and not flesh, the image of God is also spirit. Therefore, our destiny is to become spirit just like God. But first God made us flesh so that we could go through trials and tests to learn lessons to become like Him. Different people will endure different tests and trials – but the result is the same – we someday will become just like God. They now have a difficult and terrible trial with their disease – but if they are willing to search for God and His True Way of Life – then they will be on the right path to reaching their ultimate destiny. This is the hope the Creator God holds out to the world.

Gloria then spoke briefly and told them that the way to the Kingdom of God is narrow and difficult, but that they should endure and never give up hope. And she encouraged them to read the Bible to be their guide and for encouragement.

Mr. Rajendran also spoke. I think you will find the transcript of his speech very revealing: "Mr. and Mrs. Sexton and our dear friend Hubert,

Let me thank you all for coming here to meet us. This day should be called the day of blessing and goodness for us. We men and women living in this area were mostly under pressure, discouragement and attack, just for the reason of a disease called AIDS. HIV affects most of us and many cases of our family, which means the wife and children too have been infected. The worst scenario takes mostly in the villages and towns where you would witness where the family looses respect, their livelihood, and where the children loose their education and finally are pushed to the verge of suicide. As a personal example, I am an educated civil engineer and am infected by this disease and also my wife and children. Even though I stand as a leader to fight against these prejudices, many times I feel like closing my life. Nobody to share well words or even a smile. We have been looked on as unwanted dust. Why, Sir, in such a situation, do we know that our Creator still love us and care for us? When we were in such a bad trauma, we met Mr. M. R. Hubert and he was our only source of contact toward love and compassion. He gave us all the care and support in the times of ebb and sadness. He shared the message how the spirit is more important than physical body. He stated the message of Utopia, the Kingdom of God and we would enjoy physical happiness and spiritual blessings when Jesus Christ returns to the world where He would replace all the leaders and His administration would take over and bring harmony. He shared the message to all our people where most of them are ready to commit to a new way of life. Sir, we do have many plans to concern and care for

the HIV affected brethren and care givers. WE want to create an herbal village which would give these brethren a better place to live with their family and some income to live and education for their children. Sir, the most of all we would like to commit to Christ and His true teachings. Please help us. Thanks".

They want us to return on the 29th and will gather a much larger group to hear us. We do not know where all this is headed, but we continue to follow the lead of the Holy Spirit!

VI: Legacy Newsletter, May 16, 2003
Report from India

There is also a lot of activity taking place in southern India, mostly in the area of Madras (Chennai) where the Apostle Thomas evangelized and was eventually martyred over 1900 years ago.

Michael Hubert, a deacon in God's Church has been very active evangelizing in Madras and outlying areas of Tamil Nadu State, and now 2 groups of Hindus have become quite interested in the Gospel Message brought to this earth by The Messenger Jesus Christ. The first group consists of approximately 10 men and their families living near a village called Tirivannamalai, a drive of over 5 hours from Madras. The second group consists of AIDS patients and caregivers centered at a clinic in Gudiyatham – 5 hours in a different direction.

Gloria and I have visited both these groups several times and believe that the Holy Spirit is actively working with some among them that God has chosen to enter the Kingdom.

Here is Wade Fransson's inspiring report:

"About a year ago, Michael met two ladies, Jayanthi, and Shibra, at the home of a local student volunteer tutor working in his Street Children program. Jayanthi, and Shibra became interested in discussing the Bible and spiritual matters, and attended most services at the Feast last year.

Since then Michael has continued to conduct local Sabbath lessons and discussions 2-3 weeks each month. I met with them and Jayanthi's adult daughter, Lavanya. They had all been seeking baptism for some time, and Michael encouraged them to study, ask questions and wait. I took the opportunity to visit with them and counsel them for baptism for an hour and a half. Later, we also counseled with another lady, Mrs. Kumari, who has been attending for some time.

I am pleased to report that *Jayanthi, Shibra, Lavanya and Kumari* were all baptized. It was the most unusual baptisms I ever participated in up until that point, being conducted in the water cistern for Michael's house. They all attended Passover. There were 7 of us, and I'm sure this was not a coincidence.

We then traveled to Tirivannamalai (five hours) and counseled and baptized *Selvam* and *Annamalai* – two former Hindu men who had kept the Feast of Tabernacles with us last year.

This was another unusual baptism, being done in a public swimming pool during open hours. The three of us had to pretend to be there to swim to avoid suspicions, especially with the current law in Tamil Nadu against evangelism.

We celebrated night to be much observed with these two men, their wives and children. These men and their families are wonderful people, and I'm convinced they will all be at this year's Feast of Tabernacles, God willing. We had planned to take the men back with us to Madras after the Night to be Much Observed meal, but God had other plans.

We developed car trouble and while repairs were made, we spent over two hours with the family on the streets of the village. We got to know them closer as we sat together on a big pile of sand at an intersection, fighting off mosquitoes. As a result, there was a bond formed. Then we told the men that they should accompany their families back to their home village by bus since it was already dark and not good for the women to travel home alone. While this meant that the men could not accompany us to Madras for UB services, I believe that their wives perceived that Love was our first law. I'm convinced that there will be two strong Church Families in Tirivannamalai as an augmentation to the growing group in Madras.

We spent two more hours at a mechanic's shop in Tirivannamalai and somehow made it back to Madras on a sputtering engine after a grueling 7-hour trip. I managed 90 minutes sleep before services on the 1st Day of Unleavened Bread, attended by 10 people.

Friday we were supposed to travel to visit the AIDS village and counsel people interested in baptism. But I began to have stomach problems Thursday evening and this turned into a strong fever which kept me up all night. I was drenched in sweat, cramping stomach and miserable. I suspect the green slimy water of the public swimming pool was the culprit. So instead of traveling to the AIDS village I rested and read the Bible.

I had earlier had trouble with my flight back to the U.S. – due to a reservation I let lapse, so I had to extend my stay an extra day (against my will) by booking a return flight early Monday morning instead of Sunday morning. I did NOT want to do this because I couldn't afford to miss that Monday at work. But God's will is done. Because of the delay of my departure, the next day I was able to visit the AIDS village, where there were people who wanted to discuss baptism.

Sunday the 20th was the day I "wasn't supposed to be here", but for having a problem with my reservation and flights cancelled because of the SARS crisis. But now, here I was, about to travel to the "Aids Village". We rose at about 4:30 to leave at 5:30 to make the 5-hour trip. Again, the winding roads and sights, sounds and smells of third world existence were almost overwhelming. Riding in the comfort of an air conditioned chauffeured vehicle is a virtual necessity for a westerner like myself, but God saw fit to make sure I was humbled by going on 70 hours of fruit and juice fasting for my stomach. This was the only way for me to keep my bout of "Vishnu's Revenge" under control. In this weakened state I was very aware of being outside my "comfort zone" in terms of being in control of my circumstances and future, but also very much at peace in being where God wanted me to be, traveling through India towards Gudiyatham, the "Aids Village".

Michael and Leon had previously made several visits to these groups of AIDS-infected outcasts. These groups are connected through Rajendran s/o Selvam (the "s/o" is a Tamil naming convention that means "son of"). When Rajendran, a former engineer, became infected with the AIDS virus he lost not only his job but was shunned by his family.

Rajendran has worked with government agencies to fund hospices with beds and medical supplies. The resulting program now assists about 300 people who form five groups, whose primary purpose is moral support to help combat the high suicide rate among the HIV positive in India.

Rajendran had assembled 12 people who had been studying the Bible truth as outlined by Michael and Leon on their various visits. After introductions, Rajendran, who's English is fairly good, explained that they wanted to be baptized to become members of God's family. He also explained that they wanted to have God as their healer.

In spite of not being prepared for what amounted to an impromptu Bible Study, having expected to meet with perhaps two or three people for baptismal counseling, these words provided an introduction, and I felt God inspire me as I proceeded.

I started by explaining that during a serious health crisis I had a number of years ago,God revealed to me that the most important healing is of the heart and mind. I explained that disease and suffering on this planet is a result of sickness of heart and mind of all people, and that God was in the process of providing this healing. I gave a number of examples and covered some related concepts before turning to Isaiah 66.

We looked at Isaiah 66:1-2 that shows that the powerful creator of the universe will look to the man that is humble and contrite, and trembles at His word. I explained that the good news about their unfortunate circumstances is that it had brought them to this humble and contrite attitude, where they were beginning to learn what His word is, and were showing an appropriate response. I encouraged them to continue to learn what His word says, and to continue to "tremble" in that they should continue to put it into practice. I concluded by saying that Michael and Leon would return to continue to teach, and that God and His Spirit would continue to guide and open their minds.

Rajendran was visibly disappointed in this outcome. It was clear that He wanted to be baptized, and explained that he did not think it was good to wait another several months, as he and the others had already been waiting several months for my visit. The truth is, I did not want to go ahead with these baptisms, and it just seemed like "too-much-too-fast" to me. Michael and I conferred briefly about what they did and did not know.

Michael explained that they had been keeping the Sabbath and had been learning about the Holy Days and many other matters. I began to question Rajendran about these points, and he confirmed what Michael had told me by explaining clearly what the Ten Commandments were and other biblical truths. This led to a lively exchange about obedience and submission to God.

The more I tried to find a way to "get out of" baptizing these people, the more it became clear to me that God had prepared them to baptism. After another 20 minutes or so of discussion we agreed to hold a private audience with each of them to make sure that each individual understood what was involved and wanted to proceed.

By the time these discussions were over there were still 13 people who wanted to be baptized. I was in for one more big surprise. It turned out that Rajendran had commissioned a baptismal pool to be built on the grounds of the hospice. This was a 5-by-five foot, four feet deep pool, clean and filled with clean water. He had also commissioned a photographer to be present to record this event.

What a joyous experience it was to participate in the baptism of these 13 people, picturing the cleansing of their sins. My arms grew heavy and tired as I laid hands on them, asking God to send His spirit to guide, teach, protect and nurture them, but I was ecstatic. On my first visit to India six months earlier for the Feast of Tabernacles, Michael shared his hope that God would once again grant him a church family so he, Terrencia and their son Ben could enjoy the wonderful times they had experienced in the Chennai congregation. It was heartrending to know that he and his family were all alone spiritually, even as he was giving so much to serve his brothers and sisters amongst the poor and lonely of Chennai.

On this trip it became very clear that God is at Work in India. God has granted Michael favor, and has blessed his efforts. Now I was elated to have been able to play a small part in all of this. On the trip back to Chennai we talked about what Michael would need to do to be an older brother to all of these new brothers and sisters. I'd like to ask all of you to please keep *Rajendran* and the others in Gudiyatham, as well as Michael, in your prayers."

www.ingramcontent.com/pod-product-compliance
Lightning Source LLC
Chambersburg PA
CBHW080527090426
42733CB00015B/2510